THE
CELEBRATION
OF
SCANDAL

$\mathcal{T}$HE CELEBRATION OF SCANDAL

TOWARD

THE SUBLIME

IN

VICTORIAN

URBAN

FICTION

CAROL L. BERNSTEIN

THE PENNSYLVANIA STATE UNIVERSITY PRESS

UNIVERSITY PARK, PENNSYLVANIA

Library of Congress Cataloging-in-Publication Data

Bernstein, Carol L., 1933–
    The celebration of scandal : toward the sublime in Victorian
    urban fiction / Carol L. Bernstein.
          p.   cm.
    Includes bibliographical references and index.
    ISBN 0-271-00718-4 (alk. paper)
    1. English fiction—19th century—History and criticism.   2. City
    and town life in literature.   3. Sublime, The, in literature.
    4. Scandals in literature.   I. Title.
    PR878.C53B47   1991
    823'.809321732—dc20   90–7281

It is the policy of The Pennsylvania State University Press to use acid-free
paper for the first printing of all clothbound books. Publications on uncoated
stock satisfy the minimum requirements of American National Standard for
Information Sciences—Permanence of Paper for Printed Library Materials,
ANSI Z39.48–1984.

For Robin, Andrea, Jeffrey, and Daniel

Contents

Acknowledgments

Some of the early research for this study was carried out in the London Library, the British Library, and the library of the Victoria and Albert Museum, whose collections include rare texts recording the responses of novelists, journalists, and clerics to urban matters. These materials helped to shape chapter 1, which originally appeared in a slightly different form in *Prose Studies* 3 (December 1980). I am grateful to the publisher for permission to use the text. Richard Bernstein was at many stages of the manuscript the most discerning of readers. This book is dedicated to my children, who have always celebrated cities.

Introduction

his study of the representation of the city originates
in two observations: that the growth of the nineteenth-century city was
as mythical as it was undeniable, and that any representation of the
city, any gesture of the verbal toward the material, is perforce a contradiction in terms. The Victorian shibboleth of progress concealed
an immense amount of human misery and social repression; although
its self-constituted narrative focuses on the material growth of the city,
other accounts are more problematic. Wordsworth's apostrophe to
London, "Rise up, thou monstrous ant-hill on the plain / Of a too busy
world!" conveys both points: the city is an excrescence in nature,
gigantic and unclassifiable, an oxymoron; recognition of the city requires a direct address that halts and cuts across the path of narrative.
That the city should rise in response to invocation marks it both as

the product of humanity, whose attempts to rival nature result in the monstrous, and as a massive presence that eludes verbal imitation. Where Wordsworth attempts satire in response to the mystifications of the city, others celebrate its mysteries. Whatever the terms of its fascination, the city appears to be scandalous, a challenge to the natural and a contradiction to conventions of representation in fiction as well as nonfiction. It is this scandal at the origins of urban representation that invites critical scrutiny. In the wake of structuralism, critics have pursued and identified the scandalous in literary texts. The crossing from nature to culture in social formations, which ought to be clearly accomplished and definitively marked, is incompletely achieved: the crucial originary instance is the prohibition against incest. When law, the sign of culture, is invoked against a universal natural desire, it seems that no society can avoid a central scar, the mark of an irresolvable social and theoretical confusion of categories. The relation between nature and culture presents only the founding scandal: in its light it is possible to see how often our myths, our humanisms, our literary methodologies incorporate and mystify such confusions. Social practices that reflect upon or appropriate desire, or descriptive procedures that impose themselves upon lived experience, are scandalous to the degree that they veil the very differences that they intend to resolve between the natural and the conventional. The double fold, the duplicity of discourse, turns out to be both gratuitous and necessary, a way of illuminating the enigmas of literary representation and demonstrating their centrality and endurance.

Urban scandals have generally been understood as socially caused and thus comprehensible, all the more shocking for their clarity: the slums that lie at the heart of a city and contradict its myths of progress, the corruption that festers in self-celebrating governments, the secrets and betrayals that belie bourgeois as well as aristocratic solidarities. All these scandals are only intensified in certain methods of representation. Foucault's chiasmus, "It is in vain that we say what we see; what we see never resides in what we say,"[1] records the chasm between word and thing that generates differing structures of representation and becomes a source of rhetorical power. Studies in ideology, the superstructures of ideas by which societies account for their economic conditions, remind us that existing conditions are rarely represented without distortion. As explanation, superstructures cannot

1. Michel Foucault, *The Order of Things* (London: Tavistock, 1970), 9.

simply mirror the material conditions of life. When ideologies justify themselves in the name of representation, this is no justification at all. As if grammatical structures are not sufficient to maintain the disparity between word and city, ideologies maintain the distortion by suppressing alternative forms of knowledge.[2]

Histories of nineteenth-century urban representation often present a scenario in which the early material growth of the city evokes both massive metaphors (many of them biological) and a penchant for concrete and literal description, to be succeeded by a functionalism that deemphasizes the visual and instead charts the networks of urban power and communication. In this latter stage, what defines the city is not its architecture, its labyrinthine streets, its crowds or its typical characters of ragpickers, "gents," dandies, bohemians, clerks. (The man of the crowd is a liminal figure, simply because he can vanish into the crowd.) The dynamics of the city depend upon intricate networks of journalism and communication, upon economic structures in which the abstractions of money and stocks are the dominant forms of exchange, and upon their unofficial counterparts in private life, such as the circulation of secrets. Any reader of urban fictions must be indebted to such histories, although she must also be alert to the scandals and contradictions that are masked by certain methods of representation. Insofar as a mimetic model is still in place, the criterion for successful representation of the material or the functional city depends upon some form of correspondence. But suppose we were to entertain a history of representation in which the earlier confidence in material objects gives way to a scene of writing in which urban characters exist in and through the objects that bear their traces, or in which the objects themselves cede their materiality to such sign systems as advertising? Or, what if we were to think of the city as resisting representation, refusing to mark the boundaries between the true and the fictive, defying narrative momentum with the repetitions of the typical, insisting upon an impossible intimacy between its structures and memory or mind itself? One figure for the urban poet, Walter Benjamin points out, is that of the fencer, who "wrests" his booty of words from city streets.[3] The artist of the city is engaged in a continuing

2. For an illuminating discussion of ideology in relation to representation, see T. J. Clark, *The Painting of Modern Life: Paris in the Art of Manet and His Followers* (Princeton: Princeton University Press, 1984), 8.

3. Walter Benjamin, "On Some Motifs in Baudelaire," in *Illuminations*, trans. Harry Zohn. (New York: Schocken Books, 1969), 165.

agon, and whether he appears as observer or adventurer, he often adopts surrogate personae, and he is always a strategist. To cast the city as his antagonist is to find in it the same power and even "volition" that thinkers have found in such abstract categories as "thought": if full personification for the impersonal is figuratively scandalous, nevertheless cities, like thought, collect themselves into veiled entities that are both challenging and elusive. Such a personification locates thought or power in the abstract or systemic, while retaining the rhetorical strength of the person. So too with cities, which have a history of such personifications from ancient times, and which assume their modern figures in the language of power on the one hand, and in the kind of images that make city streets the site of memory or self-confrontation. This latter approach to urban novels is attractive because it seems so close to the spirit of urban novelists and poets, as well as such imaginative critics as Walter Benjamin. The questions we encounter in their texts make representation and its scandals a continuing problem. The urban artist does not always point an accusatory finger, as scandals of subject matter demand, nor does he necessarily identify the failures of an urban art. If anything, his forays celebrate an art whose strength depends upon the scandalous mutual involvement of text and city.

Since cities have always figured as the polar opposite to the natural—buildings to deserts, Jerusalem to Eden, community to isolation—they would seem impervious at least to the scandal that crosses nature and culture. Yet urban writers, whether from a culturally induced nostalgia, or a desire to control the city by distancing it, or an ideological denial of the city's material pressures, have often invoked the natural. Nature is a sublime metaphor that links cities with forests and floods, with anything vast and threatening. It offers a taxonomical frame that identifies the most quintessential urban figures, the flâneur, for example, with the botanizer. Grand schemes of natural history make asphalt and brick into flora and fauna; rivers and dust heaps frame cityscapes. To view the city under the aegis of the natural (or from the perspective of the natural, the point outside the city) is to engage in a scandal of categories. After such writers as Barthes,[4] we have become only too aware of the ideological agendas hidden in such "naturalizing" moves: constructed, historical, and contingent,

---

4. See Roland Barthes, "Myth Today," in *Mythologies*, trans. Annette Lavers (New York: Hill and Wang, 1972), 109–59.

the city is removed from considerations of change or revolution. In order to be perpetuated, the city must be denied its very history, what makes it distinctive. The indeterminacy in these passive constructions indicates how mysterious and difficult it is to locate these naturalizing forces, secret agents that, like the denizens of Conrad's novel, try in paradoxical ways to protect the city against social change, trafficking promiscuously in both law and lawlessness.

If this originary scandal is replicated in urban representation, it is nevertheless only one of the many forms that scandal assumes. It inhabits the social: in the crossing of class lines in relationships and in social spaces or city districts; in the juncture of the political and the ultra-aesthetic in the dandy; in the slums that lie adjacent to the dwellings of a middle class unaware of their existence. Ideology, a necessarily interested structure of ideas that accounts for the city, is itself a theoretical scandal. Scandal determines the privileged figures for urban representation: catachreses, oxymorons, hyperboles and errant metaphors. It offers one way of viewing the quest for the real, the attempt to render the referential city, that appears in so much urban fiction. The very crossing from site to language, from the physical to the conventional, can only be negotiated in a scandalous manner. The recourse to signs confirms this. The street signs noted by Wordsworth in *The Prelude* (1805 and 1850) and by Jo, the crossing sweeper, in Dickens's *Bleak House* (1853) signify alienation. The advertising signs in Gissing's *In the Year of Jubilee* (1894) are only a more sophisticated way of marking the separation of individuals from things, the distortions of representation, the ironic abandonment of the natural. The scandal of signs, then, is both local and pervasive, a consequence of advertising practice, of self-advertisement, and of urban representation itself.

If one pole of this study is the scandal, its opposite appears in the sublime. I approach it by way of the parodic mode of the dandy, whose term of absolute approval is "sublime." Seeking to represent the quintessence of urban style, the dandy carries refinement to a hyperbolic extreme, virtually removing himself from the chart of sensory description for the sake of a *je ne sais quoi.* But the sublime also takes a more serious turn in narration and description. Theories of the sublime arise out of an incommensurability, a rupture between the space of the senses and the space of the mind. Not surprisingly, the sublime is coupled with revolution, since both defy continuity, whether natural or historical. Certain striking nineteenth-century fictional images of revolution are in effect afterimages, where, for example, empty squares evoke reflections upon past terrors. (Ironically, nineteenth-century projects of slum clearance followed a similar pattern: slum districts were razed and large avenues constructed in their place. Architecturally speaking, the boulevards and vistas constitute gestures toward the sublime, at the expense of suppressing the "unacceptable" slums.) Opposed to the world of the sensory and concrete, of what Susan Stewart calls "the bourgeois idealization of the concrete as the real,"[5] the urban sublime records urban experience in its ambiguity, its narcissism, its negativity and, finally, its strength. Its vocabulary invokes terror and vastness; it sinks them into the theater of urban spectacles and the labyrinths of urban streets, which then evoke reflections upon subjectivity. Here the urban sublime revolves to validate those massive natural figures that initially helped to authorize it. If such scandals give rise to the sublime, the sublime contains the scandalous.

Nineteenth-century accounts of the city record a fascination with its objects, its phenomena, whatever is present to the sight, the sense that determines other sensory experiences. Surfaces and appearances are privileged, although they must be related one to another, arranged, charted, categorized. The casual art of the walker in urban streets conceals the method of the botanizer. The proliferating natural metaphors serve also as modes of control: to categorize the city as a natural phenomenon is to claim that it has an accessible natural history. Similarly, urban sketches, whether journalistic or fictional, present objects and activities in a kind of verbal museum. Although the transient—spatially speaking, trains and omnibuses; temporally speaking, the vanishing types and professions of the city—is one component, another is the permanent, the types that persist and address themselves to straightforward description. What was for Lukács a form of reification in which the described objects of a bourgeois culture signify its political stasis,[6] becomes, in the sketch, the sign of an attempt to grasp and fix an all-too-complex phenomenal world. Such a compartmentalization, a response to flux, can give rise to its own distortions or phantasmagorias. Sala's *Twice Round the Clock*, with its two dozen typical scenes and activities, for every hour of the day and night, implies an eternal recurrence of the same. The utterly banal

---

5. Susan Stewart, *On Longing* (Baltimore: Johns Hopkins University Press, 1984), 174.
6. See Georg Lukács, "Narrate or Describe?" in *Writer and Critic and other essays*, ed. and trans. Arthur Kahn (London: Merlin, 1970). 110–48.

and demystified, a quasi-sociological guidebook to the city, becomes the other, the exergue, to a more uncanny "unthought" that is suppressed by the commonplace. Repetition can be merely banal, or it can be uncanny. The urban sketches stand at some threshold with a double vision.

Walter Benjamin observes that objects are not transparent, that one does not see through them to some kind of meaning. On the contrary, they reveal their true natures only when they are wrested from their original, encrusted contexts and placed in some new order by the collector or the critic.[7] One comprehends the city through its transient objects or its detritus. If the repositioning of objects constitutes a mode of historical critique for Benjamin, for the urban writer it affords a step toward metaphor and eventually narrative. This study starts with the sketch and its penchant for the catalogue, its attempt to seize and record the ephemera of daily existence. It ends with the representation of urban London's "dust" heaps, those piles of debris that contain treasures and at the same time level or homogenize and obscure the landscape. In between, errant metaphors transport the object life of London and chart the connections between high life and low life or transpose the life of phenomena into the life of signs. The collector, like the archaeologist or the entrepreneur of the dust heaps, plays a role commensurate with that of the artist of the city, whose objects take their places in some revealing metaphorical order. If Dickens's vision in *Our Mutual Friend* is eschatological, intimating the apocalypse of capitalism, it is also, at some intermediate level, a vision of the life and death of objects. Like the stuff of fables, his characters often confuse object and person, whether in the river or the dust heap or the "articulation" shop.

What is errancy in the sketches, a relatively benign process of visually charting the city or of metaphorical transformation, develops into scandal in the slum novels. The process is nascent in some of the slum sketches, in which the narrators/writers are in effect "slumming," situating their responses somewhere along the spectrum from curiosity to sympathy but substituting their words for the inarticulateness of the slum-dwellers. The double scandal of the slum novels lies in the crossing of class lines on the one hand,[8] and the appropriation

---

7. Walter Benjamin, *Das Passagen-Werk*, in *Gessamelten Schriften*, vols. 1 and 2, ed. Rolf Tiedemann (Frankfurt am Main: Suhrkamp, 1982). See the discussion in David Frisby, *Fragments of Modernity* (Cambridge: MIT Press, 1986), 226.

8. Cf. Fredric Jameson, *The Political Unconscious* (Ithaca: Cornell University Press, 1981).

of slum lives into the trajectories of narrative on the other. What the slum novels encode is a fundamental antagonism between the forging of connections in narrative (which cannot escape ideological tincture) and the repetition of the ordinary and the typical (which resists the imposition of a form that can only distort them).

While the plan here is roughly historical, insofar as it proceeds from earlier to later, from the material problems of the slums to more elusive and less immediately visible problems of the city, from problems of class and economy to those of bourgeois culture, this is not the determining structure. In fact, the treatment of urban sketches, in which the fictional and the journalistic are organized around problems of representation and ideology in a somewhat chiastic manner, should suggest that the central problems of representation are not those contained within a historical schema. To say that the city progresses from a material to a functional structure for which corresponding modes of representation develop is to subscribe to a largely mimetic model. Yet it is precisely this model that the first two chapters call into question, first by their recognition of the formative roles of ideology and figurative language, neither of which allows "urban reality" to take the upper hand; and second, by focusing on the quest for the real. The weak form of the quest is one in which language tries to approximate the referent. In the strong form, language seeks to identify the referent and cannot therefore be shaped by it; if anything, it creates the referent as it goes along. The most obvious example is the way in which passion comes to be situated in the slums, whether love in *Thyrza* or class war in *Demos* or the familial-political in *A Child of the Jago*, whose women fuse the revolutionary with the sexual in their violent territorial conflicts. What this suggests in turn is that the city is not an inert mass awaiting verbal articulation; it is both the dream of its artist and an enigmatic structure that requires some form of engagement.

To thematize the quest for the referent, to make the slums symbolic of some bedrock reality, is to subject them to the contrivances of fiction. Plot and quest then stand opposed to the unnarratable incidents and trivia of slum life. It is a commonplace to claim that the effect of the real is a function of the unmotivated, unaccommodated detail. Under such circumstances, no narrative can ever fully serve the real. It is at this point that we may rethink the role of the detail or the shock of the moment (and the connections between these two) and suggest that they represent the "real" not by sheer irrelevancy but

by interruption, by making the fictive and ideological nature of narrative all the more evident. For Gissing, the details of slum life need
to be wrested from their quotidian contexts so that they appear in
darkness, contextless. Like the music of the slum, they need to be
placed under the scrutiny of the artist, only to be refigured in tension
with a narrative line. It is easy to normalize the typical, but this is to
divest it of meaning. The wilder, more powerful symbolizing processes
generated by such scenes as the Saturday-night markets both reveal
and legitimate them.

Many early nineteenth-century constructions of the city divide it
between the poles of high life and low life. While the division invites
a theatrical approach (if not caricature), it also highlights a certain
aspect of urban writing. What can be seen is visible from the perspective of a bourgeois class that is unwilling itself to be seen; the
alterity of the slums finds a counterpart in the alterity of high life, and
the two in turn exclude the bourgeois. In that important subgenre of
the novels of high life, the dandy novels, the hidden connections
between the dandies and the underworld are frequently brought into
the light. The dandies are also the figures who bring being seen to
the edge of abstraction: the cultivation of self, the refinement of fashion
and style, engenders a mode of hyperbole that eventually cancels the
very world it pretends to enhance. The recurrence of the word "sublime," therefore, gestures to a conventional sublime scenario even as
it parodies it. In this study, the sublime leaves its conventional natural
contexts and enters the city by way of the implicitly parodic, eventually
to inhabit a more distinctive urban mode that will be the concern of
the last chapter. The body of the dandy, or the dandies as a body,
therefore, occupy another scandalous site that crosses high and low,
aristocrat and criminal, the private and the political. The heroism that
Baudelaire attributes to him, at least in part a resistance to ennui, may
be read as a last stand against the leveling of experience by the
bourgeoisie. If sensationalism was to be a later answer to the threat
of boredom, dandyism is an earlier avatar. The artist of the city, oc-
cupying the space ceded to him by the bourgeois, projects these scandalous pairings that only seem possible in the hyperbolic figure of the
dandy.

Chapter 4 focuses upon the abandonment of a visual model in the
quest for the city. Ironically, it is at this point that social history and
text seem most complicit, even conspiratorial, insofar as thematics
and fictional methods are virtually inseparable. In the novels con-

cerned with the late nineteenth-century city, the quest for a material referent revolves into the acceptance of ambiguity on the one hand, and of spectacle on the other: instead of being analogous to urban experience, theater or carnival plays a constitutive role. As high life ostensibly foregrounds surfaces, so does bourgeois life, but only, paradoxically, to mark the crucial role of the unseen, the scandals and secrets that constitute the very stuff of urban life. Visual emptiness—the poverty of surfaces—becomes the condition for an ironic re-vision of the hiddenness and functionalism of the city. Here the privileged figure is advertising, which emphasizes the visible only to insist upon its image-making, signifying function. The abstraction of advertising follows the logic of the spectacle, which seems to celebrate life (especially its visual aspects) but which in reality negates it by valorizing the image and the passive acceptance it demands of the viewer.[9] The overturning of social hierarchy, one of the ends of carnival, slips here into the sinister social leveling of the spectacle.

Because city life is prone to adopt inauthentic forms, urban character tends accordingly to appear in modes of negative figuration. The rhetoric of indeterminacy and of displacement, as well as a focus that blurs the margins between self and scene, makes urban character into a virtual oxymoron, an impossible figuring of the figures that inhabit every text. " 'She's nothing,' " declares the servant Affery of Little Dorrit, situating herself at the threshold between plot and theory.

Traditionally, it is nature that evokes a sublime experience, not the city: an urban sublime seems to be a contradiction in terms, a theoretical scandal. The fall in value of the visual, however, together with the importing of a sublime lexicon into city matters, situates the sublime in urban texts. The experience of the vast, the obscure, and the terrible, so endemic in the city, occasions self-distancing as well as the estrangement of the object-world. From its central squares to its dust heaps, the city becomes a scene of writing whose mysteries empower the metaphorical freedom of the urban artist. Yet the urban sublime is unstable. Like Benjamin's aura, which fades with the advent of modernity, urban writing often records a moment of experience that can be known only as it vanishes. Writing about the city transforms the seen into the scene, sight into site, the visual into the verbal, the spatial into the temporal. Like photography, it is prone to conceal its

9. Cf. Guy Debord, *Society of the Spectacle* (Detroit: Black and Red, 1970; repr. 1977 and 1983).

art: it insists upon its veracity, its ability to uncover hidden relations, but it retains its right to casual observation and errancy. Urban representation emerges as a site on which politics and aesthetics meet, on which errancy and indirection figure the forms of the polis.

In the essay referred to earlier, Georg Lukács poises the forward direction of the narrative of social change against the commitment to things as they are that informs sheer description. From this perspective, description or reification is a minimal and suspect form of representation. The catalogue is so frequent a tool in the urban sketches because it purports to deliver the raw materials of the city. Its resistance to narrative, however, opens the way for an insurgent metaphorical economy: not the totalizing metaphors that hold the city in some kind of stasis, but rather errant figures that chart the urban landscape. But if metaphors unseat the false stabilities of description and display its ideologies, they require other strategies to initiate narrative. Urban representation dallies with objects, images, and metaphors, eventually to break the surface and call up narrative from some temporal depth. The problematic of urban representation must be played out within the labyrinthine vicissitudes of narrative. The fate of narrative is intertwined with the fortunes of the city. To recognize this is to transform scandal itself into cause for celebration in an urban art.

1

Nineteenth-Century Urban Sketches: Thresholds to Fiction

*W*riting about the city, especially since 1800, has been as heterogeneous as the city itself. On the one hand, an urban space offers itself to the observer's gaze: that space is replete with objects, houses, crowds, vehicles, types of people, monuments of culture. Beyond the visible hover the abstractions—among them profession, disease, poverty, wealth—that constitute the urban ambiance. The presence of the material world, striking in daylight, may solicit attention even more in a nocturnal atmosphere, when those phenomena may also be veiled. On the other hand, the city is the site of the encounter between mind and world. Engagement with the city involves an act of reading or of "re-presentation," even when the gaze is directed outward.[1] The city can be the locus for an act of self-recognition,

1. See Steven Marcus, "Reading the Illegible," in *The Victorian City: Images and Realities*,

as in Wordsworth's well-known encounter with the blind Beggar in *The Prelude*, or as in James's *The Princess Casamassima*, where London and Paris are most prominent because of the conflicting cultural claims they exert upon the mind of Hyacinth Robinson during his quest for identity.

Urban sketches share this heterogeneity. They include both the polemical outcry against urban misery and the more dispassionate, sociologically oriented journalism (of Mayhew, for example). Intersecting this plane of social orientation are the sketches apparently meant for entertainment, the products of a curious flâneur or wanderer about the city, the journalistic work of Sala or the more imaginative pieces of Dickens. These are not two utterly distinct traditions. Each impinges upon the other: the image of society is apt to be a rhetorical product, shaped by the demands of language and form. Conversely, the fictional sketch is not immune to claims that it represents the actual city, that it reveals hidden or unknown aspects of the urban milieu, or that it expresses a particular ideology. The sketch offers a formal or thematic ground, as much as a historical or cultural one, for the encounter with the city. Its concern with particularity or locale memorializes an urban scene or scenario. But its very form tends to make its space abstract or conceptual. In Foucault, an "operating table" is both a real table and a "*tabula*, that enables thought to operate upon the entities of our world . . . the table upon which, since the beginning of time, language has intersected space."[2] Just so the sketch, as the space for representing the experience of the city, looks toward both the concrete and the conceptual. The urban sketch is at once the locus of memory and the attempt to fix objects and events in the memory. It is the site of the picturesque and the ground for social outcry; it is the place of illusion and the loss of illusion. It marks the mysterious, unknown, and even uncanny aspects of the city, and yet it reassures by externalizing one's anxieties about the city; it evokes a world of bourgeois materialism, although it gives free play to the imagination.[3] It prefigures the novel, and yet its relation to the novel is characterized by

ed. H. J. Dyos and Michael Wolff, 2 vols. (London: Routledge and Kegan Paul, 1973) 1:257–76; and Philip Fisher, "City Matters: City Minds," in *The Worlds of Victorian Fiction*, ed. Jerome H. Buckley, *Harvard English Studies* 6 (Cambridge: Harvard University Press, 1975), 371–89.

2. Michel Foucault, *The Order of Things* (London: Tavistock, 1970), xvii.

3. Cf. Walter Benjamin's *Charles Baudelaire: A Lyric Poet in the Era of High Capitalism*, trans. Harry Zohn (London: New Left Books, 1973), for a discussion of similar functions of the physiologies in nineteenth-century Paris.

displacement; as the materials of the sketch enter the larger world of the novel, for example, they often become peripheral. More generally, the sketch offers figures for narrativity itself, texts in which the artist inscribes himself and appropriates the city. Any such exchange, however, must be predicated upon a form of representation. It is in this area that the most basic problem of the sketch emerges.

I

Straightforward mimetic models for representing the city are in bad repute these days, and, as we shall see, there is good reason for considering nonfictional sketches as suspect as fictional sketches. As J. Hillis Miller has shown, if mimesis survives at all in Dickens's *Sketches by Boz*, it is only as imitation of what is itself inauthentic, so that "society" is not real but rather a series of repetitions of forms of behavior, dress, and even "lives" that are always based on prior models that are fictive or conventional rather than historically grounded.[4] The city becomes, from this perspective, a text. The problematic for the writer then shifts: instead of rendering the materiality, the object-ness, the resistance of the city, the writer must read the signs, metaphors, representations-as-maps that the city offers. If it is strange or different, it is not because it contains new or unknown aspects of reality but because it is in a continual process of representing itself. Reading the city-as-text might put one in touch with the material reality of the city—though there is some question whether this is even a desideratum for such an approach—but it is just as likely to involve one in a continual reading of signs that would never bring one to the true city, the "true" point of origin. There is still another possibility, one which would involve a passage through mimesis, where the material objects, the "flora and fauna" of the city, can be described, but must then be interpreted in terms which are in some way nonmaterial or transcendent.[5] Whatever the representa-

4. J. Hillis Miller, "The Fiction of Realism: Sketches by Boz, Oliver Twist, and Cruikshank's Illustrations, " in *Dickens Centennial Essays*, ed. Ada Nisbet and Blake Nevius (Berkeley: University of California Press, 1971), 85–153. Miller's essay is seminal reading in this area, and this chapter is indebted to it at several points.

5. Cf. Peter Brooks, "Romantic Antipastoral and Urban Allegories," *Yale Review*, n.s. 64 (1974): 11–26.

tional strategy, it must be concerned with the choice of language. This precedes the additional problem of rendering the city culturally intelligible.

We can approach this problem of representation by examining a series of texts about London's slums. One way of regarding writing about the city has been to divide it into two traditions: (1) serious description, especially of the poor and the slums, and (2) low-life writing, which originated considerably before the nineteenth century and which appears in such works as Pierce Egan's *Life in London* (1821) as well as in a number of books by such writers as G. H. A. Sala.[6] The phrase "serious description" implies a high degree of representational accuracy, a subordination of the writer to the materials he must render in words. The low-life tradition, intended to entertain, allows more verbal freedom. Such a division depends in part upon motivation; the rhetorical differences are not so clearly antithetical. That the material conditions of the poor beg to be recognized is also of some relevance.

P. J. Keating applies the term "social explorers" to the writers who investigated England's slums. Many of the documents they produced focus on London.[7] For those who lived outside the slums, especially those of the East End, the slums were unknown territory, their inhabitants cast out from civilization. Andrew Mearns's *The Bitter Cry of Outcast London*, a pamphlet published in 1883, describes the conditions of the poor:

> Every room in these rotten and reeking tenements houses a family, often two. In one cellar a sanitary inspector reports finding a father, mother, three children, and four pigs! In another room a missionary found a man ill with small-pox, his wife just recovering from her eighth confinement, and the children running about half-naked and covered with dirt. Here are seven people living in one underground kitchen and a little dead child lying in the same room. Elsewhere is a poor widow, her three children, and a child who had been dead thirteen days. Her husband, who was a cabman, had shortly before committed suicide. Here lives a widow and her six children,

6. See Eileen Yeo, "Mayhew as a Social Investigator," in *The Unknown Mayhew*, ed. E. P. Thompson and Eileen Yeo (London: Merlin, 1971), 66–68, for this view of the tradition.

7. *Into Unknown England, 1866–1913: Selections from the Social Explorers*, ed. P. J. Keating (London: Fontana, 1976).

including one daughter of 29, another of 21, and a son of 27. Another apartment contains father, mother and six children, two of whom are ill with scarlet fever. In another nine brothers and sisters, from 29 years of age downwards, live, eat and sleep together. Here is a mother who turns her children into the street in the early evening because she lets her room for immoral purposes until long after midnight, when the poor little wretches creep back again if they have not found some miserable shelter elsewhere. Where there are beds they are simply heaps of dirty rags, shavings or straw, but for the most part these miserable beings find rest only upon the filthy boards. The tenant of this room is a widow who herself occupies the only bed, and lets the floor to a married couple for 2s 6d per week. In many cases matters are made worse by the unhealthy occupations followed by those who dwell in these habitations. Here you are choked as you enter by the air laden with particles of the superfluous fur pulled from the skins of rabbits, rats, dogs and other animals in their preparation for the furrier. Here the smell of paste and of drying match-boxes, mingling with other sickly odours, overpowers you; or it may be the fragrance of stale fish or vegetables, not sold on the previous day, and kept in the room overnight. Even when it is possible to do so the people seldom open their windows, but if they did it is questionable whether much would be gained for the external air is scarcely less heavily charged with poison than the atmosphere within.[8]

A passage like this one presents its appalling items straightforwardly enough. The catalogue amasses its representative horrors, not overvisual in its detail, but strongly anchored to the visual and the present by the localizing repetition of "here." The judgmental words are few, and of a similar cast: "miserable," "immoral," "poison." In fact, their proximity to such terms as "unhealthy" and "sickly" (metaphors following words denoting actual sickness) suggests that judgment and fact are closely interrelated. Moral and physical pestilence become virtually indistinguishable; even description may be understood within the framing metaphors of corruption, health, and exploration. The

---

8. Andrew Mearns, *The Bitter Cry of Outcast London*, (1883), repr. in *Into Unknown England*, 95–96.

new-found lands of urban explorers often belie their discoverers' expectations.

The image of travel and exploration of the city has both cultural and literary antecedents, although the interpretive possibilities vary. Sidonia's advice to Coningsby to travel not to the ancient world but to Manchester places that city among the wonders of the world.[9] Wilderness and sea as metaphors for the city are more ambiguous (they appear in Balzac) insofar as they are outside the pale of moral civilization.[10] But when a part of the city, a part that is literally adjacent to the world of the explorers, becomes the unknown, there are even more serious implications. Thus in *The Bitter Cry of Outcast London* Andrew Mearns writes that "the churches are making the discovery that seething in the very centre of our great cities, concealed by the thinnest crust of civilization and decency, is a vast mass of moral corruption, of heart-breaking misery and absolute godlessness, and that scarcely anything has been done to take into this awful slough the only influences that can purify or remove it" (92). The heart of darkness lies not in the Congo, but in London. Yet there is a "gulf" between the lowest classes and civilization, and a "TERRIBLE FLOOD OF SIN AND MISERY" threatens to engulf those who are on the side of decency and civilization and religion (92). Such figures are enabling: they mark the space of exploration in a new way and suggest an altered focus. If, in addition, urban objects do signify beyond their materiality, Mearns provides the allegorical figure that will interpret the scenes of misery he describes. An urban pilgrim, he comes upon the Slough of Despond. The flood, a literary as well as a biblical figure of engulfment, threatens to destroy the city. Mearns reveals his interpretive strategy at the beginning of the pamphlet: it moves any perspective on the city beyond the visual. And it is the visual that Mearns finds difficult to convey. What might be a gentler mode of expression in other contexts becomes a comment on the inadequacy of representation: "The misery and sin caused by drink in these districts have often been told, but these horrors can never be set forth either by pen

---

9. Benjamin Disraeli, *Coningsby* (New York: Century, 1904), 107.

10. The following passages are representative: "But Paris is an ocean. Throw in the plummet, you will never reach bottom"(37). "Paris, you see, is like a forest in the New World where a score of savage tribes, the Illinois, the Hurons, struggle for existence: each group lives on what it can get by hunting throughout society"(133). Honoré de Balzac, *Old Goriot*, trans. Marion Aytoun Crawford (Baltimore: Penguin, 1969).

or artist's pencil" (98).[11] The reader may be shocked by all these instances he names; nevertheless, Mearns has "sketched only in faintest outline." Truth requires, paradoxically, the artistic heightening that the writer cannot supply: "Far more vivid must be our colours, deeper and darker far the shades, if we are to present a truth picture of 'Outcast London'; and so far as we have been able to go we are prepared with evidence, not only to prove every statement, but to show that these statements represent the general conditions of thousands upon thousands in this metropolis" (105). The writer's predicament is analogous to that of the workers in the slums, where "the misery they actually see suggests to them the certain existence of so much more which no human eye discovers" (102). Such metonymies stand in danger of being overwhelmed by the untold horrors they signify, as those horrors threaten to overwhelm workers and writer alike; all three become mediating figures for the deluge that threatens civilization itself. These bleak allegories are limiting and demonic instances of an urban sublime.

In this precarious situation, language stands outside the series of the deluge: released from the constraints of mimesis, or of metonymy, it is a bulwark against the flood. Allegory is as much a defensive strategy as it is a signifying one. Mearns finds that he can describe the "human rookeries," the "lower depths" to readers who have no prior conceptions of such misery only by approaching the horrors through other forms of figurative language. Slum conditions are worse than the lair of a wild animal, more like "the middle passage of the slave ship" (94). Language itself can only be a form of displacement. "What goes by the name of a window" has no adequate signifier in civilized discourse. If "putrifying carcasses of dead cats or birds" can be named, the "viler abominations" that surpass them are blanketed in abstraction. Paratactical phrasing emphasizes the ubiquity of filth: "it is exuding through cracks in the boards overhead; it is running down the walls; it is everywhere" (95). The "sickly air" is the prelude to a grim fantasy: "The buildings are in such miserable repair as to

11. One might call this the convention of the indescribable, through which whatever offends or horrifies may be signified but neither named nor described. Dickens and other novelists, as well as the writers of nonfiction, employ it. But while it may authenticate their claims not to step outside the bounds of civilized discourse, no matter how uncivilized the subject, it may also place that subject beyond the limits of representational language. For a different perspective on this problem, see Steven Marcus, "Reading the Illegible," 265. Marcus finds a "saving function" in language that "refuse[s] to domesticate these actualities with syntax and imagery."

suggest the thought that if the wind could only reach them they would soon be toppling about the heads of their occupants" (95). Rhetorical strategies like these allow Mearns to present the "facts," which compose a "revolting spectacle," a "ghastly reality" that transcends any meretricious drama that "spectacle" might imply.[12] In fact, many of the essays of the social explorers stress the necessity for spectators, for the lives of the poor must be seen, indeed confronted, as appalling spectacles. But Mearns's writing suggests a puzzling inference: the language of representation can only exist in oblique relation to that which it represents; that very obliquity, however, enables Mearns to find meaning in the visual, to escape an apparent impasse. Thus Mearns ends by denying the primacy of ocular vision in favor of a vision of God. One's eyes can convince one that there is nothing illusory about the condition of the poor. But since such sights can only be signs of a more general situation, the imagination must reach out as the heart must be moved. This is a step toward the still-higher vision of a compassionate God.

Thus Mearns's progress through the slums is framed by the threat of apocalypse on the one hand and the reassuring vision of God on the other. This vision of sin, not atypically, blames slumlords, drink, and poverty itself, even though from a contemporary perspective, temperance and religion will seem like somewhat naive and even indirect solutions. (Only one passage in *The Bitter Cry of Outcast London* mentions the need for the state to institute reforms.) Indeed, there is a paradoxical thrust to Mearns's pamphlet. On the one hand, it attempts to make accessible, for purposes of social reform, what is vile and unknown, and it does so in ways that may shock but not alienate the nineteenth-century reader. On the other hand, the metaphorical frame that displaces the visual has some startling implications. The distinction between "civilization" and "slough" or "wild animal's lair" or "middle passage of a slave-ship," is double-edged. Instead of focusing on a common humanity, it seems rather to emphasize the division between civilization and savagery, "we" and "they."[13] Reform

12. "We shall not wonder if some, shuddering at the revolting spectacle, try to persuade ourselves that such things cannot be in Christian England, and that what they have looked upon is some dark vision conjured by a morbid pity and a responding faith. To such we can only say, Will you venture to come with us and see for yourselves the ghastly reality?"(111).

13. The fact—and the irony—of a common humanity is, however, a concern of other social explorers. Mearns's own pity and horror at the plight of the poor are apparent, though they should not cancel out the implications of his choice of language.

may be tantamount to "purification" or "conversion." It appears, there-fore, that the savages may be rescued only into the very system that "produced" them. There is no interrogation of the premises of that civilized system. If the initial image of Mearns suggested something like a volcano, "seething" beneath the "thinnest crust of civilization," and raised the possibility of revolution, that possibility has been avoided by an alternative metaphor.[14]

Even the most factual representation of the city—and there are many essays like Mearns's on outcast London—is apt to be embedded in an ideology. That it should often be Christian should not be surpris-ing.[15] Social reform is conceived of in the context of religious re-sponsibility, that is, of rescuing the heathen. Because, however, the language of such reforming tracts distributes sin indifferently among the poor and, say, their landlords, or among gin and its imbibers, it becomes that much more difficult to identify, in order to eradicate, the evils of the East End. If "Babylon" was so widespread as to be virtually a dead metaphor for London, it was also a blanket metaphor. Yet Mearns's confession that language is inadequate to describe what he has seen could be a sign of a different cultural predicament. There is the concern for the sensibilities of readers who have no prior ac-quaintance with the dark vision of the slums, thus the attempt to cross boundaries gradually in order to allow for a type of recognition that violence could only thwart. But to cross boundaries gradually can be reduced to a variant of extending the bounds of civilization; there seems to be an underlying desire for cultural preservation, a desire to show the adequacy of traditional ways of thinking about society. Reform goes hand in hand with charity; in both enterprises, Christian sympathy can recognize proximity and at the same time preserve a certain distance.

A similar admixture of horror and conservatism appears in the lan-guage of a classic piece of occasional journalism by James Green-wood, "A Night in a Workhouse."[16] Greenwood has himself admitted to the Lambeth workhouse one wintry night in the guise of a pauper

14. The image of the volcano had been linked with the idea of social upheaval earlier in the century. See, for example, G. M. Matthews, "A Volcano's Voice in Shelley," *ELH*, 24 (1957): 191–228.

15. Two representative pamphlets are Thomas Beames's *The Rookeries of London*, 1850 (repr. Cass, 1970); and Bishop Roden Noel's *The Spiritual State of the Metropolis*, 1836.

16. James Greenwood, "A Night in a Workhouse" (1866), repr. in *Into Unknown England*, 33–54.

come to seek a night's shelter. His identity is known neither to the staff nor to the paupers. Greenwood observes himself along with the paupers: he must eat the meager food and spend the night on a mattress in an unheated shelter that is not entirely closed in. But his language places him at a more distanced point of judgment: the inmates are divided into the "decent poor" and the "blackguards." Those who will not turn the wheel in the morning to mill flour in return for their food and lodging are condemned as "lazy." There are, in addition, "unnamed horrors" that he cannot mention to his middle-class readers. Nevertheless, two "quiet elderly gentlemen" are received back into thinking humanity by virtue of their discussion on "the merits of the English language" (52). Yet Greenwood is as sensitive as Mearns to "outcast humanity," here "lying around you like covered corpses in a railway shed." His catalogue of the coughs he hears while he lies on his mattress can surely be read as an ironic commentary on the finer urban discriminations.[17]

Greenwood's account of his experience relies upon an order of fact, but at the same time that experience becomes meaningful in the light of conventional attitudes. The division into good and evil is less absolute than socially determined. Greenwood's terms invite a Nietzschean reading.[18] (It is possible to claim, for example, that society owes its paupers food and shelter, rather than that the paupers must pay for them with their own labor; ironically, the term "outcast" places the paupers in the position of victims.) It is Greenwood who makes certain acts and language unnameable except in the category of the unnameable: "I have avoided the detail of horrors infinitely more revolting than anything that appears in these papers" (54). By making the world of the outcast unspeakable, or by "speaking" it in certain figures, Greenwood affirms the very distance that he intends to diminish. The possibility arises, then, that figurative language in nonfictional contexts functions as a strategy of displacement. The language that ought to convey the concrete or to affirm the real becomes locked into a social contract. Perhaps no forms of language can neu-

17. "[As] for the coughing, to lie on the flagstones in what was nothing better than an open shed, and listen to that, hour after hour, chilled one's very heart with pity. Every variety of cough that I ever heard was to be heard there: the hollow cough; the short cough; the hysterical cough; the bark that comes at regular intervals, like the quarter-chime of a clock, as if to mark off the progress of decay; coughing from vast hollow chests, coughing from little narrow ones—now one, now another, now two or three together" (45–46).

18. See Friedrich Nietzsche, On The Genealogy of Morals, trans. Walter Kaufmann and R. J. Hollingdale (New York: Vintage, 1966).

trally represent a world that contains the other, as object of exploration. But the tendency to exclude ("I had seen the show—gladly I
escaped into the open streets") or to divide (into missionaries and
heathens, for example), or to employ terms that have an unexpected
ironic resonance ("outcast" London) results in a paradox within the
very figures of social exploration. The word "outcast," for example,
is extremely appropriate for a group that is barred from the benefits
of nineteenth-century "progress"; those who use it demand that society
take responsibility for those who are cast out, but not for having cast
them out. Society is blind to the process by which it creates its victims.
Moving forward into the unknown results in an impasse: the reader
confronts limiting choices. He may (1) imagine the unnamed horrors
of the slums, (2) accept the report on trust without necessarily imagining greater horrors, or (3) meditate on the necessary gap between
language and representation. It is not only within a mode of linear
argument, one that allows for "pure" motives and uncomplicated reforms, that such problems arise. What the novels and sketches attest
to is the complexity and ambivalence of societal self-knowledge on
the one hand, and of knowledge of society on the other. It is because
of this that allegorical or quasi-allegorical models for urban representation in the nineteenth century often seem both powerful and
inadequate or defensive at the same time.

One might argue that reforming intentions, simply because they
point to action, would always demand an interpretive stance toward
the city in order to make it intelligible. An attempt merely to exhibit
the city might bring us closer to pure representation. A sketch of the
notorious rookery or slum of St. Giles, by George Henry Augustus Sala,
belongs in this category. A number of Sala's books—*Twice Round the
Clock*, *Gaslight and Daylight*, *London Up to Date*—intend ostensibly
to record London life. On the surface, Sala's exploratory stance is less
selective and more rudimentary. He does not need to explore because
he is assailed by the sights, sounds, and objects of St. Giles:

> Where the long lane from St. Giles's to the Strand divides the
> many-branching slums; where flares the gas over coarse scraps
> of meat in cheap butchers' shops; where brokers pile up motley
> heaps of second-hand wares—from fishing-rods and bird-
> cages to flat-irons and blankets; from cornet-a-pistons and
> 'Family Encyclopaedias' to corkscrews and fowling-pieces;
> where linen-drapers are invaded by poorly-clad women and

girls, demanding penn'orths of needles, ha'porths of buttons, and farthing-worths of thread; where jean stays flap against door jamps, and 'men's stout hose' gleam gaunt in the shop-windows; where grimy dames sit in coal and potato-sheds, and Jew clothesmen wrestle for the custom of passengers who don't want to buy anything; where little dens, with reminders of à-la-mode beef and hot eel soup, offer suppers, cheap and nasty to the poor in pocket; where, in low coffee-shops, newspapers a fortnight old, with coffee-cup rings on them, suggest an intellectual pabulum, combined with bodily refreshment; where gaping public-houses receive or disgorge their crowds of tattered topers; where 'general shops' are packed to overflowing with heterogenous odds and ends—soap, candles, Bath brick, tobacco, Dutch cheese, red herrings, firewood, black lead, streaky bacon, brown sugar, birch brooms, lucifer matches, tops, marbles, hoops, brandy balls, pockets of cocoa, steel pens, cheap periodicals, Everton toffy, and penny canes; where on each side, peeping down each narrow thoroughfare, you see a repetition only of these scenes of poverty and misery; where you have to elbow and jostle your way through a teeming, ragged, ill-favoured, shrieking, fighting population—by oyster-stalls and costermongers' barrows—by orange-women and organ-grinders—by flower-girls and match-sellers—by hulking labourers and brandy-faced viragos, squabbling at tavern-doors—by innumerable children in every phase of weazened, hungry, semi-nakedness, who pullulate at every corner, and seem cast up on the pavement like pebbles on the sea-shore. Here, at last, we find the hostelry of the three golden balls, where the capitalist, whom men familiarly term 'my uncle,' lends money.[19]

Syntactic structure virtually recedes before the onslaught of language in this passage. There is, to be sure, some structure: the broader catalogue has its subdivisions, as the supper-dens, coffee shops, and public houses, each with its separate list of characteristics. Or, there are the antitheses, somewhat spurious in this context, of the oyster-stalls and costermongers' barrows, orange-women and organ-grinders.

19. George Henry Augustus Sala, *Twice Round the Clock; or the Hours of the Day And Night in London* (London: Houlston and Wright, 1859), 264–66.

All phrases are subordinate to "where," which offers only a temporary closure to the sheer crowdedness of the scene; that "where" will be repeated in all the side streets. The real "closure," which can promise only a deferral of misery, lies in the pawnbroker's shop, that place to which, it is implied, all objects will go. The very structure of the passage makes the point for Sala: the catalogue, indiscriminately mingling people and objects, makes him passive, almost an object. He is, in fact, inundated with language. Words and objects are held in uneasy suspension, on the edge of linguistic and social chaos. What the passage points to, then, is the sheer difficulty of any pure representation of the city. Here the assumption is that the city is a collection of objects and rituals: the objects exist as spatial adjuncts to the activities, repeated nightly, of wrestling, demanding, squabbling, etc. This vision of the surface is itself a dubious key to adequate representation; to assume that each object and each action must be represented by a specific word is to put oneself in the power of an endless cascade of language. Even if one were to posit some sort of closure by the representation of a segment of the city, more or less homogeneous and ordered, there remains the possibility of a continuing series of segments, limited only by the totality of objects and actions, of further conceivable series, in the city itself. (Mayhew's massive *London Labour and the London Poor* projects the length of such representation-by-segment, especially if one adds, to the descriptions of each class of worker in those four volumes, the additional essays by Mayhew on the life of the poor.)[20] A completed project in these terms is, of course, inconceivable. We might, therefore, seek another motivation for such a complex catalogue. One possibility is that the catalogue represents the sheer heterogeneity of the raw materials that the writer must then order.[21] It becomes in this way a figure for representation itself. Catalogues, especially in prose, occupy a space between recording what exists and offering rudimentary figures for order. Yet Sala's catalogue suggests still another possibility. The lane along which Sala walks contains a type of life that is to be found in all the side streets; it thus stands in a metonymic relation to the area. It represents the repetition of the vitality as well as the forms of tension that are to be found in St. Giles. If children are like pebbles cast up by the tide, they will also

20. Henry Mayhew, *London Labour and the London Poor*, 4 vols. (1861; rpt. Cass, 1967); *The Unknown Mayhew* adds a selection of pieces Mayhew wrote for *The Morning Chronicle* in 1849 and 1850.
21. Cf. J. Hillis Miller, "The Fiction of Realism," 94.

be dragged by the tide to those side streets of repeated, though unseen, existence. Beyond the initial disorder, therefore, the passage makes the lane into a focal point for the slum life that surrounds it. Sala's own position is, however, a curious and self-effacing one, aside from the reference to having to "elbow and jostle." That phrase, along with the allusion to the tide, carries us back to the theme of inundation; it threatens the neutrality of the observer. No more than Greenwood or Mearns is he immune from some atmospheric contagion. Here the stakes involve autonomy and linguistic control: the writer is in danger of being displaced from the scene.

How, then, can one assert one's presence and control? One way is to invoke what is absent; Sala tries this method in a passage about third-class railway passengers:

> The seven o'clock trainbands are not exactly of the class who drink sherry and play cards; they are more given to selling walnuts than to eating them. They are, for the most part, hard-faced, hard-handed, poorly-clad creatures; men in patched, time-worn garments; women in pinched bonnets and coarse shawls, carrying a plenitude of baskets and bundles, but very slightly troubled with trunks or portmanteaus. You might count a hundred heads and not one hat-box; of two hundred crowding round the pay-place to purchase their third-class tickets for Manchester, or Liverpool, or even further north, you would have to look again, and perhaps vainly after all, for the possessor of a railway rug, or even an extra overcoat. Umbrellas, indeed, are somewhat plentiful; but they are not the slim, aristocratic trifles with ivory handles and varnished covers—enchanter's wands to ward off the spells of St. Swithin, which moustached dandies daintily insert between the roof and the hat-straps of first-class carriages. Third-class umbrellas are dubious in colour, frequently patched, bulgy in the body, broken in the ribs, once much given to absence from the nozzle. Swarming about the pay-place, which their parents are anxiously investing, thirteen-and-fourpence or sixteen-and-ninepence in hand, are crowds of third-class children. I am constrained to acknowledge that the majority of these juvenile travellers cannot be called handsome children, well-dressed children, even tolerably good-looking children. Poor little wan faces you see here, overshadowed by mis-shapen caps, and bonnets nine bauble

square; poor little thin hands, feebly clutching the scant gowns of their mothers; weazened little bodies, shrunken little limbs, distorted often by early hardship, by the penury which pounced on them—not in their cradles—they never had any—but in the baker's jacket in which they were wrapped when they were born, and which will keep by them, their only faithful friend, until they die, and are buried by the parish—poor ailing little children are these, and among them who shall tell how many hungry little bellies! Ah! judges of Amontillado sherry; crushers of walnuts with silver nut-crackers; connoisseurs who prefer French to Spanish olives, and are curious about the yellow seal; gay riders in padded chariots; proud cavaliers of blood-horses, you don't know how painfully and slowly, almost agonisingly, the poor have to scrape, and save, and deny themselves the necessaries of life, to gather together the penny-a-mile fare. (61–62)

This passage contains more figurative and rhetorical constructions than the previous one. The railway journey allows Sala to envisage the journey of life; the evocation of an absent upper class provides the contrasting elements for a rigid social system that closes out the possibility of another fate for the poor. The imagining of what is absent largely cancels out the depiction of the scene in merely picturesque terms, which would avoid questions of concealed meanings or of judgments. The social conscience of the railway passage, however sentimental, is prominent compared with the virtually parenthetical conscience in the description of St. Giles, where poverty and misery are items in a catalogue. Nevertheless, the dandies, with their characteristic material objects, belong more to the rhetorical antithesis of high life versus low life and thus preserve the mode of the picturesque; behind them lie the vaster exclusions of the class system. In the passage on the slum, Sala's world of surfaces, of plenitude become congestion, of a variety so intense that it is on the verge of collapsing back into sameness, disallows the dominance of any ideational system. The very materiality of the city blocks other forms of awareness in a moment of a strange urban antisublime. Like Greenwood, Sala has crossed a threshold into an unknown part of the city; but where Greenwood maintains his sense of identity by adhering to convention, Sala suspends overt interpretation: reduced to a figure elbowing his way through the crowd, he becomes, in some minimal way, his own double.[22]

Sala's description of St. Giles demonstrates the dangers and seductions of objectivity, as it leads the narrating consciousness close to self-effacement. But self-effacement can, in the end, be a figure of concealment that calls attention to itself. Even the nonfictional representation of the city, therefore, is likely to implicate the figure of a narrator who traverses the scene, more or less obscured. While it may be threatened, his stance is always privileged, in the simple sense that he possesses a mobility, a difference, a capacity to withdraw and enter at will. Thus the figures of disguise, the protean narrative personae, are appropriate for the urban artist. Sala, moreover, places himself in an explicit relation to fiction; *Twice Round the Clock* is dedicated to Augustus Mayhew, whose novel *Paved with Gold* incorporates episodes that are "picturesque but eminently faithful photographs of fact."[23] Some of those "photographs" had first appeared as Mayhew's contributions to his brother Henry's documentary *London Labour and the London Poor*. The descriptions of a rat fight; of the life of chimney sweeps, into whose society the protagonist enters for a time; of the watercress trade, a marginal occupation that becomes symbolic of the threshold between a life of crime and a life of honest poverty (crime becomes, on this scale, a limiting economic condition): all are incorporated nearly verbatim into the text of the novel.[24] Sala himself had connections with Dickens's circle, and in parts of his books he abandons the perspective of the journalist to adopt a more comic or fanciful mode that is apparently derived from the *Sketches by Boz*. Sala, who casts himself as Asmodeus, peering through the rooftops of London, assumes a persona that appears in a number of contemporaneous novels.[25] The writer thus places himself in a border zone between fiction and fact in which even the metaphor of the photograph is unstable, the camera eye complicit with an Asmodeus.

22. Cf. Walter Benjamin's discussion of Poe's "The Man of the Crowd" in "On Some Motifs in Baudelaire" in *Illuminations*, trans. Harry Zohn (New York: Schocken Books, 1969), 170–73. The "force" of the crowd in Sala, however, is virtually equated with the force of words.

23. *Twice Round the Clock*, vi.

24. Augustus Mayhew, *Paved with Gold, or The Romance and Reality of the London Streets* (London: Chapman and Hall, 1858; repr. Cass, 1971).

25. For a discussion of the use of Asmodeus figures in the nineteenth century, see Jonathan Arac, *Commissioned Spirits* (New Brunswick: Rutgers University Press, 1979). Tom Eaves in Thackeray's *Vanity Fair* is a kindred spirit.

In the sketches, the impetus toward narrative or fiction appears to be nearly irresistible. Some of James Grant's begging-letter writers in *Sketches of London* are master fiction-makers, protonovelists.[26] In other sketches in that book, the workhouse and the debtors' prisons turn into sites not only of biography but also of romance. All of these instances would support the familiar thesis that writers were finding in the city an ever-widening range of raw materials. In that urban setting the presumably superior claims of truth could accommodate themselves to the felicities of romance. Nevertheless, such work embodies a problematic that opposes the possibilities of narrative. The materiality of the city, especially as Sala conveys it in his sketches, comes close to a fixation upon objects. To represent the city in all its objectness could become an exercise in description, a survey of urban objects whose only meaning lies in their plenitude. There is no necessary connection between description and narrative, as Lukács argues so persuasively; it is the novelist's task to endow the object-world with some authentic human signification that in turn enables narrative to develop.[27] But to write truthfully about the city seems to entail a commitment to the visible, at whatever cost to narrative relevance, or to that which is most striking about the city: monuments, theaters, distinct professions. Thus the writer would be as much threatened by, as supported with, an endless progression of observed details, whether they appear as catalogues or as more sophisticated descriptions of street markets, slums, railway stations, lawyers. The street elevation, which appears in certain nineteenth-century documents, is from this perspective a more complex and abstract form of the catalogue or the outside view.[28] Significantly, it appears in early parts of the *Sketches by Boz* as an image for the external and proprietary interest in the city. Later it is transformed, in "Shops and their Tenants," into a metaphor for the imaginative history of the city. But this is to anticipate. In the various forms of the catalogue, the city is observed from a spatial and synchronic perspective. The urban carnival of objects and signs, to which the recurring descriptions of fairs and theaters in urban

26. James Grant, *Sketches in London* (London, 1840).

27. George Lukács, "Narrate or Describe?" in *Writer and Critic and Other Essays*, ed. and trans. Arthur Kahn (London: Merlin Press, 1970), 110–48.

28. See, for example *John Tallis's London Street Views, 1838–1840* (London: Nattali and Maurice, 1969). Each of Tallis's plates has a map, a view, and an elevation of a particular building or street. Because the prints are concerned mainly with commercial establishments, that aspect of middle-class London is dominant in the collection.

sketches testify, presents that challenge to narrative that Wordsworth anticipated in the seventh book of *The Prelude*, on his sojourn in London.

Despite his professed allegiance to an ideal that blends fact with romance, Sala stands on a threshold that resists his crossing. The passage on St. Giles reveals, we remember, a lack of discrimination not only in the catalogues, but in the absence of syntactical closure. As the figure who elbows his way through the crowd, Sala quite literally lacks the perspective that would enable him to organize his notations into more than a tableau. Lukács's comments on the novel oriented to description are applicable to Sala, for whom the "contemporaneity of description transforms the novel into a kaleidoscopic chaos."[29] But the alternative contained in the railway-station passage is only a shade more promising. There the interplay between presence and absence, the modified antithesis between high life and low life, and the allusion to narrativity, organize the chaotic matter of the city, present an ethical stance, and give meaning to the life of the crowd. Certain great Victorian paintings of crowds, including those of Frith, embody the principle that Sala is on the verge of actualizing, that of the individual destiny emerging from the undifferentiated mass.[30]

Yet the obstructions to narrative in Sala are equally great. One is the sheer dominance of convention. We can see this indirectly by a glance at one of the most popular texts of the nineteenth century, Pierce Egan's *Life in London*, first published in 1821. Egan's book recounts the adventures in London of the country cousin, Jerry, who comes to visit his city cousin, Tom. Although it has been called the archetypal urban novel of the early nineteenth century, the adventures are little more than excuses for the copious description of the language and rituals of high life and low life in London.[31] For example, a chapter on Almack's, that exclusive weekly assembly to which only the most favored received invitations from a committee of controlling matrons, is followed by one on All-Max, the site of a riotous gathering at the other end of town—and of the social scale. Entertaining as the book

---

29. "Narrate or Describe?" 133.

30. A number of Frith's paintings, among them "The Railway Station" and "Derby Day," imply this tension between the individual and the crowd. Jem Wilson's heroic rescue of his father and another worker from the burning factory in *Mary Barton* presents a fictional analogue, because Jem separates himself from the watching crowd and then, as if to underscore this process of individuation, emerges twice from the fire.

31. See P. J. Keating, *The Working Classes in Victorian Fiction* (New York: Barnes and Noble, 1971), 13.

was, and still is, its dominant structure is spatial. Its art excludes the middle: a middle line of narrative as well as the middle class. If every place evokes its opposite, or the present poor suggest the absent rich, then the city becomes a closed system. While the contrasts are not so stark, Sala's sketches imply a similar order. Despite its gesture toward temporality, even the "typical" narrative, exemplified in the life of the poor child, becomes part of that system. Thus the concern for representing the city in its various aspects, for finding some principle of order, for displaying the typical, can be as much a threat to fictionality as the apparently undifferentiated kaleidoscopic "presence" of the city. If any text on the city must inevitably move away from the neutral point of absolute imitation, then some directions might be less propitious for fiction than others. If conventions like the antithesis between high life and low life are to work, some different mode of representation is necessary.

II

While this brief survey of nonfictional sketches does not call into question their documentary intentions, it should be clear that even writing with the strongest referential motives and leanings finds a purely descriptive language impossible and slips inevitably toward figure. There are, of course, major consequences for an understanding of the novel, as the documents used to measure the novel's historical veracity or the fictional departures from history may now appear themselves to be displaced from absolute fact. Previously, one might have said that the description of Jacob's Island in *Oliver Twist*, measured against Mayhew's journalistic report on that notorious slum, or Dickens's description of Tom-all-Alone's in *Bleak House*, compared to a documentary rendering by Mearns or Sims or Booth of any East End slum, would make Dickens's rhetoric, now referentially anchored, seem less exaggerated.[32] The procedures for determining a level of rhetoric that distinguishes the novel from nonfiction still have some value, but one should also consider the alternative possibility of a

---

32. Mayhew's description was printed in *The Morning Chronicle*, 24 September 1849. See also George R. Sims, *How the Poor Live* (1883); and William Booth, *Darkest England and the Way Out* (1890).

common resort to figural representation. Here, for example, is Henry James's comment on the workers who come to the tavern called the "Sun and Moon" in *The Princess Casamassima* (1885–86): "They came oftener this second winter, for the season was terribly hard; and as in that lower world one walked with one's ear nearer the ground the deep perpetual groan of London misery seemed to swell and swell and form the whole undertone of life." And in 1902, C. F. G. Masterman wrote in the nonfictional *From the Abyss*: "Without warning or observation, a movement and a sound have arisen in those unknown regions surrounding the kindly, familiar London that we know. As the Red Indian, putting his ear to the ground, could hear murmurs beyond the horizon inaudible to the bystander, so the trained ear could discern the turmoil of the coming flood and the tramp of many footsteps."[33] Both passages inevitably resort to metaphor to represent the unknown. But in the sketch, there is a thin line between referential claims and ideological assumptions; the latter endow the urban scene with meanings that are both comprehensive and yet disputable from the perspective of the reader.

How easily, then, the city may come to be regarded as a storehouse of images for the novelist. This is, to be sure, no peculiar distinction of the city. Nevertheless, it is a matter of history that the nineteenth-century novel gradually extended its scope to include urban scenes and characters that had been beyond its notice previously. As soon as those images appear in the sketches, however, they are tantamount to prior texts. In its first appearance in written discourse the city becomes, as it were, textualized. But to say this is to repeat a commonplace and to ignore the problems that arise from this heap of available images. These include the heterogeneity and the conventions we have already observed: one pole represents chaos, the other a closed system. From neither pole does the transition to temporality seem easily negotiated. The collections of nineteenth-century sketches offer a view of the city as more or less fixed in its rituals, endlessly amassing objects. The spatial spread of the city becomes one more perverse figure for the spatiality of urban representation, fixed in maps as in all other conventional notations. Ironically, the spatial images in the

33. Henry James, *The Princess Casamassima* (New York: Charles Scribner's Sons, 1908), 1:343 (I use the New York Edition for consistency. Where dating matters, as it does here, there is no substantial difference from the Macmillan edition of 1886); C. F. G. Masterman, "A Weird and Uncanny People," from *From the Abyss* (1902), repr. in *Into Unknown England*, 241.

passages from James and Masterman anticipate, even announce the temporal and thus the narrative possibility of uprising or revolution. The form of the sketch might revel in its distinctiveness; but it might also seem doomed to the wilderness, forever in sight of the promised land of fiction but forever barred from it. Such an Arnoldian perspective overlooks the possibility that Dickens realizes in the *Sketches by Boz*. One could claim that as most of the urban sketches were written later than those of Dickens, they are regressive rather than problematic from the perspective of fiction. But insofar as the problem of representation is not necessarily temporal in itself, we can think of the sketches as forming a play of forces that generates illuminating contrasts.

Suppose we look at the issue another way. It might seem as if the discussion thus far has served not only to call into question the innocence of the nonfictional sketch, but also to assert its pre-fictional qualities, or its compatibility with more overtly fictional modes of representation. On such a linear course, the differences among urban sketches would be a matter of degree: all of them would be more or less ideologically motivated, more or less metaphorical, more or less systematic in their presentation of urban matters. But it is precisely at this point that we would be justified in doing a double-take, in breaking the line. Instead of an easy slide into fiction, we encounter a problematic of fiction, a by-product of the narrative perspective. One need not discard the metaphors and the catalogues, or the exuberance and latent violence of the material crowding or linguistic plenitude: all of these are elements in fiction. Nevertheless, neither the strict observance of convention, or metaphor-become-convention, nor the sheer giving of oneself to the matter of the city, promises an easy transition to narrative. Rather they would seem to result in a rigid antithesis, a perpetual standstill between self and the city-as-other, or an obliteration of self within an urban milieu. What we need is a breaking of the figure, a swerve into an alternative stance toward the city. And this is what we find in Dickens. His sketches project the forms of displacement in two ways. First, those very factors on the original line that seemed to be precursors of fiction now appear, but in an oblique fashion; metaphor has a different quality, and conventions, like illusions, are as often as not played with or violated. But this still characterizes only the surface of the text. If we think of the sketches as presenting incipient narratives about the city, then a second form of displacement appears when we move from the urban explorers and journalists to Dickens. Here the terms of interpretation change, and with them the relation of the narrator, or Boz, to the city. In this second form of interpretation, this second swerve, we find the emblem of a genuine urban narrative.

It should be apparent that the theme of urban exploration is implicated with a thematics of the maze: Mearns's repeated "here," which serves in one way to dislocate, Sala's repetitive side streets, and even Greenwood's sense of relief at leaving the workhouse with its unfamiliar topography: all testify to the experiences of dislocation, disorientation, or entrapment for which the maze is the emblem. Dickens's "Seven Dials" makes explicit those balancing motifs:

> Look at the construction of the place. The gordian knot was all very well in its way: so was the maze of Hampton Court: so is the maze at the Beulah Spa: so were the ties of stiff white neckcloths, when the difficulty of getting one on was only to be equalled by the apparent impossibility of ever getting it off again. But what involutions can ever compare with those of Seven Dials? Where is there such another maze of streets, courts, lanes, and alleys. . . . The stranger who finds himself in 'The Dials' for the first time, and stands Belzoni-like, at the entrance of seven obscure passages, uncertain which to take, will see enough around him to keep his curiosity and attention awake for no inconsiderable time. From the irregular square into which he has plunged, the streets and courts dart in all directions, until they are lost in the unwholesome vapour which hangs over the house-tops, and renders the dirty perspective uncertain and confined; and lounging at every corner, as if they came there to take a few gasps of such fresh air as has found its way so far, but is too much exhausted already, to be enabled to force itself into the narrow alleys around, are groups of people, whose appearance and dwellings would fill any mind but a regular Londoner's with astonishment. . . .
>
> The peculiar character of these streets, and the close resemblance each one bears to its neighbour, by no means tends to decrease the bewilderment in which the unexperienced wayfarer through 'the Dials' finds himself involved. He traverses streets of dirty, straggling houses, with now and then an unexpected court composed of buildings as ill-proportioned and

deformed as the half-naked children that wallow in the ken-
nels.[34]

The fact that the Seven Dials is a slum emerges only after a meditation on mazes and a comment on the uncertainty and astonishment
experienced by the stranger who confronts this maze and is unable
to interpret it. The series to which the Seven Dials belongs—Gordian
knots, Hampton Court, neckcloths—demands the placing of this new
member. At the same time, the stranger, himself a slight enigma, almost displaces the unwholesome vapors to find his way into the labyrinth along with the fresh air. These two movements anterior to the
description of the world of the slum mark the first steps over the
threshold into fiction. The first is a siting in a context that is primarily
cultural, although it may also be memorial; this siting transcends the
immediately visible not so much through a totalizing metaphor (as
one finds in Mearns) as through a horizontal series of figures that
open up a space for speculative exploration.[35] The doubleness of the
figural direction is crucial: it is not just the thematics of the maze but
the incongruity of neckcloths and buildings, palace and slum, which
are nevertheless yoked together, that is central. There is a similar
movement in "Gin-Shops." The opening evinces an ostensible concern
with a "madness" that has appeared in trade, a madness concerned
with display and ostentation in shops, which began "among the linen-
drapers and haberdashers" and spread to other trades, including the
publicans, "with unprecedented rapidity." What is essentially a "disease" of trade, of the middle class, spreads to the slums of London:

> Although places of this description are to be met with in every
> second street, they are invariably numerous and splendid in
> precise proportion to the dirt and poverty of the surrounding
> neighbourhood. The gin-shops in and near Drury Lane, Hol-
> born, St. Giles's, Covent Garden, and Clare Market, are the

34. Charles Dickens, "Seven Dials," in *Sketches by Boz* (London: Oxford University Press,
1969), 69–70, 71. The mutual reference of houses and children at the end of the passage
is additionally unsettling.

35. For a discussion of totalizing metaphors in nineteenth-century novels, see J. Hillis
Miller, "Optic and Semiotic in Middlemarch," in *The Worlds of Victorian Fiction*, ed. Jerome
H. Buckley, Harvard English Studies 6 (Cambridge: Harvard University Press, 1975), 125–
45.

> handsomest in town. There is more of fish and squalid misery
> near those great thoroughfares than in any part of this mighty
> city.[36]

It is only after this introduction that there is a paragraph on the misery of the slums, followed by a more complete sketch of the gin-shop. Here too, then, we find incongruity in the adjacency of the "splendid mansions" to "wretched houses with broken windows patched with rags and paper" (184), but there is a hidden incongruity as well in the metonymic series for madness that links haberdashers and gin-shops. Dickens is presenting figures for culture, but presenting them in such a way that one aspect of the figure is hidden or covert. At the same time, culture itself is no longer that which is immediately observable or visible (which might then be tantamount to "Nature" in some abstract scheme), but that which partakes of the figural. The very terms for representation then stand in need of radical alteration. The accompanying enigmas or paradoxes also open up the space for exploration, for a quest for some hidden secret. To do so is to enable narration, for whether it will be the stranger, or Boz, or some other narrative voice, his quest will consist of the traversal of this cultural space.

Returning to "Seven Dials," we can see that the single figure of the labyrinth joins a series of images drawn from theater, art, language, and writing. An observed scuffle "became general, and terminates, in minor playbill phraseology, with 'arrival of the policeman, interior of the station-house, and impressive *dénouement*' " (71).[37] A long descriptive catalogue of the street completes a " 'still life' of the subject" (72). The language of the sketch thus hovers between apparent referentiality (now at least a partial fiction) and a representation fully conscious of the artifices and the nonreferential models which it employs. The same dubious series appears in minor catalogues: "dirty men, filthy women, squalid children, fluttering shuttlecocks, noisy battledores, reeking pipes, bad fruit, more than doubtful oysters, attenuated cats, depressed dogs, and anatomical fowls, are its cheerful accompaniments" (72). Not only the order of the catalogue but the choice of adjectives (some repetitive, some echoing, some flirting with

---

36. "Gin-Shops," in *Sketches by Boz*, 184.
37. Cf. "The Fiction of Realism," 117–18, for a discussion of the conventions of drama, art, and literature as sources for the *Sketches by Boz*.

assonance) indicates that this is the meeting-place of language and space. A deeper knowledge contradicts the evidence of the eye:

> Now anybody who passed through the Dials on a hot summer's evening, and saw the different women of the houses gossiping on the steps, would be apt to think that all was harmony among them, and that a more primitive set of people than the native Diallers could not be imagined. Alas! the man in the shop ill-treats his family; the carpet-beater extends his professional pursuits to his wife. . . . Animosities spring up between floor and floor; the very cellar asserts his equality. (72–73)

Houses and people share bad proportions; houses or parts of them act as signs to betray their inhabitants. Reading these signs, however, is often an oblique or deceptive process, as the end of the sketch implies.[38] The evidence of the eye may feed statistics, but it baffles the interpreter. What he *can* discover is the ways in which the slum and its inhabitants represent themselves; among those ways are the figurative displacements. The process of figuration here is a move not toward abstraction or distancing—as it was in Mearns—but toward humanizing, toward recognizing an active volition among the poor.

The interpreter's own moves to place himself within the scene constitute the second step toward realizing the possibility of narration. If his initial entry into the maze is one form of displacement, the further displacements he effects are acts of inscribing himself upon the city. Here the surrogate figure of the literary man is crucial:

> The second floor front, and the rest of the lodgers, are just a second edition of the people below, except a shabby-genteel man in the back attic. . . . The shabby-genteel man is an object of some mystery, but as he leads a life of seclusion, and never was known to buy anything beyond an occasional pen, except half-pints of coffee, penny loaves, and ha'porths of ink, his fellow-lodgers very naturally suppose him to be an author; and

38. The ultimate discrepancy appears in Arthur Clennam's perception of Casby in Dickens's *Little Dorrit* (London: Oxford University Press, 1967): "He was aware of motes and specks of suspicion, in the atmosphere of that time; seen through which medium, Christopher Casby was a mere Inn signpost without any Inn—an invitation to rest and be thankful, when there was no place to put up at, and nothing whatever to be thankful for" (149).

rumours are current in the Dials, that he writes poems for Mr.
Warren. (72)

Somewhat withdrawn and mysterious, the shabby-genteel man, an
author only by dint of surmise, of rumor, seems to stand for the difficulties inherent in representation itself: he is a sign for an indeterminate signified, his ink no more than a possible metonymy for authorship. The mystery that surrounds him argues a limit to
representation. And yet, could not his very indeterminacy be an emblem of the presence of the author in the urban milieu? No art can
identify him as more than he appears, as the city for its part declares
its unalterable yet mysterious presence. Yet that very mystery generates
interpretation of the city. It is as if by entering the Seven Dials, and
even by making that shabby-genteel man a signature figure for the
artist, Boz has prepared a linguistic ground for urban fiction. If one
of the figures in Cruikshank's illustration for "Public Dinners" represents Dickens, then Boz, also a representation of Dickens, appears in
a still further displacement in the shabby-genteel man. Boz figuratively
displaces the self-representing figures of the Seven Dials to become
an authorial figure for that area.

That process of self-inscription, of coming to terms with the otherness of the city in such a way that it is held in a delicate balance
with the self, appears even more clearly and paradigmatically in the
"Meditations in Monmouth Street." As in "Seven Dials," what is apt
to impress readers most is not the presence of the narrator so much
as the speculations (a recurring word in the *Sketches*) on an observed
locale. The description of secondhand clothes develops into a fantasy
about their history or the histories of the wearers, or about the way
in which a pair of boots, surmised to be the former possession of a
jovial market-gardener, engages in a courtship pantomime with a pair
of Denmark satin shoes that once adorned the feet of a servant girl.
A more elegant pair of grey cloth boots becomes the property of a
smart female; the boots then mime a dialogue with a gallant gentleman
in list shoes, to the amusement of an imagined young fellow in long-
quartered pumps. High life and low life meet in Monmouth Street and
in Boz's imagination the scene develops, thanks to all the secondhand shoes, into a dance, replete with corps de ballet.

Such lively meditations occupy a good part of the sketch; they indicate, as Miller has suggested, the way in which even the inferences
about history and causality that one may derive from a realistic mode

recede before the pressures of the exuberant imagination.[39] But the passages that frame the central part of the sketch are puzzling simply because they have little apparent relation to that center. Here is the second paragraph:

> The inhabitants of Monmouth Street are a distinct class; a peaceable and retiring race, who immure themselves for the most part in deep cellars, or small back parlours, and who seldom come forth into the world, except in the dusk and coolness of the evening, when they may be seen seated, in chairs on the pavement, smoking their pipes, or watching the gambols of their engaging children as they revel in the gutter, a happy troop of infantine scavengers. Their countenances bear a thoughtful and a dirty cast, certain indications of their love of traffic; and their habitations are distinguished by that disregard of outward appearance and neglect of personal comfort, so common among people who are constantly immersed in profound speculations, and deeply engaged in sedentary pursuits.[40]

One might regard these people as a species of urban mole; what is more important, however, is the quality of their withdrawal, their peaceful and sedentary ways, their "profound speculations." The fantasy-provoking old clothes are more prominent than the shopowners, whose recessiveness appears in their retiring (rather than attiring) qualities, and whose "disregard of outward appearance" contrasts with the clothes that are all appearance. The clothes take the place of the proprietors, who then give themselves to their mysterious profundities. Of course, not all connections are effaced: "thoughtfulness" may retain a trace of its disinterested connotation, but it is also a sign of a "love of [commercial] traffic"; "speculations" has a double meaning in this context; even "pursuits" must sacrifice some of its innocence to the pun. Yet these signs of proprietary interest are by and large supplanted by the presence of the clothes, which are in turn displaced by the conjuring imagination of Boz. That this series is not strained may appear from the final paragraph, where Boz alludes to the "depths of his meditations," which have in fact so eclipsed the

---

39. Cf. "The Fiction of Realism," 96–98.
40. "Meditations in Monmouth Street," in *Sketches by Boz*, 74.

visual that "we might have been rudely staring at [an] old lady for half an hour without knowing it" (80). Proprietorship, a term not explicitly used, passes from the shopowners to the author, as their "profound speculations" traverse the dusk of the street to the twilight zone of writing. Indeed, Boz's final "flight" to become "immersed in the deepest obscurity of the adjacent 'Dials' " (80) has imaginative implications. The form of immersion and self-revelation of the Monmouth Street inhabitants has now been assumed by the narrator. The presence of the narrator, at first recessive in its encounter with the visual, eventually signifies a deepening of the inner gaze: the artist comes to master all speculation, all imaginative traffic. The sketch offers, then, a figure for the activity of writing itself, where the clothes constitute the pre-text.

The clothes contain still another hidden figure. The one life which Boz does infer from a series of outfits (metonymically placed side by side, in such a way that Boz's narrative imagination may supply the continuities) takes a downward course from respectability to crime and poverty. The more cheerful antidote involves incipient narrative that bursts out into a miniature carnival of dance, pantomime, ritual. But there is a tension with the actual emptiness of the shoes, or with the subsequent flight of the imagined occupants when the barrel-organ stops playing. The hidden figure may thus be that of the *Totentanz*, or, more ambiguously, the attempt to ward off death.[41] The interplay between presence and absence, life and death, artifact and nature, gaiety and despair, implies that the sketch is a determined effort—if not desperate then not merely genial—to assert the power of the self. At the same time, the city on its part is threatened with a form of death, as the clothes-as-artifacts may testify to a vanished life or civilization. The image of the necropolis does not appear in strength until the later Dickens novels, but even in *Sketches by Boz* Dickens reckons the ways of discerning life in a still city.[42] "Meditations on Monmouth Street," with its transferences and displacements, its recessive and emergent figures, its dialectic of writer or self and city, becomes a signature piece for the Dickensian mode of writing.

41. Cf. Tzvetan Todorov's discussion of the relations between narrative and life, and absence of narrative and death, in "Narrative-Men," in *The Poetics of Prose*, trans. Richard Howard (Ithaca: Cornell University Press, 1977), 66–79.

42. For a discussion of London as a city of death in Dickens's novels, see Alexander Welsh, *The City of Dickens* (Oxford: Clarendon, 1971).

III

If we return to the point of origin, that of representation of the city, we are now in a position to note more fully the problematic this involves. In the first place, the issue of culture (and ideology) is perceivable in comprehensive metaphors, in serial metaphors that chart a hidden relation among parts of the city, in allusions to a vanishing past, and in central episodes that resemble the encounter between two cultures.[43] In the second place, the presence of the observer on the scene of cultural encounter is translated into the confrontation of self and other. That presence, as much as any other factor, generates questions about the possibilities of narrative. While the formal problem common to Dickens and the writers of the nonfictional sketches arises from the impact of the visible and the consequent ways of containing or transcending it, the social problem concerns the preservation of a culture. If the most obvious signs of urban blight, for example, are conveyed in religious, moral, or other conventional terms, then the cure is one prescribed by that very terminology. Various forms of the sketch embody, therefore, modes of acculturation, whether that of the externally directed colonial explorer or missionary, or that of the internally motivated flâneur who seeks, through the act of strolling itself, to establish the continuities and connections of the city, to re-incorporate the outcast other into the knowable city.[44] But the project of making the city known can set up false directives, turn the city into a museum containing collections of objects that are neatly classifiable, or from which one might reasonably infer histories or meanings. It is here that the novelist might part with the journalist, the sociologist, or the statistician, insofar as the latter three share in an enterprise of collecting and classifying on the one hand, and of reassuring the public about the possibility of knowledge on the other.[45]

Literature of the city is prone to execute a double movement: the intense observation and exploration of the unknown are followed by

43. The awareness of antithetical cultures within London itself is apparent even in the titles of some books. See, for example, *St. James and St. Giles*, which refers to the adjacent districts of the aristocracy and the poor.

44. See Benjamin's description of the Parisian flâneur in *Charles Baudelaire: A Lyric Poet in the Era of High Capitalism.*

45. In the book on Baudelaire, Benjamin notes that the French physiologies—in some respects a counterpart to the English sketches—helped to reassure those readers who felt threatened by the uncanny and secret aspects of the big city: "The more uncanny a big city becomes, the more knowledge of human nature . . . it takes to operate in it"(40).

a swerve into a metaphor or a systemic pattern meant to account for the visible. This move toward interpretation constitutes a displacement from the observable scene, so that the final image of the city may appear as a palimpsest. Missionaries and heathens, Vanity Fair, the world threatened by the flood, or high and low, East End and West End, West End and City, even light and dark, are central terms for ways of regarding the city that are as significant for their exclusions as for their inclusions. Certain metaphors, when examined carefully, disrupt those comprehensive views of the city. The fear of violence and the continuing awareness of the otherness of parts of the city, tend also to undermine that system of comprehension. That the city is as ultimately knowable as these first explorers assumed now becomes questionable: it is the ambiguities rather than the availability of cultural metaphors or schemas that allow the turn toward narrative.

With the possible exception of the labyrinth, urban metaphors may be most efficacious for narrative when they abjure the comprehensive or the systematic. Some of the major metaphors for the city are "horizontal": the madness for decoration that spreads over the city in "Gin-Shops" is noticeably spatial. Eventually juxtaposed with the slums that lie at the heart of the sketch, the madness for decoration represents the gin palaces as dream palaces, fantasies where one can drink gin as an alternative to the waters of Lethe (much as gambling is a fantasy about fate).[46] Such figures are more modest in their claims than the totalizing metaphors: they are provisional figures for culture, and they permit the exchange, transgression, and discontinuity that set a Dickensian narrative in motion. But a more casual stroll or a simple excursion can also connote a move toward the figurative. The move of the Tuggses to Ramsgate, Mr. Minns's trip to the suburbs, Mr. Dumps's trip to Bloomsbury in "A Bloomsbury Christening"—all journeys that cross boundaries—are steps toward narrative.

Many of the urban sketches feature the presence, implicit or explicit, of an observer on the scene. The roles in which these observers cast themselves are significant. Sala is Asmodeus, the invisible figure who sees everything that goes on beneath the rooftops; he is also a night-watchman, one who is familiar with the secrets of the night and at the same time a guardian of order, a source of reassurance. As ex-

---

46. Cf. Benjamin's comments on the gambler's "phantasmagoria of time," which corresponds to the flâneur's "phantasmagoria of space," in *Charles Baudelaire: A Lyric Poet in the Era of High Capitalism*, 174.

cavator—still another persona—he will unearth the artifacts of the city and construct from them an intelligible picture of urban life. Even if he were to depict only the publicly observable life of the city, like the flâneur, he would, as Benjamin notes in another context, turn the exteriors into interiors, impart to them a degree of intimacy and make all forms of external life potentially comprehensible.[47] All of these personae are observers whose very strategies maintain some separation from the scene. In many of the nonnarrative sketches, alternatively, Dickens—or Boz—inscribes himself on the scene, translates a cultural encounter into a meeting of self and other. Thus his "speculations" constitute that act of transgression or exchange that marks out the scene as a space for narrative.[48] While this is by no means necessary (it does not happen in all of the *Sketches*), it marks one way of going beyond the impasses created by the systems, antitheses, and catalogues that close around the scenes of urban life. This merging into the scene, like the figures for transgression and discontinuity—the beggar-woman singing with her baby who breaks the fabric of the night street scene, the mysterious figure in Scotland Yard who represents the persistence of memory as well as the distance from all conventional history—becomes a figure for narrativity.[49]

If urban culture is to be preserved, then it would seem necessary to take cognizance of the ruptures that threaten culture. But if culture is seen not only as the phenomenon of the present but also as that which is continuous with the past, then preservation is a still more precarious enterprise, if it is possible at all. Leigh Hunt strolls about London, meditating on the histories of certain houses and thus incorporating those histories into the facade of the present.[50] In *Twice Round the Clock*, Sala's evocation of Regent Street, changed considerably between its Regency beginnings and the midcentury at which Sala writes, is charged with the *ubi sunt* motif: even as the mores of the street are changing, the figures who would formerly have inspired Thackeray's novels are nowhere to be seen. In fact, the historical consciousness becomes an awareness of decline: it is not only the

47. See *Charles Baudelaire: A Lyric Poet in the Era of High Capitalism*, 36–37.
48. On the relation of transgression to narrative, see Roland Barthes, *S/Z*, trans. Richard Miller (New York: Hill and Wang, 1974).
49. See "The Streets—Night" in *Sketches by Boz*, 55–56, and "Scotland Yard," in *Sketches By Boz*, 67–68.
50. See Leigh Hunt, *Political and Occasional Essays*, ed. Lawrence Huston Houtchens and Carolyn Washburn Houtchens (New York: Columbia University Press, 1962).

loss of illusion that Dickens's "Vauxhall by Day" chronicles, but also the decline of the pleasure garden itself from its eighteenth-century heyday. The decay of small houses (an implicit counterpart to the decay of greater houses) is chronicled in "Shops and their Tenants."[51] Several sketches, however, question the very notion of history. In "The First of May," the pastoral glory of May Day acquires the status of a dream of childhood, even as it metamorphoses into the urban celebration of the chimney sweeps and then into a motley ceremony. Boz ends his sketch of Scotland Yard by observing that no ordinary history will help the antiquarian of the future to locate the landmarks of that area. The consciousness of what is transitory must, therefore, be caught in the sketch; the newspaper account of the balloon race in "Vauxhall by Day" is emblematic of the process. If writing about the city becomes a sign, as Benjamin suggests, for externalized memory, then the sketch becomes the site for a collector of objects that represent both the cultural past and individual memory.[52]

This returns us to the mode of textuality. The vanishing of forms of urban life can be conceived of as a source of narrative. It is, to be sure, oblique. For example, buses and coaches in nineteenth-century novels are more or less thematic or peripheral; they are symbols, but not actual materials, of narrative. The "Lads of the Village," an errant omnibus in "The Bloomsbury Christening," is exemplary: its wayward progress over the space of the city forms a figure for urban narrative.[53] The city, to be sure, has no exclusive rights over literary vehicles: the stagecoaches of *The Heart of Midlothian* and *Felix Holt*, symbols of a more leisurely past, of a different conception of temporality as well as entrées into narrative, are sufficient evidence. Nevertheless, the abundance of vehicles in *Sketches by Boz* is linked to a receding past that can only be halted or transfixed within a text. The not entirely nominal metamorphosis or corruption of William Barker into "Bill Boorker" and then "Aggerawatin Bill" in "The Last Cab-Driver, and the First Omnibus Cad" offers a human counterpart. His early life is obscure, his "restlessness of purpose" evident: his "feverish attachment to change and variety nothing could repress" (147). As a cab-driver

51. Alexander Welsh comments that "the passing of time is more perceptible in the city than in the village" in *The City of Dickens*, 7.

52. The idea is central in Benjamin's writings about the city. One version appears in "A Berlin Chronicle," in *Reflections*, trans. Edmund Jephcott (New York: Harcourt Brace Jovanovich, 1978), 3–60.

53. Cf. Patricia Parker's exploration of the idea of errancy in narrative in *Inescapable Romance* (Princeton: Princeton University Press, 1979).

symbolizes the shifting of self into assumed characters that is so much a part of an urban poetics,[54] so nonlinearity of narrative is symbolized in the movement of the buses, which constantly change their origins and destinations. Like the social madness in "Gin-Shops" or the speculative exuberance in "Meditations in Monmouth Street," which ends with Boz fleeing from his own imaginative violence, there is an apprehension of things getting out of hand, of unpredictability and madness.

Dickens's sketches, then, tend to break away from the taxonomy, articulation, and system that govern so many of the nonfictional sketches and instead regard the city as a more mysterious text. The nonfictional sketches are more closely related in other ways: in their oblique comments on language—the implication that London is a city of words, whether they are spoken by lawyers (Sala's sketch of the legal profession in *Twice Round the Clock* focuses on legal diction and rhetoric) or written in begging letters; in the containment of a problematic of fiction, as in the comments on the relation of romance to reality; in the use of figures that in one way or another remove the sketch from the scene of representation. The city may be the common ground of encounter, but it also contains an underworld of representation. Wordsworth's reading of the city as a chaos of signs was in one sense entirely accurate, but the city was also a destructive element in which he refused to immerse himself. That immersion, as Sala's own moment of impasse suggests, is no guarantee of a successful emergence and appropriation of the city. One liberating recognition, however, which goes beyond the materiality of the city, was that of new correspondences between urban and verbal creation, and of the artist's capacity to insert himself into a city now conceived of as a text. That immersion, that tolerance of mystery, that recognition of language's displaced relation to the object-world of the city, can be seen as the very factors that allowed the urban novel to come into being.

---

54. The importance of masquerades (and of theatricality in general) in an urban poetics is in part an outgrowth of earlier satirical views of the city. John Corry's A *Satirical View of London at the Commencement of the Nineteenth Century* (London: printed for G. Kearsley, T. Hurst, 1801) is representative: "The two most powerful motives that keep this vast community in continual agitation, like the undulations of the ocean, are the love of pleasure and the love of gain. Venus and her auxilliary, Bacchus, reign in the fashionable circles. Masquerades, balls, fetes, public and private theatres, and all the luxurious delights that fancy can devise, minister to the passions and appetites of those sons and daughters of pride" (7). Here the masquerade appears as an upper-class version of carnival.

2

Rewriting the Slums: Ambivalence and Reversal

*O*ne motif of chapter 1 has persisted in popular thought: that the life of the slums is closer to "reality" than the more insulated and artificial life of the upper classes. Slum life must in some way be free from the inevitable distortions of convention; one goes to the slums to find "nature" in the city. In the representation of the city, a touchstone for the urban artist would be the ability to capture the slums, to render them narratable. An urban project would have to be aware of the object, of a need for referential accuracy; at the same time, however, it would be an enterprise of self-authentification. The doubleness of the enterprise then argues that while culture is the object of narrative, narrative determines its own cultural concerns. This is nowhere more evident than in Gissing's early novels. Gissing's life entwines the strands of literary-artistic culture and low life: the novels thematize culture as a mode of knowing and penetrating the slums. Gissing discovers, like Boz, that culture must be enshrouded in mystery (often, literally, darkness) before one can, narratively speaking, cross the threshold into the slums.

I

> Shooter's Gardens [was] a picturesque locality which demolition and rebuilding have of late transformed. It was a winding alley, with paving raised a foot above the level of the street whence was its main approach. To enter from the obscurer end, you descended a flight of steps, under a low archway, in a court itself not easily discovered. From without, only a glimpse of the Gardens was obtainable; the houses curved out of sight after the first few yards, and left surmise to busy itself with the characteristics of the hidden portion. A stranger bold enough to explore would have discovered that the Gardens had a blind offshoot, known simply as 'The Court.' Needless to burden description with further detail; the slum was like any other slum; filth, rottenness, evil odours, possessed these dens of superfluous mankind and made them gruesome to the peering imagination.[1]

This passage, which appears near the opening of *The Nether World*, offers a seemingly restrained and innocent introduction to the most physically scandalous locale in the novel. Gissing will in fact "burden description" several times, because Shooter's Gardens is the site of the denouement of one of the novel's narrative lines—a narrative of degradation, as well as a bitter thematics of poverty, drink, and "superfluity." There is a further irony, however, because description will not be able to call upon the catalogue of visible objects, that staple of urban writing. A mattress, a heap of rags, a teakettle, a few coals: one could not add much more to the inventories of these rooms in which seven families live. Where sight is deprived, hearing intervenes. The explorer (a common enough metaphor in the late nineteenth century, as we have seen) will instead have to listen to the drunken cries,

---

1. George Gissing, *The Nether World* (London: Smith, Elder, 1907), 74.

the horrendous invectives, the deranged psalms and speeches of one "Mad Jack." Toward evening, baked-potato ovens, which will afterwards be wheeled away to streetcorners, are lighted in this Court, which is then filled with smoke. We learn that a "single lamp existed for the purpose of giving light to the alley, and at no time did this serve much more than to make darkness visible . . ." (344). Here, just before the denouement of that narrative line, Mad Jack will relate his vision to a gathering crowd, a vision which will identify the poor as those formerly rich who are now suffering for their selfishness and hard-heartedness. He makes explicit what we have suspected all along: that Shooter's Gardens, the heart of darkness, is hell.

Why does Gissing place a burden of description upon the slums? They are located topographically and historically, in a sequence of urban improvement (which later descriptions, of public housing in Farringdon Road and suburban villas at Crouch End will make ironic[2]). Shooter's Gardens are in Clerkenwell, but four other novels—*Workers in the Dawn*, *The Unclassed*, *Demos*, and *Thyrza*—locate the slums with equal precision in Lambeth, or Hoxton, or Islington, or the East End. The ironies of social indignation with their "literary" overtones that frame the passage from *The Nether World*—"picturesque," "dens of superfluous mankind," "darkness visible"—spread to the summarizing "filth" and "rottenness" and intensify the fact that this slum existed, that it was accessible ("To enter . . . you descended"), that it was "like any other."

What makes Gissing's obsessive return to slum life so puzzling in these five early novels is his accompanying (and frequently noted)

---

2. Cf. *The Nether World*, 273–74, 364. Here is the description of the Farringdon Road Buildings: "The economy prevailing in to-day's architecture takes good care that no depressing circumstance shall be absent from the dwellings in which the poor find shelter. What terrible barracks, those Farringdon Road Buildings! Vast, sheer walls, unbroken by even an attempt at ornament; row above row of windows in the mud-coloured surface, upwards, upwards, lifeless eyes, murky openings that tell of bareness, disorder, comfortlessness within. One is tempted to say that Shooter's Gardens are a preferable abode. An inner courtyard, asphalted, swept clean—looking up to the sky as from a prison. Acres of these edifices, the tinge of grime declaring the relative dates of their erection; millions of tons of brute brick and mortar, crushing the spirit as you gaze. Barracks, in truth; housing for the army of industrialism, an army fighting with itself, rank against rank, man against man, that the survivors may have whereon to feed. Pass by in the night, and strain imagination to picture the weltering mass of human weariness, of bestiality, of unmerited dolour, of hopeless hope, of crushed surrender, tumbled together within those forbidding walls." The Crouch End villas, which appear at the end of the narrative and at the spatial limits of the city, in effect remove temporal limits from the spread of the slum.

ambivalence. Gissing's slums can be as "bestial" as those of any social explorer: he uses this term and similar ones without irony, even in novels like *The Nether World*, where he is most sympathetic to the poor. Nor is it sufficient to distinguish between the world of the "respectable" poor and the slum; that sociologically grounded distinction can be found, to be sure, but it does not explain Gissing's mingled attraction and revulsion. The clue comes, rather, from the challenge the slums present to the narrative imagination, which must reconstruct what history has demolished, go beyond the "glimpse" afforded by the obscure, surmise and imagine what is "hidden" and "out of sight." Even "realistic" novels, we know, seem less concerned with referentiality than with the acts and gestures of narration itself. Insofar as they go beyond the role of explorer, Gissing and his narrators do reveal their imaginative strategies. But even if this is an ultimate concern of the novels, we can best understand it by interpreting them first at some intermediate level where we can view the uncertainties of Gissing's project, his struggle with a referent that resists easy identification. The slums present a supreme challenge to the artist of the city, who must devise some verbal medium to account for their massive phenomenal presence, some way of absorbing their otherness into the space of fiction. He must view the slums not only as context (which would, after all, yield a great deal to description) but also as the container of narrative energies. But then there arise the ancillary problems of focus, of how the collective life of the slums can confront the individual lives that form the traditional materials of narrative. What results are moments of crisis where the two approaches exist in a central tension with each other. It is these moments, however, that allow one to view the slums as synecdoches for the city. Thus the art of the urban novelist, at least as Gissing conceives of it, depends upon what amounts to a perceptual uncertainty. It may also help to account for a series of puzzling double moves: to enter the slums is to traverse the spaces of London, the named streets, the distinctive areas, and then to abandon the visual. Here is Gissing on the music of the street-organ:

> Do you know that music of the obscure ways, to which children dance? Not if you have only heard it ground to your ears' affliction beneath your windows in the square. To hear it aright you must stand in the darkness of such a by-street as this, and for the moment be at one with those who dwell around, in the

blear-eyed houses, in the dim burrows of poverty, in the un-mapped haunts of the semi-human. Then you will know the significance of that vulgar clanging of melody; a pathos of which you did not dream will touch you, and therein the secret of hidden London will be half revealed.[3]

Such a passage, with its emphasis on the importance of sound and sympathetic identification, raises the specter of the Romantic artist.[4] Gissing will do what the social explorers could not do. (In contrast, Charles Booth, the great urban sociologist of the late nineteenth century, did not enter the houses of the London poor until after he had completed his demographic and statistical analyses.[5]) Conventional language, which hears only "vulgar clanging,"must be made trans-parent, if one is to heal the scandalous rift between the language of the upper world and the presence of the slums. Nevertheless, to listen to the voice of the poor is not to transcribe it directly in the novel. Gissing insists that the narrator's voice must mediate for the inar-ticulate voices of the slum. He cannot, like Wordsworth, only listen in darkness,[6] but must become the impresario of a darkness made audible and variegated.

II

Getting into the heart of the slums has a complex signification for Gissing. He must find and give voice to the hitherto inarticulate slum-dwellers, delivering them, as it were, into humanity. At the same time, he must come to grips with the independent, transhuman presence of the city. The writer is caught in the double bind of having to nat-uralize what is already all too natural, and of having to recuperate that

3. George Gissing, *Thyrza* (Rutherford: Fairleigh Dickinson University Press, 1974), 111.

4. Shelley is the Romantic poet to whom Gissing refers most explicitly in his novels, often as the political idealist. The more implicit issues concern imaginative apprehension and identification, and here both Wordsworth and Shelley may serve as models.

5. See *Charles Booth's London*, ed. Albert Fried and Richard Elman (Middlesex, Eng-land: Penguin, 1971), 24.

6. William Wordsworth, *The Prelude, 1799, 1805, 1850*, ed. J. Wordsworth, M. H. Abrams, and S. Gill (New York: W. W. Norton, 1979), Book II, lines 306–10.

natural entity into the order of art. These imperatives require that he confront or transform the conventions of both nonfiction and fiction. Such an enterprise may help us to uncover the contradictions that run through Gissing's slum novels, contradictions that emerge in special sharpness at key points. Gissing uses philanthropy, and the relationships it entails, as a means of entering the slums; art becomes the means of escaping them. Analogously, he tries to represent the collective passions of the slum world and at the same time to depict individual desires. This leads him to develop structural paradigms involving ambivalence and reversal. An ambivalent structure imposes two narrative patterns upon a single referent. A reversal inverts the metaphorical structure of a narrative as well as the nature of the referent. Thus in a novel of social exploration whose ostensible referent is the slum and the lives of the poor, where the powers of narrative should be directed toward illuminating and giving voice to the lives of the poor, that collective life may become the vehicle for communicating the qualities of individual lives, individual passions. The referent of such a novel may then seem either problematic or reversible, and as a result it may be both necessary and irrelevant at the same time. These narrative lines would then have to cross the barriers between middle- and upper-class worlds (which are more apt to privilege individual lives) and the slums. But they also evoke the clash between civilization's language for the slums and the voice of the slums itself. If conventional metaphors place them outside the margins of discourse about civilized society, how then can discourse represent the unfamiliar? (One would be justified in construing that word in a radical sense: a number of the novels contain narrative puns on families that try, with varying success, to transgress class barriers.) The attempt to systematize the relation between upper and nether worlds is at stake here. Finally, there is the contradiction between the phenomenal city—an apparent chaos of objects and actions that demands order and interpretation—and the city that is already a prior text in the novels of Dickens and others, so that writing is necessarily re-viewing or re-writing. Such a process may be seen in the various "revisions" of *Oliver Twist*, first in Augustus Mayhew's *Paved with Gold*, then in Gissing's *Workers in the Dawn*. Each novel alters the narrative as well as the language of slum description to be found in its precursor(s); the succession takes on the quality of a palimpsest.[7] Gissing's revisions,

---

7. The narrator of *Paved with Gold* (London: Chapman and Hall, 1858; repr. London:

however, more often become forms of displacement; the repeated return to the slums, as if to a primal scene, could be written in textual terms, to be sure, but Gissing seems to have been compelled to confront and appropriate some real space on which to inscribe his own artistic presence.

III

In Gissing's novels, philanthropy and art oppose each other. Philanthropy, which figures in some form in all five slum novels, provides a narrative means of entering the slums with its projects of active engagement and reform, both physical and moral. By allowing its advocates to have a point of origin outside the slums, however, it maintains a certain distance from its object. Art is more complex, because it is both thematized in the attempts of a group of slum characters to escape or surmount their environment by means of art— high or low art, craft or performance—and represented as the approach that is antithetical to philanthropy. In this respect, art regards the slums as mere subject matter, elevates the picturesque over the moral, and allows the artist or narrator to have a distanced and neutral stance.

Whatever the social valorization of philanthropy in the late nineteenth century, the novels do not offer any final judgment about it. The sheer misery, brutality, and benightedness of life in the slums invite several kinds of philanthropic projects, ranging from soup kitchens (*The Nether World*) to classes in reading and writing (*Workers in the Dawn*) to lectures on English literature (*Thyrza*) to model socialist communities (*Demos*). Every project encounters the resistance of the poor (except the last, in which the novel, by a plot device, allows the project to be overthrown by the resistance of the rich). From the perspective of the outside, it seems as if the nether world is locked into

Frank Cass, 1971) refers to a course alternative to Oliver Twist's, which the protagonist may follow when he comes to London. Adrian Poole calls Arthur Golding of *Workers in the Dawn* "the Oliver Twist of Gissing's first novel" (2), in *Gissing in Context* (Totowa, N.J.: Rowan and Littlefield, 1975). P. J. Keating notes the similarity of certain characters, the Blatherwicks, to the workhouse crones of *Oliver Twist*. (See *The Working Classes in Victorian Fiction* [New York: Barnes and Noble, 1971], 74–75.) But the revisionary sequence involves more than characterization; it has important narrative implications as well.

ι.. a closed, repetitive circuit of custom and behavior.|As Helen Norman discovers in *Workers in the Dawn*, a half-naked family that has sold its possessions for drink will also sell any replacements for more drink. Where Dickens exposed the self-gratifying impulses of the philanthropist in such characters as Mrs. Pardiggle of *Bleak House*, Gissing adds the intractability of philanthropy's object, even when it receives material aid rather than the religious tracts that Mrs. Pardiggle distributes.[8] This would seem a trivial point to make over and over again; it becomes more illuminating in the contexts of the interpretation and narratability of the slums. If we think of the philanthropist as projecting an ideal narrative involving the simple and straightforward giving and acceptance of a gift, and of the defeat of both project and narrative because they are based upon an inadequate interpretation of the donee, then we can begin to grasp the problematic of Gissing's slum novels. Gissing's skepticism about the idealism and eventual fanaticism of the philanthropist, either of which can create its own closed circle of perception, is manifest in these collapsing narratives. Egremont's literary lectures in *Thyrza* fail to take account of the practical interests of the majority of working men, while Michael Snowdon's vision in *The Nether World* founders on its inadequate understanding of its chosen instruments, the people who are to put his philanthropic idea into practice. In effect, Snowdon's scenario treats people as instruments and subordinates them to his grand vision, thereby negating the very end of philanthropy. What is prominent, then, is a cycle of fascination and defeat, a clash, at some conceptual threshold, of two modes of being and perceiving: the clash generates narrative by its deviance from preconceived models. In *Workers in the Dawn*, extensive poverty and illness, as well as the unwillingness of the poor collectively to "improve," thwart Helen Norman's attempts to educate. Her narrative is fixed in a dawn that threatens to become a false dawn. The structural counterpart is Arthur Golding's marriage to the lower-class Carrie Mitchell, whose alcoholism and indifference to learning cancel the Pygmalion-narrative into which Arthur has cast himself. Even the modest project of a soup kitchen in *The Nether World* en-

---

8. The poor show no gratitude for Mrs. Pardiggle's tracts, but the material situation in Gissing's novels displays more inclusively the shortcomings of philanthropy. Cf. also Jacques Lacan's discussion of apparently charitable motives and responses to them in "Aggressivity in Psychoanalysis," in *Ecrits*, trans. Alan Sheridan (New York: W. W. Norton, 1977): "After all, do we not point out the aggressive motives that lie hidden in all so-called philanthropic activity?" (13).

counters the resistance of the slum-dwellers to the changes it would entail in their eating habits.[9] The success, in *The Unclassed*, of the former prostitute Ida Starr's philanthropic activities seems to be the exception; her success is rendered ironic, however, by the source of her money: her grandfather's rack-renting. In this instance, then, surface philanthropy may be understood as a kind of monetary recycling.

It seems as if philanthropy's usefulness to narrative increases in proportion to its failures, to its misrepresentations of the slums. One version is that the plot that philanthropy projects is rejected by the materials upon which it should work; two modes of life are out of line. In other terms, it maintains a distance between the donor (who is a character but who may, within the limits of his own activity, play a quasi-authorial role) and his object. The repeated acts of entering the slums to do good, which often involve crossing a physical boundary, gesture toward the incorporation of new material into narrative. When Walter Egremont, the Oxford-educated intellectual, crosses from Bloomsbury to Lambeth to give lectures and found a library, the voices of Lambeth's poor become for the most part articulate in proportion to their suspicion, to their resistance to his projects. In fact, the charitable relation distances the object; pastoral and idealizing in nature, it neutralizes the slums in the very instances where it seeks them out.[10] Both parties are locked into a donor–object relationship that establishes their difference. This difference has a formal analogy to the process of defamiliarization: if the donors belong to the middle or upper class, the "exotic" material of the slums is freshly perceived, as something like an order of nature that exists outside of stale and unperceptive cultural conventions. Freshness of perception would then depend upon the difference between the middle-class expectations of the perceiver and the slum world itself, which defies conventional categorization.[11] If this is so, then it happens despite the phil-

9. See *The Nether World*, 250–53. The project becomes exemplary: "It is significant, and shall take the place of abstract comment on Miss Lant's philanthropic enterprises."

10. Cf. William Empson's comments on the "essential trick of the old pastoral, which was felt to imply a beautiful relation between rich and poor," and on "the pastoral process of putting the complex into the simple" in *Some Versions of Pastoral* (Harmondsworth: Penguin, 1966), 17, 25. See also "The Charities and the Poor of London," *Quarterly Review*, 97 (1855): 407–50; Gareth Stedman Jones, *Outcast London: A Study in the Relationship between Classes in Victorian Society* (Oxford: Clarendon Press, 1971); and Alexander Welsh, *The City of Dickens* (Oxford: Clarendon Press, 1971).

11. Cf. Victor Shklovsky, "Art as Technique," in *Russian Formalist Criticism; Four Essays*, trans. Lee T. Lemon and Marion J. Reis (Lincoln: University of Nebraska Press, 1965), 3–24.

anthropic relation, which absorbs the other into the conventional (pastoralism or one of its analogues) and elides the challenge posed by these new urban materials. Philanthropy's true formal analogues then appear in the rural or provincial novels as the charitable gestures of the squirearchy toward the poor, gestures from which not even the principled Dorothea Brooke of *Middlemarch* is exempted. From a narrative point of view, if philanthropy does not constitute a threat to the urban novel, it is no more than a negative asset.[12] The frequent appearance of the "substitute hero," a middle- or upper-class person who, openly or in disguise, enacts the focal part of the slum drama in place of the slum-dwellers, and who often engages in philanthropic activity, underlines the point: if one cannot trust the inhabitant of the slums to be sufficiently articulate, then one is placing the slums at a remove.[13] Gissing is, to be sure, ambivalent in this respect. Arthur Golding, the son of a middle-class father, grows up in the slums and distinguishes himself by his artistic talent; in *Demos*, Richard Mutimer is a working man, but his rhetorical skills make him exceptional; Thyrza is a working girl, but her beauty and talent remove her from the ordinary. Only in *The Nether World* does Gissing fully abandon the model and grant authority to a working-class hero, and even Sidney Kirkwood is made unusual by his artistic skill. In general, Gissing seems close to many of the social explorers of the late nineteenth century, whose modes of exploration, ranging from the statistical to the rhetorical, brought the slums into the realm of the known but granted full consciousness only to their own judging and interpreting minds. But Gissing, like Dickens before him, diverges from them. Gissing's novels are less tracts on the shortcomings of philanthropy than explorations of its narrative potentiality. In this respect, failure seems more like postponement, the enactment of a quest for the real where the real is continually approached but obscured by the mediating terms of the quest.

Conceived of as a mode of access, as a transposition of the exploratory situation (which turns out to be a covert exercise of power

---

12. For a somewhat different view of the narrative role of philanthropy, cf. Fredric Jameson's discussion of the new narrative paradigms which derive from the philanthropic situation and replace the paradigms of the Dickensian novel in *The Political Unconscious* (Ithaca: Cornell University Press, 1981), 185–205.

13. See P. J. Keating's *The Working Classes in Victorian Fiction* for a discussion of the substitute hero.

operating across distance), philanthopy would have seemed to be the most direct approach. In light of its failure, the artistic approach would seem to offer a more promising alternative. Art would at least be neutral. This is the burden of a passage from *The Unclassed*, the declaration of the novelist Waymark. If art has brought him "increased knowledge" of suffering, it has provoked no commensurate social conscience.

> 'I often amuse myself with taking to pieces my former self. I was not a conscious hypocrite in those days of violent radicalism, working-man's-club lecturing, and the like; the fault was that I understood myself as yet so imperfectly. That zeal on behalf of the suffering masses was nothing more nor less than disguised zeal on behalf of my own starved passions. I was poor and desperate, life had no pleasures, the future seemed hopeless, yet I was overflowing with vehement desires, every nerve in me was a hunger which cried to be appeased. I identified myself with the poor and ignorant; I did not make their cause my own, but my own cause theirs. I raved for freedom because I was myself in the bondage of unsatisfiable longing.'[14]

The disjunction between art and conscience, analogous to the disjunction between economic survival (Waymark collects rents for a rack-renting landlord) and ethics on one level, is analogous to the distance of the writer from his subjects, whose plight has been subordinated (to the "real" subject of individual passions and desires). Art's neutrality is thus a fiction for another kind of distancing that transforms the referent into a signifier for individual passions.

If even an art that looks most openly at the slums—a verbal, narrative art—turns out to be a way of turning one's back on them, it is not surprising that art, as it is thematized in these novels, is so often indifferent to the slum world. That it cannot be ultimately indifferent is the result of its juxtaposition with philanthropic concerns. Its practitioners, like Gilbert Gresham, the society portrait painter of *Workers*

14. George Gissing, *The Unclassed* (Rutherford: Fairleigh Dickinson University Press, 1976), 211. The passage has been interpreted as a statement of Gissing's own views; this discussion questions that reading. In a different context, Waymark's crossed motives resemble those of James's *Princess Casamassima*, whose concern for the poor seems to come from her own "starved passions."

in the Dawn, or its votaries, like Hubert Eldon, who studies Continental art, and Stella Westlake, whose devotion to poetry and art has Pre-Raphaelite overtones in *Demos*, are affluent and occasionally aristo-cratic. The names of their neighborhoods, streets and squares (St. John's Wood and Portland Place, for example) ring out in the texts almost in counterpoint to the bells, which so often symbolize misery.[15] The subjects of such an upper-class art, if they are not literary, his-torical, or neutral landscapes, are members of the artist's own class. Such art bespeaks ease and culture, and cultivates the urbane rather than the urban. At the same time, it is an art of both constriction and exclusion, depending as it does upon a certain superficiality and ig-norance of the urgencies of Demos (as the novel of that name sug-gests). To exclude the world of the slums from the order of art becomes tantamount to making it a subculture; to place it in the order of nature is to relieve it of any claims to representation. The position has some similarity to the linguistic mode of assigning the slums to the order of the indescribable, which, for all its rhetorical force, has the social effect of condemning them to inarticulateness.[16]

Such a gulf between a socially prominent art and a slum world that has no acceptable mode of representation is explicit in both *Workers in the Dawn* and *Demos*. Thus Arthur Golding feels he must choose between helping the poor and devoting his life to painting; he rejects a Hogarthian middle way.[17] His choice of high art is apparently sealed when he illustrates two landscapes from Tennyson's "The Palace of Art." In *Demos*, we must associate Hubert Eldon's affinity for European art with the squirearchic concern for natural beauty, which causes him to demolish Mutimer's "ugly" socialist village.[18] If we are to believe in the authenticity of such high art, which is not identical with the superficialities of the fashionable world, then we must see it in the

15. See, for example, *The Nether World*: "The sound of church-bells—most depressing of all sounds that mingle in the voice of London . . ." (391).

16. See the discussion of a related rhetorical problem in chapter 1.

17. See George Gissing, *Workers in the Dawn* (Garden City, N.Y.: Doubleday, Doran, 1935), 1: 163–70.

18. Eldon is explicit about the reasons for his actions: " 'It may be inevitable that the green and beautiful spots of the world shall give place to furnaces and mechanics' dwellings. For my own part, in this little corner, at all events, the ruin shall be delayed. In this matter I will give my instincts free play. Of New Wanley not one brick shall remain on another. I will close the mines, and grass shall grow over them. . . .' " And later: " 'The ruling motive in my life is the love of beautiful things; I fight against ugliness because it's the only work in which I can engage with all my heart. I have nothing of the enthusiasm of humanity.' " See *Demos* (New York: Dutton, n.d.), 338, 339.

context to which the titles of both these novels refer. Even if the dawn of *Workers in the Dawn* is in danger of being a false one, and "demos" is reduced to a mob, the problem of representing the slums is no less urgent. If the slums function as a thematic other to the traditional modes of art, they supply a persistent challenge to the adequacy of that art which, like the alternative mode of philanthropy but for other reasons, deflects them as subject.

No wonder that the reverse process seems so attractive: why not turn one's back on the slums and use art as a means of escape? Gissing is trying to undo the philanthropic relationship in Clara Hewett, who attempts to escape from the nether world of the Clerkenwell slums by acting in traveling provincial companies, and Thyrza Trent, whose talent for singing promises a career in a more cultured society. Both drama and music, cheap melodrama and art song, are secondary here in that they make no verbal pretense to articulate the lives of the poor. But there are also narrative signs of their failure. Her face disfigured by acid thrown by a rival actress who is jealous of her comparative success, Clara must return to her milieu; as she moves from the flat in the Farringdon Road buildings (an early instance of public low-cost housing) to the suburban villa in Crouch End, the disfigurements of the slums move with her. Rarely venturing outside, her face covered by a black veil, she is confined to the narrow spaces of the poor. The end of Thyrza's singing career is more ambiguous, though it is connected with her thwarted love for Egremont. The narrative problems raised here concern the difference between an art that takes the slums as its subject, and an art that seeks to disengage its subject from the slums. At this point, an erotics of art becomes entwined with the failure of its social promise.[19]

The complex problem of the subject, the origin, and the neutrality of art arises in the most powerful episode of *The Unclassed*. Waymark is on his weekly round of rent-collecting when he is captured (tied up and fastened to iron stakes on the floor of a flat) by Slimy, who is the quintessential creature of the slums. One-eyed, barely articulate, clad in a "semblance of clothing," Slimy is a jack of many trades, and a type of the debased artist. In one episode, he stands on his head

---

19. Thyrza Trent is in some ways comparable to Lizzie Hexam, in Dickens's *Our Mutual Friend*. Both have middle-class professional or intellectual lovers who are attracted to them as slum girls: they represent the attractions of the other, as well as the energies lost to the enervated middle class. The narrative thrust—aided in Thyrza's case by her singing—seeks to remove them from the slums.

and sings for money, only to have mud thrown in his mouth; the walls of his flat are "all scribbled over with obscene words and drawings" (101). He is a marginal creature:

> Among others, the man named Slimy just managed to hold his footing. Times were hard with Slimy, that was clear; still, he somehow contrived to keep no more than a fortnight behind with his rent. Waymark was studying this creature, and found in him the strangest matter for observation; in Slimy there were depths beyond Caliban, and, at the same time, curious points of contact with average humanity, unexpectedly occurring. He was not ungrateful for the collector's frequent forbearance, and, when able to speak coherently, tried at times to show this. Waymark had got into the habit of sitting with him in his room for a little time, whenever he found him at home. Of late, Slimy had seemed not quite in his usual health; this exhibited itself much as it would in some repulsive animal, which suffers in captivity, and tries to find a remote corner when pains come on. At times Waymark experienced a certain fear in the man's presence; if ever he met the dull glare of that one bleared blood-shot eye, a chill ran through him for a moment, and he drew back a little. Personal uncleanliness made Slimy's proximity at all times unpleasant; and occasionally his gaunt, grimed face grew to an expression suggestive of disagreeable possibilities. (229)

When those "disagreeable possibilities" are realized, Slimy is still not malevolent: he wants the rent monies from Waymark for the binge on which he plans to drink himself to death. The captivity, which is accidentally prolonged, is meant merely to give Slimy time to go on that final binge. While everything in this passage (and in the entire episode) endows Waymark with cultural superiority—his language, his aloofness (in part a function of the language[20]), his interpretive categories—there are nevertheless signs of what is to come. Slimy will rise up like a return of the repressed and take his narrative revenge. What happens argues for the impossibility of conventional artistic and philanthropic distance. Waymark is the artist imprisoned by his own ma-

---

20. In *Gissing in Context*, Adrian Poole comments for different reasons on the distance between observer and observed, which is in part a function of style (53–59).

terials. His self-assured interpretive categories are inadequate; Prospero in Milan, his powers abandoned, could not have controlled this Caliban. During the long hours of his imprisonment, Waymark listens to the games of children in the court below, games consisting of such things as riddles, "strange incantations" (237), the fitting of letters to objects (" 'I sent my daughter to the oil-shop, and the first thing she saw was C' " [236]). These sounds, and Slimy's brief monologue when he explains his plans (there is a simple practical syllogism: he has never been happy, money means happiness, therefore he will take the money for a full supply of his friends Brandy, Whiskey, Rum, and Gin), suggest that Waymark has observed but not heard, that the slums are his riddle, that they demand to be voiced, and that that voicing will be the only true way for the novelist to put his mark on the city. To solve the riddle of the city, one must hear it first.[21]

Thus far, it seems as if what is thematically prominent in the novels has led to narrative impasses. Philanthropy, which initially seems a reasonable method for uncovering the existence—the scandals—of the slums and for "improving" them, turns out to affirm the distance between donor and recipient, a distance which denies the poor an active or generative role in either philanthropy or narrative. Thematized, philanthropy would foreclose the very referent it seeks to engage; it is only if we view it as an approach to be tested, as one narrative strategy among others, that it becomes indeterminate or open enough to be fictionally useful. Although philanthropy itself might, depending on the rigidity or blindness with which it is practiced, invite a satirical eye, the aesthetic question has more to do with the way its interpretive system is cast into narrative categories. It is as if Gissing were transposing the spatial premises of the urban sketches into the more temporal terms of the novel. But to do that demands a constriction of the absolute claims of philanthropy into more tentative, heterogeneous terms. Philanthropy itself runs the risk of becoming a scandal.

The alternatives of art are also suspect, however. Its traditional mode simply excludes the slums, consigns them to a perpetual otherness, and denies them access to a cultural semiotic. An aesthetic of the

21. Waymark is eventually rescued into philanthropy by his marriage to Ida Starr. But this doubly elides the authorial problem: Waymark's future as a writer is left open, and, even more important, Gissing shifts into a romance mode where slum improvement substitutes for representation. Nevertheless, Waymark's experience during his captivity has similarities to the situation of the narrator in *Thyrza* listening to street music.

beautiful, of order and containment, has no affinity for the slums. Nor is an ethically disinterested art that takes the slums for its subject any more promising, because that very subject turns out to be unstable. Only the juxtaposition—a kind of syncrisis[22]—of philanthropy and art in narrative lines, a juxtaposition that appears in different forms in each of Gissing's slum novels, attests to the slums as an undifferentiated or preverbal presence. The slums are known obliquely, by dint of the mutual resistance between their voices and the language(s) of conventional art. What looks strangely like an antithesis between culture and nature can be overcome by introducing a third term into the problematic, that of the indigenous or natural art of the slums. Let us return to that passage about street music, now in its complete version:

> Do you know the music of the obscure ways, to which children dance? Not if you have only heard it ground to your ears' affliction beneath your windows in the square. To hear it aright you must stand in the darkness of such a by-street as this, and for the moment be at one with those who dwell around, in the blear-eyed houses, in the dim burrows of poverty, in the unmapped haunts of the semi-human. Then you will know the significance of that vulgar clanging of melody; a pathos of which you did not dream will touch you, and therein the secret of hidden London will be half revealed. The life of men who toil without hope, yet with the hunger of an unshaped desire; of women in whom the sweetness of their sex is perishing under labour and misery; the laugh, the song of the girl who strives to enjoy her year or two of youthful vigour, knowing the darkness of the years to come; the careless defiance of the youth who feels his blood and revolts against the lot which would tame it; all that is purely human in these darkened multitudes speaks to you as you listen. It is the half-conscious striving of a nature which knows not what it would attain, which deforms a true thought by gross expression, which clutches at the beautiful and soils it with foul hands. (*Thyrza*, 111–12)

22. The term is adopted from Mikhail Bakhtin's generalized use of it in *Problems of Dostoevsky's Poetics*, ed. and trans. Caryl Emerson (Minneapolis: University of Minnesota Press, 1984). Syncrisis, "the juxtaposition of various points of view toward a given object" (110–11), characterizes the mode of implicit dialogue in Gissing, even without the explicit context of carnivalization.

The street-organ, together with the dancing children, appears in several of Gissing's works, as well as in novels by Meredith and James.[23] The dancers are dirty, ragged, barefoot children, but here, as in the other passages in his novels, Gissing cannot tell the dancers from the dance, nor music from its meaning. Both nature and art, the expression of the beautiful in the ugly, they are essentially oxymoronic. The privileged art form of the slums is one that by its nature distances the urban artist, if it does not exclude him altogether. He must situate himself in a darkness that is both literal and figurative, and listen. The figure that will then represent the slums most authentically is one of de-formation: of the true and the beautiful, of prior artistic texts, of conventional codes and relationships, even of language and voice. Gissing apprehends the slums through tropes that convey varieties of antithesis. At the same time, the artist's recessive awareness offers through those very tropes, figures of disfigurement, access to the hidden sweetness and vigor of the slum-dwellers. The process is not dissimilar to the way in which Browning uses the alloy of the imagination in *The Ring and the Book*, which is, after all, an urban narrative.

In the slums, high art must undergo a process of deformation in order to emerge as the authentic art of the poor. (The only traditional artist mentioned in the slums is Hogarth; rejected as a model by Arthur Golding, he returns as an adjective describing the faces of two women of no culture and fewer morals in *Workers in the Dawn*.[24]) In the friendly lead[25] at the pub where Thryza first sings publicly, ballads are

23. See Henry James, *The Princess Casamassima* (New York: Charles Scribner's Sons, 1908): "A hand-organ droned in front of a neighbouring house and the cart of the local washerwoman, to which a donkey was harnessed, was drawn up opposite. The local children as well were dancing on the pavement to the music of the organ, and the scene was surveyed from one of the windows by a gentleman in a dirty dressing-gown, smoking a pipe, who made Hyacinth think of Mr. Micawber" (2:176). See also George Meredith, *Diana of the Crossways* (New York: Charles Scribner's Sons, 1910): "the ridiculous intervention of a street-organ, that ground its pipes in a sprawling roar of one of the *I Puritani* marches . . ." (439). Each of these passages questions the authenticity of the art mode, which diminishes or parodies the original context of feeling. Gissing's reversal consists of trying to discover the literary mode that will render the authenticity of the art of the streets.

24. See *Workers in the Dawn*, 2:335 "The two faces were a study for Hogarth: that of Polly Hemp, round, fair, marked with an incomparably vicious smile, the nose very thin and well-shaped, the lips brutally sensual, the forehead narrow and receding; that of Mrs. Pole altogether coarser and more vulgar, the nose swollen at the end and red, the mouth bestial and sullen, the eyes watery and somewhat inflamed, the chin marked by a slight growth of reddish hair. At the present moment both faces, different as were their outlines, vied in giving expression to the meanest phase of the meanest vice, that of avarice."

25. The *OED* defines a *friendly lead* as "among the poorer classes in London, an

more or less mauled by the other singers. Similarly, the sounds of a concertina and of Mr. Boddy's violin scrape and wheeze through the air of Lambeth. In *The Nether World*, art forms are also parodic, or they may be so apparently unmotivated as to seem antithetical to their contexts. Sidney Kirkwood's sketches are the sign of his failure, of his thwarted desire for art, love, the countryside, even of irresponsibility— of everything that is not connected with the slums. The best one can say of Mad Jack's psalms, which rise from the depths of Clerkenwell, is that they are a form of semiconscious religious parody.[26] Alternatively, Bob Hewett's turn to counterfeiting, the obverse of his talent for casting medals, approaches the debased and the vicious. Its very deviousness becomes embodied in the flight from the law that leads him into the heart of the slums (Shooter's Gardens) and to his death. One may contrast the rather elegant settings for the tableaux of *Vanity Fair* and *Daniel Deronda* with the *tableaux vivants* of *Workers in the Dawn*: a form of pornographic art in which young women clothed in flesh-colored material and posed in some allegorical scene, such as Adam and Eve with the apple, revolve on a "stage" before the stares and obscene remarks of male viewers.[27]

The figures of antithesis, catachresis, and oxymoron, to say nothing of the presence of debased and vicious forms of art, restore the necessity of the mediating figure of the narrator. If one needed more evidence, it would come from the frequent privileging of oratory as a representation of the voices of the slums. Once again, however, it entails the figures of deviance. *Demos* is in part a novel about voice;

---

entertainment given by friends for the benefit of a person in distress." A street reciter tells Henry Mayhew, " 'We went to a public-house where they were having a "lead," that is a collection for a friend who is ill, and the company throw down what they can for a subscription, and they have in a fiddle and make it social' " (*London Labour and the London Poor*, vol. 3 [New York: Dover Publications, 1968], 154).

26. Neither the audience nor the setting can be said to motivate Mad Jack's "performance": ". . . a wild, discordant voice suddenly broke forth somewhere in the darkness, singing in a high key, 'All ye works of the Lord, bless ye the Lord, praise Him and magnify Him for ever!' It was Mad Jack, who had his dwelling in the Court [in Shooter's Gardens], and at all hours was wont to practise the psalmody which made him notorious throughout Clerkenwell. A burst of laughter followed from a group of men and boys gathered near the archway" (*The Nether World*, 75).

27. *Workers in the Dawn* 2:381–82. The music accompanying the scene is that of a "wailing hand-organ playing a waltz in the time of a psalm-tune." Another index of the debasement of the art may be found in Benjamin's remark on *tableaux vivants*, the enjoyment of which is related to the "art of seeing." Further, "edifying sayings provide the interpretation" ("On Some Motifs in Baudelaire," in *Illuminations*, trans. Harry Zohn [New York: Schocken Books, 1969], 173).

Richard Mutimer's oratory has made him a leader of men, and it is opposed to the inarticulate roar of the mob, of demos: "On all sides was the thud of blows, . . . the clamour of those who combated. Demos was having his way; civilisation was blotted out" (*Demos*, 454). Mutimer's oratory, however, is suspect because it is now self-serving, now altruistic, sometimes like the performance of "a conscientious actor who plays night after night in a part that he enjoys" (416), sometimes sincere. It is a figure for the instability of voice itself: authentic as heard, it nevertheless demands figuration and interpretation. Similarly, John Hewett joins the crowd of Sunday-night orators on Clerkenwell Green, that public rostrum for the nether world. What is utterly sincere Radicalism on his part dwindles to incoherence over the years. But even when Hewett can speak well for the plight of the poor, he, too, is a performer in the crowd's eyes; ironically, his direct utterances speak less eloquently than his life, which must be cast in the words of the novelist.

There are moments in *The Nether World* where oratory and rhetoric recede into something like pure voice. Clara Hewett's richly moving voice, all that remains after her disfigurement (doubly symbolic in this context), becomes the vehicle by which she induces Kirkwood to marry her: it is her best performance, intended to evoke desire where her major desire is for security. But this is still a threshold phenomenon, where voice, although it is not only expressive, approaches art. From that point we may trace a gradually descending line of voices in the poor, from the fully self-conscious, which the narrator can overhear (especially in *The Nether World*), to the "brutal voice" and "atrocious language" of a Clem Peckover (*The Nether World*, 362) or the drunken cries of a Mrs. Candy.

It is the paradox of voice, then, that authorizes both the obscuring and the subsequent reemergence of the author. Here is the narrative voice speaking out of the twilight of Clerkenwell:

> A strange enough region wherein to wander and muse. Inextinguishable laughter were perchance the fittest result of such musing; yet somehow the heart grows heavy, somehow the blood is troubled in its course, and the pulses begin to throb hotly. (*The Nether World*, 11)

The narrator's interests are engaged, but he seems indistinct by virtue of both the infinitives and the synecdoches. This appears to be a move to effacement, the counterpart of the move into darkness in *Thyrza*, which nevertheless allows a generalized language to speak for the slums, whose own mode of speech can be so inarticulate, some sort of communicative noise from the perspective of civilization. The narrator has placed himself in the midst of his subject, but he must employ two modes of language, the heard and the impersonal, to represent it.[28] It is such double moments that Gissing inscribes in his novels as grounds for an urban poetics; against the directedness and the conventions of both philanthropy and art, Gissing offers the way of indirection, the figures of deviation, the impersonality of engagement.

IV

By recognizing the strangeness and otherness of the slums, the tradition of social exploration designates them as an area to be discovered and recuperated into language. Thus the hypothetical "stranger bold enough to explore" in the passage on Shooter's Gardens becomes a figure for the writer. From his standpoint, the slums offer immediacy and energy despite the visible signs of entropy and decay. Although Gissing's general vision of the city has been compared to Charles Booth's,[29] there is surely a divergence from Booth's systematic approach, his statistical reticence. What Booth tries to summarize and encode, Gissing tries to open up. This is a problem of narrative, to be sure, but it is also one of language, which inverts the spareness of sociological accounts. It seems puzzling, then, that despite his sympathy for the slum-dwellers and, even more important, the re-situating of the narrator within the space of the fictional text, Gissing resorts to the conventional metaphors of disease, bestiality, and hell to depict the slums. Any one of these relegates the world of the poor to the other-than-human, to a domain to be avoided rather than ex-

28. One should distinguish this doubling in the modes of language from the distinction Adrian Poole makes in *Gissing in Context*. For Poole, the narrator's language—and thus his narrative distance—is a function of class or even ideological differences.

29. See John Goode, *George Gissing: Ideology and Fiction* (New York: Barnes and Noble, 1979), 93–100. The importance of Goode's analogy lies in another direction, however: Booth's interpretive concern is with "urbanisation," with a process inferred from the abstract analysis of the city. This may be compared with Gissing's own imaginative mapping of London.

plored. Together, they have been taken as evidence for a latent Toryism that disdains its subjects and that rescinds the very sympathies the novels have been willing to offer in other ways.[30] Another reason, however, lies in the distribution of metaphors. These metaphors are not determinate; rather, they challenge the very constructions that they ascribe to the slums.

The later representations of Shooter's Gardens in *The Nether World* reveal one way in which Gissing's language works. Gissing does finally "burden description" with the austere materiality of poverty: the bare rooms, the dark passages, the voices rising out of that darkness— drunken cries, the hyperbolic invective of one Mr. Hope, petty but violent quarrels, the wandering prophecies of Mad Jack. Poverty, drink, and crime appear to situate Shooter's Gardens at the center of an urban labyrinth from which there is no escape. The place seems to be a metaphorical gloss upon the title of the novel. Yet from the perspective of the labyrinth, Shooter's Gardens is a blind alley, rather than the center of the slums, despite Bob Hewett's flight there which ends in his death, or Mad Jack's apocalyptic dream. It stands as a parodic version of the community that exists elsewhere in the slums; that genuine community finds a place not in this abstract, quasi-allegorical ending but in the narrative lines and endings concerned with Jane Snowdon and Sidney Kirkwood. Both renounce love and ambition, but both embrace an ideal of service:

> Unmarked, unencouraged save by their love of uprightness and mercy, they stood by the side of those more hapless, brought some comfort to hearts less courageous than their own. Where they abode it was not all dark. (392)

Gissing's narratives, then, question their metaphorical premises. The fate of the ironic general term "superfluous mankind" is significant. A meditation on superfluity runs throughout the novel, most often settling upon the passive, victimized Pennyloaf Candy (and her lack of superfluities), but also raising the abstract question of when or in what context an ironic term may be understood literally. Because the

---

30. See P. J. Keating's remarks on Gissing's mistrust of the working-class hero in *The Working Classes in Victorian Fiction*; Jacob Korg's comments on Gissing's attitudes (in his novels) to social reform in *George Gissing: A Critical Biography* (Seattle: University of Washington Press, 1963); and Fredric Jameson's reading of Gissing's ambivalence in the context of *ressentiment* in *The Political Unconscious.*

slums are superfluous from the perspective of the middle and upper classes (even when they provide labor for "the meaningless work which is demanded by the rich vulgar" [57], the necessity is dubious) in a social sense, the term depends on context. Pennyloaf is "superfluous" (356); there is little money to spend on "superfluities" in the Hewett–Kirkwood villa in Crouch End. But if the term is thematized, it also slips into narrative, insofar as Pennyloaf serves as an agent in whom slum life is foregrounded. The instability of the term "superfluous" is an index to the way in which Gissing can call into question the categories of verbal meaning.[31]

Something similar happens with Clem Peckover, the apparent personification of the brutality of the slums. Only when she is dissembling is she able to avoid violence in speech or act: every relationship—marital, familial, amorous, mistress–servant—is marked by present or projected violence put in the service of desire or hatred. Yet there is a qualifying note in the narrator's stance:

> The frankness of Clem's brutality went far towards redeeming her character. The exquisite satisfaction with which she viewed Jane's present misery, the broad joviality with which she gloated over the prospect of cruelties shortly to be inflicted, put her at once on a par with the noble savage running wild in woods. Civilisation could bring no charge against this young woman; it and she had no common criterion. (6)

If civilization casts Clem beyond its peripheries, she nevertheless represents another order of discourse which the artist may seek:

> There was no denying that Clem was handsome; at sixteen she had all her charms in apparent maturity, and they were of the coarsely magnificent order. Her forehead was low and of great width; her nose was well shapen, and had large sensual apertures; her cruel lips may be seen on certain fine antique busts; the neck that supported her heavy head was splendidly rounded. In laughing, she became a model for an artist, an embodiment of fierce life independent of morality. (8)

31. Cf. also Lear's "Our basest beggars / Are in the poorest thing superfluous" (William Shakespeare, *King Lear*, II.iv).

If the narrator sounds like the Victorian casting off the restraints of Hebraic morality for the pagan pleasures of Hellenism, more is at stake than the justification for the worldly connoisseur: Clem's is an "evilly fostered growth" (8) that belongs in an art or a narrative from which "civilisation" would exclude it. Witness to the discontinuities between civilization and savagery, morality and act, Clem's presence also proclaims a new alliance, now to be explicit, between a "fierce life" and art.

Gissing's novels presuppose a dialogue between a civilization that is complacent about its metaphors, depending upon them for the definition of its perimeters, and a narrative voice that attempts to unseat those metaphors. The method entails not excluding but contextualizing even the most traditional metaphors and casting them in a heterogeneous series. This is apparent in the beginning of Gissing's first novel, *Workers in the Dawn*. The narrator takes the reader on a guided tour of the Saturday night Whitecross Street market. The opening words, "Walk with me, reader, into Whitecross Street" (1,3), indicate that the scene is to be regarded as spatially continuous with the world of the reader. (That the market is to be interpreted under the sign of the real already questions the premises of the excluding metaphors of civilization.[32]) Such an invitation to a spectacle that cannot have been ordinary to a reader unacquainted with the slums masks cultural discontinuity with a rhetoric that establishes spatial continuity. Narrator and reader will be both observers and observed: "Now back into the street, for already we have become the observed of a little group of evil-looking fellows. . ." (1,4). Here specularity serves the referential rather than the self-reflexive. This minor labyrinth, this cacophony of sounds, this jumble of figures and objects that is ordered by the text in only the most casually metonymical way, has the atmosphere of a theater, of a shifting spectacle, of something strange and exotic. The flickering lights, the repeated intense cries, the succession of typical faces, all seem to belong to some ritual. The darkest overtones of the passage identify as a version of hell this market whose "flaring naphtha-lamps, the flames of which shoot up fiercely at each stronger gust of wind" (3) emerge from "horrible darkness" (4) beyond, with its "unspeakable abominations." In this pestilential world, brutes live in

---

32. Gissing's narrative openings frequently gesture toward the real. For a discussion of the possible ambiguities of such openings, see Victor Brombert, "Opening Signals in Narrative," *New Literary History* 11 (1980): 489–502.

dens fouler than those of animals. The dominant metaphorical structures, those of hell and bestiality, may share the same signifier, but
they are distinguished by their contraries, each one of which is to be
developed in a complex manner. With a simple shift to the third person
and to a time twenty years earlier, the slums, as hell, become the
origin of narrative. The following chapter offers in contrast the idyllic
rural home (in a village conveniently named Bloomford) of the Nor-
mans. From a narrative point of view, the mediating place is the ironically named Adam and Eve Court, a part of the slum in which the
Reverend Norman will find the child Arthur Golding by the side of his
dying father.

But if we consider the slums to be the domain of the bestial or the
subcultural, as if they were nature viewed from the perspective of
Caliban, then the contrasting world is that of culture, of education,
art, and material ease. This second metaphor is by no means stable,
however: the cultural world is often superficial, as we see in the fashionable art of Mr. Gresham and the loveless marriage of his daughter
Maud. The world of culture is linked even more directly to the slum
via the ordinand Augustus Whiffle's seduction of Carrie, the slum girl.
(Whiffle's continuing dissipation does not prevent his eventual ordi-
nation.)

Gissing's metaphorical treatment of the slum is not merely incon-
sistent, however, insofar as it opens up a space for writing. Each
metaphor limits the other, but in so doing becomes an enabling figure
for narrative and initiates a different set of narrative activities. One
does not try to educate the denizens of hell, though one can try to
transform "nature" into "culture," as both Helen Norman and Arthur
Golding proceed with their educational projects. As the realm of the
demonic, the slum may be the locus of vice; but it is also the source
of rich and hitherto undifferentiated energies that bring the novel into
being. Even by using conventional metaphors, then, Gissing alters the
relation of language to its referent and of writer to city. The terms that,
when used singly or monolithically, would have served to demystify
the city, or to fix it in a pattern of relations in nonfiction (to the point
of confirming the ideology or the superiority of the writer), together
now deepen the mystery and permit the narrator to mediate among
divergent systemic patterns. If totalizing metaphors reduce, then the
ambiguity of the slums refuses that reduction.

The function of description—nowhere more evident than in the
great set-pieces that punctuate the novels—is then to assert simul-

taneously both the reality and the metaphoric heterogenity of the slums, to make them both referentially useful and narratable. The descriptions of Litany Lane in *The Unclassed*, of the Saturday-night market, the street dancing in Lambeth, and the Caledonian Road in *Thyrza*, of the Sunday-night oratory on Clerkenwell Green in *The Nether World*, the scenes of Hoxton and Clerkenwell that virtually frame *Demos*: one is tempted to view such passages as vestigial urban sketches that confirm the reality of each locale. The use of the present tense and the reference to a present time of writing, to which the time of the novel may then be related as historical time, would then authenticate the scenes.[33] What sounds rhetorical ("Do you know the music of the obscure ways, to which children dance?") would assert rather the accessibility of the slum world outside the order of narrative. But that assertion becomes a narrative move that will break into—or break up—the closed world of convention. One important chapter in *The Nether World* portrays an excursion of a wedding party from the slums to the Crystal Palace, now the site of a pleasure garden for the poor. The rowdiness and the latent violence, the de-formed popular culture of which one now and then catches a glimpse, are framed in the language of high literary culture, of which the title, "Io Saturnalia," is a fair indication. That language is frequently considered to be the vehicle of a perspective directed ironically against the poor.[34] But it can also be read allegorically as the clash of literary language against the fierce energies of the slums. Gissing is engaged in a double project: that of writing the slums as if they were real, and of recasting the linguistic, textual, and narrative codes of an urban culture that persistently misread the nether world. New metaphors appear, for example, the spreading blot of the poor on the map as the Hewetts move from Clerkenwell Close to the Farringdon Road Buildings to Crouch End. The slums become a new text.

V

The slums, then, are at once independent and the product of a relation, the object of a discourse whose categories are unstable. Several prob-

---

33. Cf. Roland Barthes on the function of informants in "An Introduction to the Structural Analysis of Narrative," *New Literary History* 5 (1975): 249–50.

34. See, for example, Jacob Korg, *George Gissing: A Critical Biography*, 114.

lems arise from this situation. If the slums are the object, then the life of the poor is central. But how can one cast their collective life into narrative discourse, especially when that discourse, like Gissing's, largely avoids such obvious devices as crowd scenes, scenes that in the novels of Scott and Dickens do often portray the actions and destinies of a people. In contrast, Gissing's crowd scenes tend to be threshold phenomena that situate the urban novelist as much or more than his subject. Further, how can one revise the categorical absolutes (for instance, vice and its subcategories of drunkenness, deceit, thievery, and violence) so that their force as synecdoches is limited or deflected? How, too, can one differentiate the individual passions that emerge from the collective life of the lower world? That new discourse would first have to foreground the culture of the slums, including such collective rituals as the dancing, the market nights, the political meetings, the friendly leads. Against this culture, however deformed, one can then measure family loyalties, friendships, love: all the forms of desire and passion that were formerly granted only to the socially and economically privileged."[35] Gissing wrests his subject from its demonic depths in the progression of the five novels: the hellish White-cross Street market of *Workers in the Dawn* becomes, for example, the more vital communal Saturday-night market of Lambeth in *Thyrza*. Political oratory, confined and futile in *Workers in the Dawn*, then self-seeking voices that sway the mob in *Demos*, develops into a more authentic (if still futile) expression of desire in *The Nether World*.

Thyrza presents a reasonably normalized structure of slum life. The perspective from the outside does make it a unified community, to be sure. It is a geographical entity, different from Bloomsbury or Islington or Vauxhall; its streets are named, and it is traversed and in effect defined by the inhabitants. Its people work in local factories, making candles and hats; poor though they are, they are not subject to the vicissitudes of casual labor. The innocent gossip of factory workrooms, the occasional "ceremonial" meetings for tea, the meetings of courting couples on streets (which afford more privacy than crowded rooming-houses): such details appear with a frequency that establishes their normality, their ordinariness. Although voicing the world of the poor presupposes its own semiarticulateness, its inability to go

---

35. We may add these new forms of recognition and differentiation to the new forms of perception that Raymond Williams finds in urban writing of the late nineteenth century. Cf. *The Country and the City* (London: Chatto and Windus, 1973), 215–32.

beyond the sounds and cries of Lambeth, and its occasional half-illiterate writing, that voicing also makes the narrator a mediator, a specially endowed flâneur or privileged observer who discovers, in the metaphorical half-darkness of the slums, a world not so very different from the known civilized world.

All this documentation, which relies as much upon the presentation of communal mores as on the representation of external detail, appears to be directed toward transforming the otherness of the slums into a subcategory of the familiar, as we have noted. Gossip is as malicious in one as in the other;[36] husbands and prospective husbands, among the poor as among the middle class, are both granted the right to approve and direct their wives' behavior: these are signs of the impulse to restore the world of the poor to a known circuit of desires and concerns. But even this apparently innocent process may alter the moral balance and give the slum community an edge over its fashionable counterpart, which tends to lack the vitality, the intense loyalties, and the open expression of feeling (here valorized as a form of authenticity) so intrinsic to life in Lambeth. The married life of the politician Dalmaine (he is the middle-class MP for Lambeth) consists of trying to mold his wife—to suppress and transform her—into his idea of the model politician's mate, for example, while the problem envisaged in a marriage of Lambeth's Totty Nancarrow and Luke Ackroyd would be that of accommodating two such outspoken and individual personalities in the close quarters of the slum. The social expediency that motivates Dalmaine's marriage (as political expediency determines his public acts) finds a higher moral opposite in the friendship, sympathy, and unselfishness that often motivate slum marriages. Even Egrement's romantic visions of Thyrza are preceded by thoughts of the working-class home that Thyrza and Gilbert Grail, married, would share. The deficiencies of the slum with respect to education, to art, to self-representation, all that to the superficial perspective might reveal only the slum's brutishness, are thus balanced against its moral qualities, its openness, its cohesiveness. We now discover that they supply a lack: to identify this as "home" or "ethics" is to offer a somewhat sentimental formulation. The deeper logic is that of the supplement, in which the slum's moral and passional energies are crucial to society.[37]

---

36. See *Thyrza*, 236.
37. Daniel Doyce's family plays a similar role in Dickens's *Little Dorrit*. Gissing's com-

In effect, what Gissing is doing is rewriting the slums. Document supplants worn metaphor, the inner vision cancels distance, the discovery of a community, bound occasionally by expediency and malevolence, but more often by loyalty and honesty, organizes apparent chaos. One might claim that when the crowd gives way to types (even when they are figures for the crowd) and individuals, Gissing is applying in a practical way a strategy in which his perception of the slum, far from approving its mores, is under the constraints of an ideology that would neutralize it and remove its covertly revolutionary threats to established society.[38] But this thesis is debatable, especially after one recognizes first that the representation of the slum is the result of a mode of perception newly brought to bear on its materials; and second, that Gissing's version revises middle-class dreams of the slums, dreams that themselves profess variously to be enlightened, idealistic, or cynical. (Mad Jack's dream then stands as the interior, satirical text.) Those dreams are, of course, predicated on class and distance, the latter symbolized in the physical sources of the dreams: the Lake District and Westminster. The dreams become actualized in political schemes and philanthropic projects, whose inadequacies we have already examined. The resistance to the schemes is then figured in the fact that after four years, there is very little change in the self-enclosed life in Lambeth. What is more scandalous from a narrative point of view, beyond the inadequacy of the motivation for these schemes, is the inappropriate representations of the slums that they have implied.

Perhaps because there is no overriding collective concern or movement, aside from an occasional abstract identification with the community, representation is apt to assume a form analogous to that of the still life, a picture that contains, significantly for these novels, the hidden figure of death or *nature morte*. Or, representation may comprise a collection of narrative fragments: the Trent sisters' concern for

munity is more extensive than that of Bleeding Heart Yard, however, and its attractions are less likely to be enhanced by the language of the narrator. The enhancement is, rather, the result of Egremont's desires. On the logic of the supplement, see Jacques Derrida, *Of Grammatology*, trans. Gayatri Chakravorty Spivak (Baltimore: Johns Hopkins University Press, 1976).

38. Cf. Raymond Williams, *Culture and Society, 1780-1950* (New York: Columbia University Press, 1958). Williams claims that the "structure of feeling" in Elizabeth Gaskell's *Mary Barton* demonstrates a tension between sympathy and fear of violence. One might then argue that Gissing's treatment of the slums defuses, by its narrative strategies, the revolutionary threat that would be fostered by slum conditions.

the aging, crippled Mr. Boddy, who has "fathered" the orphaned girls and finds himself clinging more and more to the margins of life when he can no longer find work; the romance of Luke Ackroyd and Totty Nancarrow; the growing closeness of the widower Bunce and Totty, who cares for his children; the tensions between Christian and atheist. Combined into a network of narrative lines, these slum stories all move, in *Thyrza*, toward stability. If plots, like instincts, seek eventual quiescence,[39] that end may also be political. In this narrative sense it would be true to say that, neither volcanic nor demonic, its narrative energies apparently dispersed into fragments, the slum poses no social threat.

This would also be true of *The Nether World*, where violence is turned inward, both spatially and thematically: the victims are the slum-dwellers themselves. But to come to this point requires a reinterpretation of social codes:

> Bob's temperament was, in a certain measure, that of the artist; he felt without reasoning; he let himself go whither his moods propelled him. Not a man of evil propensities; entertain no such thought for a moment. Society produces many a monster, but the mass of those whom, after creating them, it pronounces bad are merely bad from the conventional point of view; they are guilty of weaknesses, not of crimes. (218)

Together with the fragmented narratives, such passages allow us to interpret Gissing's novels as reconstituting the crowd. Dispersed into separate narrative fragments, the crowd is then reformed not as the mob of *Demos* but rather as the still life, whose components may be will-less, or passive, or; if they are violent, the victims of their own violence. Middle-class fantasies can be defused or turned inside out; society may be unscathed physically if not ideologically.

It would not be surprising to find the representation of the community relying upon types, and Gissing does indeed evoke a typology of urban figures that rises at moments to personification. Clem Peckover is "embodiment of an fierce life." If Bob Hewett is the debased artist, Pennyloaf Candy has "that dolorous kind of prettiness which is often enough seen in the London needle-slave" (*The Nether World*,

---

39. See Peter Brooks, "Freud's Masterplot: A Model for Narrative," in *Reading for the Plot* (New York: Knopf, 1984), 90–112.

72). One can find, at the artificial-flower factory where Jane Snowdon works, "all the various types of the London crafts-girl" (127).[40]

But the difficulty of the type from the narrative perspective is that it is too predictable—it cannot generate new narratives—and thus places the urban novelists in a paradoxical situation. Identifications of the type in Gissing generally appear under the sign of the natural, as part of the claim for the real.[41] Not only is the type a threat to the deviations and mysteries of fiction, it challenges the thematic premises of Gissing's art. While he cannot avoid the type (to do so would defy description)—the déclassé intellectual, the frustrated worker, the fanatic philanthropist—he can show the individual emerging from the type. In this way, he advances the gesture made in the urban sketch. The frequent representation of marginality and of transgressive acts then acquires a new significance. The crossing from Bloomsbury to Lambeth, from intellectual quarter to slum, marks a transgression of fictional as well as class boundaries. Egremont enters Lambeth as a philanthropist and discovers a passion in himself that is irrational, almost uncanny. Egremont has in fact returned to his place of origin: his father was poor and uneducated but made a fortune as a manufacturer. Similarly, Thyrza, although she thinks of herself as a working girl, is singled out for her musical talent and her beauty. The slums are at best plain, at worst ugly, as if ugliness had a negative moral value from which all that is good in the slums would have to be distinguished. It is as if Gissing needs to find an individual emerging from a type to set narrative in motion; the slums, however, can comply only in part. Once the slums are perceived as ordinary, then something stronger is needed for the enabling act of narrative. Many of the most intense scenes in *Thyrza* occur at thresholds, margins, points of de-

40. See also the additional reference to Pennyloaf's typicality: "Like all the women of her class, utterly ignorant and helpless in the matter of preparing food, she abandoned the attempt to cook anything, and expended her few pence daily on whatever happened to tempt her in a shop, when meal-time came round" (*The Nether World*, 266). Cf. also Hyacinth Robinson's response to Millicent Henning: "She summed up the sociable humorous ignorant chatter of the masses, their capacity for offensive and defensive passion, their instinctive perception of their strength on the day they should really exercise it; and as much as any of this their ideal of something smug and prosperous, where washed hands and oiled hair and plates in rows on dressers and stuffed birds under glass and family photographs of a quite similar effect would symbolise success" (Henry James, *The Princess Casamassima* [New York: Charles Scribner's Sons, 1908], 1:164).

41. A more abstract or romantic presentation of types is far less apparent. *The Unclassed*, which seems to some readers to lean more to romance than the other slum novels, presents Maud Enderby and Ida Starr as sacred and profane love respectively.

marcation: on Lambeth Bridge (a point between two worlds); at a hedge outside a summer house; in an empty building which is being remodeled into a library; at the edge of the sea. It is at these points of emergence that a counternarrative takes shape in which individual lives and passions gain precedence over communal life.

These thresholds are also areas where individual passions detach themselves from the social and form more continuous narrative lines. It is here that the structural paradigms of ambivalence and reversal become apparent, that those novels which ostensibly narrate the lives of the poor now relegate them to background or contextual functions. The narrative project of establishing the ordinariness of the slums recedes before a focus on the extraordinary. In *Thyrza*, it is passion that is extraordinary, all the more so because at several places in the novel, characters explicitly deny that they feel any passion. Thyrza agrees to marry Grail despite her lack of passion for him; Egremont feels no passion for Annabel (a middle-class young woman), nor does Annabel admit to any for him (142–43, 161, 490), though they will eventually marry. To the contrary, Thyrza and Egremont, after a very few meetings, are aware of their passion for each other. Not only is this extraordinary (" 'You missed your chance' ", Annabel tells Egremont at the end), but it raises serious problems about one's commitments (Thyrza is about to marry Grail). These relationships are not independent of setting, because what makes the "affair" (never more than desired by Thyrza and Egremont, and imagined by the rest of the novel's world) so scandalous is that it would involve the unthinkable union of a working girl with an Oxford-educated intellectual. In late Victorian terms that union could only be interpreted as seduction. After two years of separation, however, during which time Thyrza has suppressed but "nurtured" her passion while Egremont has lost his, class issues are no longer dominant: musical training as well as some education have made Thyrza, if anything, a "better" person than Egremont.[42] Their separation and Thyrza's death seem more the frustration of conventional romance than the fulfillment of a covert authorial statement about the impossibility of crossing class lines.[43] But such a romance, with its ordeals, its separations, its crossed lovers, is ascribable to questions of individual honor, and more and more inde-

42. See *Thyrza*, 442–43.
43. Cf. Michael Collie, *The Alien Art: A Critical Study of George Gissing's Novels* (Hamden, Conn.: Archon, 1979); and Fredric Jameson, *The Political Unconscious* for differing comments on Gissing's concern with maintaining class barriers.

pendent of the slum, which seemed at first so inescapable. Even Thyrza's fondness for the sea (it is her first experience of it that predisposes her to fall in love with Egremont, and thereafter it symbolizes for her both passion and independence) elides the specifically cultural. The moments when characters become oblivious to their settings mark their abandonment of social existence:

> [Thyrza and her sister Lydia] walked quickly and without speaking as far as the lights and noise of Westminster Bridge Road. For them the everyday movement of the street had no meaning; such things were the mere husk of life; each was absorbed in her own being.[44]

It is in the return to the social that we can perceive the reversibility or the ambiguity of the narrative lines. Even as the story of individual passions detaches itself both formally and thematically from its context, it becomes a social allegory, a comment upon a lack or deficiency in contemporary society—here the lack of potentially ennobling passion. In this light, Egremont's return to Lambeth, to his origins, is predicated on the initial severance; that his return is abortive bodes a continuing lack of authenticity in a society that countenances no extreme gestures. (This is thematized in the alternative modes of life in the upper world: the political, the contemplative, or the mildly philanthropical.) The slums then become the site of a passion perceived as threatening but that could give new life and meaning to a worn society.

The Nether World varies this model: the type gives way to the individuals whose passions, desires and schemes sketch out trajectories that separate them, figuratively speaking, from the slums. Although it depicts the plight of those who have not, it also presents an underlying opposition between passion and amoral energy on the one hand, and poverty, emptiness, and suppression on the other. This tension is supported by the nearly homologous one that balances art against counterfeits, or against the vulgar jewelry made in Clerkenwell, or against money. Thematically, art is linked with passion and the individual, amoral (in a complex, anticonventional sense) life. Philan-

---

44. *Thyrza*, 465. Adrian Poole notes that "the central plot of the love complications between Gilbert, Thyrza and Egremont becomes increasingly detached from the dense physical context of Lambeth" (*Gissing in Context*, 82), but for different purposes.

thropy is linked with the collective life, and with the suppression or displacement of desire. At one moment in the novel, Sidney Kirkwood's love for Jane Snowdon seems coincident with the philanthropic project that her grandfather has envisaged for them. When Sidney cannot reconcile the two, the social is once again poised against the individual. Thus the original problematic of philanthropy and art is now interiorized in *The Nether World*, a novel that tends to interiorize its urban spaces as well as its narrative perspectives. The figure who opens the book, the strangely dressed traveler who will turn out to be Michael Snowdon, becomes a surrogate for the wandering artist and the initiator of a quest; the form it first takes, that of the search for his granddaughter Jane, will then become the larger quest to relieve slum misery through a philanthropic program. Sidney Kirkwood, whose own craft of jewelry-making foregrounds art, replaces him and the narrator as the interior observer for part of the novel. The narrative ends in a scene of death: Sidney and Jane meet annually at Michael's grave. But the ambiguous meanings of death— of passion and of art, and of a large philanthropic plan—serve to confirm the reversibility of the narrative that has led to it.[45]

VI

Gissing's project of voicing the slums retains its ambivalence, although we may now understand more easily why the slums should have had so obsessive an attraction for him. The question of their narrative status, their referentiality, is still unresolved. There is the problem of representation. One formulation of the paradox appears in Foucault: "It is in vain that we say what we see; what we see never resides in what we say."[46] To say this is to challenge the representational powers of fiction. Freed of a conventional language which, by its metaphors or by its elisions, excludes the slums from representation, Gissing seems able to approach the slums in a project with social as well as aesthetic implications. But his narrative solution—the use of a par-

45. Walter Benjamin's claim that death sanctions narrative here invites the supplementary remark that reversible narratives insist upon death's double (both literal and figurative) meaning. Cf. "The Storyteller," in *Illuminations*, 100–101.

46. Michel Foucault, *The Order of Things* (London: Tavistock, 1970), 9.

adigm of reversal—then places the very substantiality and urgency of the slums in tension with the imperatives of art. Voicing the slums (where the voices of the slums are fixed in art) amounts, in the end, to questioning or denying their referentiality. The monster lurking in the nineteenth-century slum may not be poverty or drink so much as it is referentiality itself, which Gissing must repeatedly confront and try to overcome in order to assert his powers as an artist of the city.

Insofar as Gissing's novels are exemplary, they suggest that coping with "the real" in fiction may dramatize the instability of the very referents with which it is concerned. In nineteenth-century urban novels, narrative is involved in a continuing struggle with its subject, where the strength of prose narrative itself is at stake. Here the slums stand as a metonymy for the massive phenomenal city. How can one make "superfluous" humanity not superfluous to art? Entrance into the slums involves an exchange: the demonic, pre-moral narrative energies of the slums for the discourse of the narrator. Such an exchange seems tantamount to repression, as those energies are acceptable only in disguise, channeled through the voice of the narrator.

By making the slums the subject of his narratives, however, Gissing multiplies their scandalous possibilities. The scandal doubles merely by reversing the social perspective: if the existence of the poor raises questions about society's responsibility for that world, the attempts of the poor to resist or transgress the roles into which society casts them are equally scandalous. Scandal merges with the carnivalesque, itself an antihierarchical eruption. A still deeper scandal appears at the level of representation, in which the poverty of the slums is rewritten as unconventional energies, supplementary to an urban art, that polite society and polite literature would suppress. It is Gissing's own ambivalence, which operates at each level, that allows the scandal to persist. Even if we were to bracket the possibility of the self-referential, we would still have to face the lack of fixity in what had seemed the most absolute of referents. Without that bracketing, Gissing's quest for the referent becomes an allegory about urban fiction. The search for the real lays bare the materials of art; social and aesthetic ambivalence ends by opening fiction to the unexpected, the unconventional, and the heterogeneous. If Gissing's novels too often fail to resolve the issues they raise, if his ambivalence comes dangerously close to the programmatic or the prescriptive, they may for those very reasons afford a deeper glimpse into that heart of darkness that was at once the nineteenth-century slum and the problematic of an urban fiction.

3

The Fashionable Novel and the Mode of Hyperbole

*I*n the quest for the reality of the city, the slums turn out to be an ambiguous referent. Elusive and unstable, subject to the metaphors they first engender, their appearance masks a complex idea of the urban. The exploration of the slums entails the identification of their opposites, of a series of relations in which the slums' very otherness binds them uncannily to those parts of the city that refuse to recognize them. Let us turn to their apparent antithesis, the life of fashion, where the problematic track of representation allies the material with the immaterial.

Novels of fashionable life occupy a special place in the literature of the city. Those novels, and the exemplary figure of the dandy who is so much in their foreground, are radically different from those other urban fictions that seek out the physical phenomena, the flora and fauna of the city as evidence of the city's material reality or as symbols of its social or moral structures. The fashionable novels tend to elide conventional description and to concentrate rather on extremes, on splendid interiors that can eclipse even those of the Arabian Nights (as Thackeray noted[1]) or, paradoxically, on the dens of low life. Such descriptions then imply the presence of the marvelous or the romantic, those very qualities that seem extraneous to the urban artist's search to comprehend the city. To found description on the excessive or the spectacular is to pursue a contradiction. In contrast, Wordsworth's experience of London, which deflated his romantic dreams of the city, creates the paradigm for the city as the place of the unromantic, of alienation, and even of superficiality. The exotic creatures who traverse the text of Book VII of *The Prelude* are grotesque copies, to the point of caricature, of a splendor that cannot be authentic in the carnival world of the city. How, then—national differences aside—are we to understand Baudelaire's persistent linkage of dandies and dandyism with the modern, with the "heroism of modern life," and his identification of the city as the site of the marvelous and the poetic, as the sphere of the dandy's actions?[2] It is Baudelaire who adds a third problem to those of description and romance: the dandy, despite his aspirations to spiritual elegance, to true aristocracy, seeks also "l'insensibilité." To be insensible or blasé, rather than passionate, is his ideal. Surely this is not very promising for the novel, which so often explores desire and passion. The literary problem of dandyism is, then, to become narratable, to add something to those elegant surfaces for which dandies are so notable. The fourth problem is again articulated in Baudelaire's brief essays on the heroism of modern life and on dandyism. Heroism and dandyism are not, on the face of things, linked, nor would the dandy seem to belong to a political moment. Yet these qualities are precisely what Baudelaire attributes to him. That moment is, Baudelaire claims, the time when the aristocracy is on the wane, but before the rising tide of democracy (the phrase is his) has triumphed. The fashionable world and politics: How

---

1. See Thackeray's comment on Disraeli's *The Young Duke*: "he out-duked all the dukes in the land—he invented splendours which Stafford House never can hope to equal—he dreamed better dreams than Alnaschar himself. . . ." (William Makespeace Thackeray, Review of Disraeli's *Coningsby* [13 May 1844], *Contributions to the Morning Chronicle*, ed. Gordon N. Ray. [Urbana: University of Illinois Press, 1955], 39–40).

2. Charles Baudelaire, "De l'héroïsme de la vie moderne," in *Salon de 1846*, in *Oeuvres complètes*, Bibliothèque de la Pléiade (Paris: Editions Gallimard, 1961), 951, 952.

is it possible to justify this odd couple? All of these issues form a problematic of representation. The artist of the city, seeking a way of entering it at least figuratively, is denied those very modes of description by which the city becomes accessible in other genres. Let us start, however, with an obvious threshold.

> I was ushered into a beautiful apartment, hung with rich damask, and interspersed with a profusion of mirrors, which enchanted me to the heart: beyond, to the right of this room, was a small boudoir, fitted up with books, and having, instead of carpets, soft cushions of dark green velvet, so as to supersede the necessity of chairs. This room, evidently a favourite retreat, was adorned at close intervals with girandoles of silver and mother of pearl; and the interstices of the book-cases were filled with mirrors, set in silver: the handles of the doors were of the same metal.
>
> Beyond this library (if such it might be called), and only divided from it by half-drawn curtains of the same colour and material as the cushion, was a bath room. The decorations of this room were of a delicate rose colour; the bath, which was of the most elaborate workmanship, represented, in the whitest marble, a shell, supported by two Tritons. There was, as Glanville afterwards explained to me, a machine in this room, which kept up a faint but perpetual breeze, and the light curtains, waving to and fro, scattered about perfumes of the most exquisite odour.[3]

Material felicities such as these are extreme, but they are not uncharacteristic of the dandy's environment. Mrs. Darlington Vere, styled the "Muse of the dandies" in Disraeli's *The Young Duke*,[4] has similar furnishings: her saloon is "hung with rose-coloured silk, which dispersed a delicate tint over the inlaid and costly cabinets. It was crowded with tables covered with bijouterie." Like Glanville's rooms, it represents a secular temple where art, by shutting out the natural— muslin curtains screen out the "garish light of day"—transforms a boudoir into an urban bower:

3. Edward George Bulwer-Lytton, *Pelham: or The Adventures of a Gentleman*, ed. Jerome J. McGann. (Lincoln: University of Nebraska Press, 1972), 183.
4. Benjamin Disraeli, Earl of Beaconsfield, *The Young Duke*. (New York: M. Walter Dunne, 1904), 90.

> A ravishing perfume, which was ever changing, wandered
> through the apartment. Now a violet breeze made you poetical;
> now a rosy gale called you to love. And ever and anon the
> strange but thrilling breath of some rare exotic summoned you,
> like an angel, to opening Eden. All was still and sweet, save
> that a fountain made you, as it were, more conscious of silence;
> save that the song of birds made you, as it were, more sensible
> of sweetness. (*The Young Duke*, 199)

The first passage, from Bulwer-Lytton's *Pelham*, was considered so
scandalous, so potentially negative an influence when it first appeared,
that it was partially excised from subsequent editions. Reginald Glanville himself, whose apartment Pelham sees for the first time, seems
to his guest to be a perfect "specimen of masculine beauty, at once
physical and intellectual" (184). His table is always set for three, he
dines every day at eight, he never dines elsewhere, and he has an
excellent French cook. Glanville shows Pelham two books, one on
the Catholic question and one of poetry, both dedicated to him. " 'See
what it is to furnish a house differently from other people; one becomes
a bel esprit, and a Maecenas, immediately. Believe me, if you are rich
enough to afford it, that there is no passport to fame like eccentricity' "
(184).

If there is a scandal here, it lies less in the inclusion of a few decorative details than in the privatization of public space (apartments
supersede monuments, as display replaces use or action), in the centering of the eccentric and the related inclusion of the exotic in urban
representation, and in the insistence upon excellence in both surface
and depth (as in the dual nature of Glanville's perfection). The scandal
deepens in the oxymoronic joining of the Catholic issue and poetry,
wisdom and decoration. Further, the privileging of the superlative and
the hyperbolic, the insistence upon the conventional or upon repetition (which makes living an art or a ritual and suppresses the immediacy of the natural): these too insist upon artifice as the sine qua
non of urban life. The appeal to the sense of smell, to say nothing of
the synaesthesia, assures us that the senses will be foregrounded,
even though these rosy breezes are enclosed, the products of an art
of the natural. These passages proclaim a semiotics of wealth whose
capacity to foster a language of extremes, to coin phrases and visual
puns, is prominent. The French phrases hint at the codified or exclu-

sive nature of the language of high life; and the ancillary issues of repetition and textuality inhabit this world of artifice.

To enumerate these issues is to suggest the role that the novel of fashionable life plays in the representation of the city. Traditional histories refer to a number of these novels as the "Silver Fork" school (their antitheses are the Newgate novels); social histories, depending on their perspectives, explore them for evidence of urban ways of life or dismiss them as conventional and therefore unhistorical entertainments.[5] A number of the novels, even those most committed to the city, stray well beyond its limits, to rural castles, romantic forests, even isolated madhouses.[6] But it is the very introduction of such romantic stage properties, and of an exterior perspective, that returns us to the central narrative interests of these novels, to problems that first move away from historical concerns to issues of description, of rhetoric, of convention and even of plot, but that eventually go beyond the mirror stage of Glanville's apartment to a new view of public urban life. What is intriguing and challenging about the novels of high life is not their apparent affirmation of a way of life that now seems so remote, but the double gesture they make: the valorization of the delights of the surface, of the bon mot and of *ton* is coupled with the equally important concern with the well-being of self and city. It would be possible—and facile—to say that the latter enfranchises the former: it is all right to spend time on your toilette, even to the point of self-deification, if you also deliver the crucial speech on the Catholic question. But that would not explain why the fashionable novels approach the sober center of the polis by way of its extremes, why they affirm the urban from the perspective of something closer to fantasy. Wordsworth's encounters with the cities of Cambridge and London destroy his romantic dreams and cast him into the decentered role of the alienated spectator. Do these novels return to some pre-Romantic and youthful fantasy of the city? Or do they attest to Baudelaire's discovery that the marvelous pervades the atmosphere of the modern city, in contrast to Wordsworth's disillusionment? Perhaps the writer seizes the opportunity to liberate the city from the unremitting claims of the real, to represent it by a no less essential figurality. At the same time, he must recuperate the rituals of high life into an acceptable form of

5. For a good history of the dandy and of fiction about dandies, see Ellen Moers, *The Dandy: Brummell to Beerbohm* (New York: Viking, 1960).

6. See, for example, both *Coningsby* and *Pelham*.

narrative. While fantasy would seem to be the reasonable mode of representing the occasional eccentricity of these rituals, it is more puzzling as a way of approaching the conventions of fashionable life. Such paradoxes occupy a significant part of urban fiction; the dandy novels dramatize them in their splendidly, if at times ironically, hyperbolic reach toward the limits of that fiction.

I

The contrast between high life and low life is at once one of the oldest, one of the most historically grounded, and one of the most conventional ways of structuring the city. It assumes its archetypal nineteenth century form in Pierce Egan's *Life in London*, a genial protofictional saunter around London, where each aspect of high life—Opera, Carlton Palace, Tattersall's, Almack's—has its low-life counterpart—"Sluicery" or gin palace, a meeting of the beggars or cadgers, Newgate, All-Max. The urbane Tom the Corinthian takes his country cousin, Jerry Hawthorn, on a series of tours of the city; at times they are joined by the logician, Bob Oxford. For a good part of the novel, the fiction is sustained by the liminal or spectatorial presences of the characters. There are narrative moments, to be sure: the characters get drunk, get into brawls, have amorous affairs, go to debtors' prison (toward the end of the book, Bob Logic is at home on board the Fleet[7]), which are as much occasions for displaying parts of the city as they are signs of the city's capacity to generate fictions. Those fictional moments are so thoroughly conventional that one could justifiably doubt their narrative potentialities. (Such later well-known inmates of debtors' prisons, Rawdon Crawley and William Dorrit, should, however, help to quell those doubts.) At most, the narrative episodes in *Life in London* seem like the stuff of minor melodrama whose usefulness lies in their capacity to replicate on the narrative or syntagmatic level the vision of the city as an antithetical structure of high and low places. Subsequent novels of high life, and, still later, the novels of G. M. Reynolds and Dickens, confirm these melodramatic tendencies and imply that urban plots are necessarily polar, repetitive, and at some remove from the real.

---

7. See Pierce Egan, *Life in London* (London: Sherwood, Needy and Jones, 1821). The Fleet was one of London's debtors' prisons.

Life in London opens up a series of paradoxes: first, the highly structured quality of life in the city, with its emphasis upon the typical and the visible, suspends flexible or even meaningful forms of narrative. Second, insofar as narrative is possible, it devolves upon the inconsequential or the fragmentary, on the one hand, or the melodramatic or the histrionic, on the other. Third, the attempt to represent the city by means of narrative only distances whatever it is that we take to be urban reality. The opening of the book, in which Tom establishes himself as an impresario of the urban, then settles upon a patterned space in which contingency and causality, or any of the factors that would allow a linear plot to unfold, are for the most part suppressed. It is an abstract form of the city, then, that contains narrative.

Such an abstract and antithetical spatial model of the city need not preclude descriptive plenitude, however. It is the very suppression of narrative, together with the exclusion of a mediatory middle class, that furthers such a genial, carnivalized presentation of high and low,[8] and that permits an essentially neutral description. But description itself is frequently displaced to a series of plates by the Cruikshanks that utilize the conventions of comic and satirical art. When Egan relegates a portion of the representation to the visual arts, some of the verbal remainder takes art, as much as the city, to be its referent. Now a supplement to the visual, the verbal represents the city only at two removes.

We need construe this as a deficiency, however, only if we insist that the text be a transparent record of potentially real experience. What *Life in London* records, rather, is the way in which the city has become a text. Here, the verbal is as prominent as the visual. Egan is fond of catalogues. The passage on Hyde Park, the "Show-Shop of the Metropolis," as Tom calls it, lists all the types to be seen there, among them these:

> The MAN of TON *staring* some modest female, that attracts his attention, completely out of countenance; while the *Lady of Rank*, equally *delicate* in her ideas of propriety, uses her *glass* upon the same object till her carriage removes her out of sight.

---

8. See Mikhail Bakhtin, *Problems of Dostoevsky's Poetics*, ed. and trans. Caryl Emerson. (Minneapolis: University of Minnesota Press, 1984), for an extended discussion of carnivalization. Egan's recourse to the "living present," to parody, to the "mixing of high and low" in narration, and to the verbal texture of London life all point toward carnivalization.

The DEBAUCHEE endeavouring to renovate, or brace himself up with the fine air of the Park, *ogling* all the girls that cross his path. The SWELL DANDY could not exist if he did not show himself in the Park on a Sunday. The Gambler on the *look-out* to see if any new pigeon appears in the circle, in order to plan future operations that may turn out to his advantage. The *peep-o'-day* woman of *Quality*, who, night after night, disposes of all her hours of rest in card-parties and routs, is here to be seen riding around the circle to *chit-chat* and nod to her friends, in order to get rid of her yawnings, and to appear something like being *awake* at dinner-time. The PEER relaxing from his parliamentary duties, and the Member of the Lower House. . . . The Scheming *Procuress* . . . The Wealthy CIT . . . the extravagant *Fancy*. (*Life in London*, 190)

A number of passages, whether or not they are catalogues in the strict sense, are lexical in character, presenting the vocabularies or argots of London's different groups and areas. Egan makes liberal use of italics for typical words (Tom and Jerry take a *"turn* or two in Bond Street, a *stroll* through Piccadilly, a *look in* at Tattersall's, a *ramble* through Pall Mall, and a *strut* on the Corinthian path"), for glosses in footnotes (not always straightforward), and for the more arcane or flash terms, for example *"lumbering"* (being arrested) or *"lush"* (drink). The urban lexicon appears as an alternative to both visual description and narration of physical action. Its various sociolects are a constituent of the city, the language of fashion as much as the criminal argot or the cockney dialect. The somewhat bemused Jerry Hawthorn must learn to listen as well as to see. But the persistent massing of vocabularies is the equivalent of the illustrative plate, and both are forms of the urban text. (Egan's catalogues, however more abstract, are also the equivalent of Sala's; it will remain for Dickens to move the artist-narrator into a position of more conscious control vis-à-vis his materials.) The rich urban vocabularies in *Life in London* will become, selectively, the often arcane and specialized urban dialogue of a Meredithian or Jamesian drawing-room. Such dialogue breaks down the absoluteness of the distinction between description and narration; it functions as both the primary datum and the sign of a certain milieu (and thus as description) and as the vehicle of communication and understanding, of a narrative hermeneutics.[9]

---

9. Thus the kind of distinction that Lukács makes in "Narrate or Describe?" need not hold in fiction.

Interiorization of urban dialogue belongs to a slightly later phase of the novel. Language leans more toward the openly carnivalesque in *Life in London*. In fact, that book may be said to portray one continuous carnival: Tom and Jerry set out to have a good time wherever they go, and they have one. It would be unnecessary to spell out the complex meaning of high life in this context, were it not for the fact that the excess eventually eradicates the distinction between high and low. It is not simply that a carouse is the same, whatever the accidents of costume or birth: what matters more is that the structuring antitheses of the urban world are ruptured. Exclusive idiom or criminal argot: each is still a form of specialized language opposed to the public language of the middle class. (Compare James Grant's observation, in 1837, that the upper and lower classes shared a freedom from the moral imperatives to which the middle classes by and large subjected themselves.[10]) Exuberance and excess, both social and linguistic, become the signs of that secret community which urban writers in England and France were to exploit throughout the nineteenth century; they also signify the carnivalesque and scandalous break in the rigid ways of structuring urban life which allows narrative to emerge. It is, then, not so much the antithesis between high and low life, but the scandalous cancellation of that antithesis, that is so determinant for the representation of the city and that constitutes a hidden subplot of *Life in London*. To be sure, some form of this unstable or self-cancelling antithesis is present in earlier urban satire. In the nineteenth-century city, however, it must be written anew.

Yet dandies are the quintessence of refinement. What is the relation between Tom the Corinthian, that ebullient but imperfect subscriber to the fashionable mode, and the dandy proper, or the dandies who inhabit the fictions of Bulwer-Lytton or Disraeli or Catherine Gore? Why is low life, in which Tom, Jerry, and Bob Logic are almost equally at home (especially in the more riotous forms) as they are in high life, virtually suppressed in the later fashionable novels, though it will return more indirectly as the excessive, the sinister, or the criminal? The openness, the display of text and figure in the taxonomically conceived *Life in London*, disappears from the later novels.

Several motifs of the fashionable novels are scarcely a concern of

---

10. See James Grant, *The Great Metropolis*, 2 vols. (London, 1836, 1837). This observation is from Vol. 2, a large part of which surveys London's three classes. Both higher and lower classes are prone to indulge in promiscuity, for example, and to "disregard" religion and truth. But while the lower classes utter ad hoc falsehoods, the higher classes make falsehood into a convention: "aristocracy," Grant notes, is synonymous with "hypocrisy."

Life in London. One is the motif of selfhood or, more precisely, self-perfection. Baudelaire found spiritual excellence as well as visible elegance to be the goal of the dandy. But the fashionable novels center upon those moments when perfection is not so much achieved as it is sought for. If the text of *Pelham*, especially Pelham's maxims and the letters of his mother, seems at times like a primer on how to succeed in high life, its subtext is surely that of how to expose oneself as a coxcomb—even when one has consciously assumed the mask of a coxcomb. From a narrative point of view, the dandy's reified world of the self becomes more accessible when it becomes possible critically to scrutinize that self-objectification. In this most theatrical of fictional worlds (Disraeli images life in society as a pantomime), if the self does not merge with the role it plays, then role is a means of self-revelation.

A further complication comes from the fact that no matter how much the perfected self is a desideratum, the dandy is rarely free from images of decline. Disraeli's comment in *The Young Duke* that the London Season is never so brilliant as when it is about to decline is emblematic.[11] The trajectory of Beau Brummell's life, which had started by making the self into an object of art, had already ended miserably in exile and destitution. It is at this moment of decline that Russelton, Brummell fictionalized, appears in *Pelham*.

It is at these moments of perfection undone that the costs of perfection or exclusion are revealed. What has been repressed in the name of perfection figures in the text as unacceptable or unexplainable passions that lead to duels or attempted seductions, to gambling, even to murder. All these bespeak a turn toward melodrama that would in itself provide a sufficient contrast to the elegant soirees, to the life of *ton* and esprit. But we should also add the drunken sprees, the boisterous practical jokes, the amusing self-revelations to which the dandy-as-coxcomb is prone. The fashionable novels, then, suppress the individual and collective forms of low life, where place—the gin palace or the beggars' den—becomes the external sign of a more pervasive atmosphere. What was so open in *Life in London* returns to leave its traces upon the polished surfaces of high life. But high life must be made problematic: the motifs of self-perfection masked

11. *The Young Duke*: "As people at the point of death often make a desperate rally, so this, the most brilliant of seasons, was even more lively as it nearer approached its end" (61).

or undone, of decline, and of suppressed low life are ways to realize its narrative potentialities. Let us look first, however, at the way in which the spatial schematism of *Life in London* is extended in the fashionable novels, so that it both defines and opens up the symbolic resonance of high life.

II

The exclusiveness and antithesis that inhabit the notion of high life make it easier to perceive the schematic nature of the fashionable map of the city. Such an urban map resembles the well-known Steinberg New Yorker map of the United States, which omits everything between the Hudson River and California. The fashionable quadrangle, formed by Pall Mall, St. James's Street, Piccadilly, and Regent's Street, is at the center; close by are fashionable areas such as Grosvenor Square; more to the periphery are the less fashionable but aspiring ones, such as Portman Square. Within and around these areas are the clubs (White's, Brooke's, Crockford's, Watier's, Almack's), the tailors, the jewelers of Bond Street, as well as such major edifices as Carlton House and Holland House. High life gravitates to the known: transgression beyond its boundaries (as when Disraeli's Lothair wanders through London and finds himself at a Fenian meeting in Pentonville, or when Bulwer's Pelham and his sporting friends go on a drunken carouse in the slum of St. Giles) only highlights the way in which the upper class clings to the familiar. Ordinarily, one would not suspect that a slum such as St. Giles is adjacent to the district of St. James. It is important, however, not to regard these topographical indices of urban life as entirely literal. The famous bow-window of White's, in which the dandies sat to be seen at a certain hour each day, symbolizes place as a transparent container. Place names belong to a lexicon of privileged words and phrases. The street on which one lives, one's club (distinguished according to function, say, politics, or according to its degree of exclusiveness), the type of one's carriage: all convey a social, hierarchical significance. To be part of the world of high life is to be part of a symbolic grid in which topography—or referentiality—itself is subordinate. Places of privilege, like privileged words (*ton*, bel esprit, beau, brilliant, for example), insist upon the priority of convention, or of ways of thinking about the appurtenances of one's world. Although we shall have to return later to all that has been bracketed or excluded, that is, to the more dubious neighborhoods and the slums, it should be clear that the map of the exclusive world is predicated upon a form of the superlative, or of hyperbole. The map is, in effect, a hyperbolic text, entailing suppression of that which is other than fashionable. That map both plays with limits and steps toward the fashionable sublime.

III

The figurative map of the fashionable world provides, then, one entry into the hyperbolic, which includes the insistence upon the grammatical superlative and the suppression of qualification. If not all dandies are perfect (there are imitative dandies, and Pelham modestly refers to himself as a second-rate one), there is generally at least one exemplary figure in each novel. As Bulwer's Glanville seems the image of physical and intellectual perfection to Pelham, so Disraeli's Young Duke "aspired to be society itself. In a word, his tastes were of the most magnificent description, and he sighed to be surrounded by a court" (*The Young Duke*, 27). Glanville's mother is faultless at least in public, and her house is "one of the most recherché in London" (*Pelham*, 6). " 'A young Duke,' " says May Dacre, " 'like the young lady in the fairy tale, should scarcely ever speak without producing brilliants' " (*The Young Duke*, 269). Here is Mrs. Gore's Cecil:

> Now and then, I glanced meteor-wise across the surface of London Society; and as the brilliancy of a shooting star attracts fifty million of times more attention than your matter of fact planet, whose phenomena are duly set down in the ephemeris, I gained much by the rapidity of my transit.[12]

Cecil's satisfaction with his life is boundless: "All the poetry of civilized life condenses itself into such a destiny as I was then enjoying" (29–30). Civilized life eclipses the natural: "It was the very meridian hour of fashion,—and gorgeous enough for a *coup de soleil*" (33). Civilized

---

12. Mrs. Catherine G. F. Gore, *Cecil, A Peer, A Sequel to Cecil, or the Adventures of a Coxcomb*, 3 vols. (London: T. and W. Boone, 1841), 1:11–12.

life shapes itself into an alternative solar system, "whose sunshine," in this earth, "is candlelight" (1:29–30).

Such planetary metaphors do more than dispense with qualification. What are also noticeable are the grammatical modes in which hyperbole traffics, which qualify the superlative. May Dacre's imperative "should . . . speak" or the Young Duke's aspirations and sighs, followed by the infinitive form ("to be surrounded") are equally important. The fashionable world, eclipser of suns and container of perfections, betrays a fissure in its own brilliant surface: the fissure indicative of unfulfilled desire, whether the object of that desire be another or an idealized self, or, more broadly, the forms of social life. Such idealizations, contained within hyperboles, are the counterpart to the exclusiveness of fashionable society, although it is an exclusiveness already rewritten as problematic and incomplete.

It is possible to read these hyperboles as jeux d'esprit, or as representations of desire, without claiming for them any more serious effects than those of a charmingly self-revealing parody; it is the latter genre to which the Cecil novels lay claim. But the opening chapters of *The Young Duke* contain more sinister implications. The Duke's satisfaction with himself as "the most distinguished ornament" of existence makes him a "sublime coxcomb" (18). His social debut extends the meaning of his coxcombry:

> The banquet was over; the Duke of St. James passed his examination with unqualified approval; and having been stamped at the Mint of Fashion as a sovereign of the brightest die, he was flung forth, like the rest of his golden brethren, to corrupt the society of which he was the brightest ornament. (22)

Although hyperbole starts as a figure of self-definition, as the proper metaphor for a society that realizes itself by living a form of fantasy, it develops into the vehicle of sudden reversal. As "a sovereign of the brightest die," or "the brightest ornament," the Duke is originary, centered metaphorically, socially, even mythically as an Apollo-figure. Yet the far-reachingness confirmed by that hyperbolic "flung forth" cannot obscure the passive construction which, together with "stamped," the earlier "to be surrounded," and the ornamental, make the Duke simply a copy, one of a series, who has undergone his rites of passage in a quasi-mechanical fashion. The obverse of the proper debut, the other side of the coin, is the improper; the proper name sinks into the Young

Duke, a sovereign among others, a product of the Mint. Hyperbole now seems far less innocent even as the medium of fantasy. It is the sign of corruption, just as the shooting star prefigures its own extinction.

The language of this passage, with its literary overtones ("Mint of Fashion") and its vaguely public ring, represents the idiom of the fashionable world, much as if it were the expression of a collective urban linguistic fantasy. The linguistic register of the superlative may be identified with the London of high life. Dukes, women, houses, horses, costume, dinners, conversation: all are the best, or incomparable. Action and desire themselves are oriented to the absolute. (Ironically, the young Coningsby rejects London's political idiom in his own quest for absolutes; nevertheless, this does not preclude his exaggerated admiration for the clothes of a London dandy.) The absolute, however, does not make common or middle-class discriminations: it takes greatness, Cecil remarks, to "delight in small talk" (*Cecil, A Peer*, 1:33). Despite the metaphors of visual brilliance in the quoted passage, the qualifying adjectives—"golden," "brightest"—do very little to make concrete the language of coin and ornament. Another function of hyperbole, therefore, is to make abstract and less visual the material world of fashion. Surfaces, to which the dandies seem so dedicated, recede before a generalized sensory vocabulary. Add to this (from similar passages) the importance of unconditional terms ("all," "incomparably," "sole"); of French words (to be used in moderation; it is vulgar to employ them excessively) that valorize the ineffable ("*ton*," "bel esprit") and are themselves signs of that which is inexpressible in English; of the parodic shift of object-words to proper nouns (Lord Squib, Mr. Ruby, the jeweler); even of zeugma, which justles the concrete against the abstract (the Duke "took the oaths and his seat [in Parliament]" [*The Young Duke*, 26]). The lexicon of the fashionable world dematerializes the representation of that which is dedicated to the material, or to the material as a source of selfhood.[13] Such a lexicon then becomes the representation of a self-

---

13. In *Pelham*, Russelton (a figure based on Beau Brummell) gives an account of his growing up: "I gave myself, without restraint, to the ambition that burnt within me—I cut my old friends, who were rather envious than emulous of my genius, and I employed three tradesmen to make my gloves—one for the hand, a second for the fingers, and a *third for the thumb!* These two qualities made me courted and admired by a new race—for the great secrets of being courted are, to shun others, and seem delighted with yourself" (130). The language of fashion, or of food or interior decoration, gestures beyond itself to the achieve-

representation, but it is also the medium by which that self-image can be examined. Thus it is that the ornamental, however bright and golden, comes to reveal its sensory emptiness and superfluity. Disraeli's use of "corrupt," with its physical, moral, and linguistic senses, is entirely appropriate here.

The hyperbolic, which motivates so much of the fashionable style, has wider consequences to which the collective implications of "corruption" point. A city of such incomparables hovers at the edge of community; one may wonder whether those words do not write London out of the register of description, whose terms would always be insufficient to convey the splendor of the fashionable world. If even metaphor tends toward figures for the indescribable, then the abstraction, the unrealizability, or the irreality of high life is affirmed all the more. In the fictional texts description becomes virtually self-negating, rendering problematic its referential claims.

That contradiction, however, may serve a rather simple ideological purpose, insofar as it refines the material and the vulgar, now seen as perpetual threats to genuine *ton*, out of textual existence. The object of exclusion is not only low life, which is easier to deal with because of its stark difference, but a certain part of the upper-middle class and the squirearchy. This latter object is redefined as the conglomeration of vulgar objects and manners that can be readmitted to the text only as parodies of the real, the exquisite thing. But the further contradiction to which this gives rise is that the essential threat to high life comes from within, for example, from provincials like Sir Lionel and Lady Harriet Woodstock:

> [T]hey might have been great people in the country—they preferred being little people in town. They might *have* chosen *friends* among persons of respectability and rank—they preferred *being* chosen as *acquaintance* by persons of *ton*. Society was their being's end and aim, and the only thing which brought them pleasure was the pain of attaining it. (*Pelham*, 10; Bulwer-Lytton's italics)

A form of description that centered upon the concrete, upon the material aspects of high life, would be suspect because it would represent

---

ment of selfhood (or of the stylishly beautiful), with the implication that the material is not an end in itself.

the oxymoronic aspirations of the vulgar or the social parvenu rather than the achieved *ton* of the aristocracy. Even if it fell short of parody, it would betray a bourgeois element. Description, then, in order to affirm the values of high life, must operate on the level of the general, the abstract, or the extreme. Only if one thinks of description as necessarily tied to the sensory would this be a self-negating conception of style: the flora and fauna of high life inhabit its language and form part of its ambience. The more serious threats to description come from an assumption of familiarity (those in the know need no explanation of those flora and fauna, the clubs, place names, and frequent expressions), as well as from the motifs of brilliance allied with decline and corruption, which suggest that any extended representation of fashionable life might well end in self-cancellation.

Yet there is one mode of physical description that plays a prominent if not extensive role in the dandy novels: the mode of the exotic. The passages describing the Alhambra, the pleasure palace built by the Young Duke of St. James in Regent's Park, are exemplary. The park is still, in the early nineteenth century, "a wild sequestered spot," a suburb of London whose inhabitants are a "distinct race" who cannot "speak the language of London" (*The Young Duke*, 40). As the name indicates, the Alhambra is Oriental in style: the entrance is a Saracenic cloister; the banqueting-room is "fitted up as an Eastern tent" (289). The Duke plays the role of a "Caliph" (296), clapping his hands to open the curtain that conceals the ballroom. The walls of that room "exhibited a long perspective of golden pilasters, the frequent piers of which were of looking-glass, save where, occasionally, a picture had been, as it were, in laid in its rich frame" (296). The ceiling is "richly painted, and richly gilt," and the floor is "of polished and curiously inlaid woods" (296). An orchestra plays, and the "elegant revellers waltz, at first "[s]oftly and slowly . . . like spirits of the air," but eventually like "spinning dervishes" (297). The conservatory, which is "full of rare and delicious plants and flowers, and brilliantly illuminated" (298), is a "fairy grove" that effectively blurs the distinctions between art, nature, and humanity. The repeated "now and then" formalizes the casual:

> Busts and statues were intermingled with the fairy grove; and a rich, warm hue, by a skilful arrangement of coloured lights, was thrown over many a nymph and fair divinity, many a blooming hero and beardless god. Here they lounged in different

parties, talking on such subjects as idlers ever fall upon; now and then plucking a flower, now and then listening to the fountain, now and then lingering over the distant music, and now and then strolling through a small apartment which opened to their walks, and which bore the title of the Temple of Gnidus. Here, Canova's Venus breathed an atmosphere of perfume and of light. (298)

To this passage of exotic description, one may add the allusion to the Venetian modes of architecture in the town house of the St. Jeromes in *Lothair*;[14] Catholicism, the religion of the St. Jeromes, itself has an aura of exoticism in that novel. The exotic becomes, therefore, the meeting-ground of the aesthetic and the incipiently political.

Why should urban description be open at the physical level to the exotic, when it is more or less closed to the familiar? To say that exoticism is compatible with exclusiveness and with hyperbole would be merely to reformulate the question. The premises of *Life in London*, which seeks to be as inclusive as possible in its descriptions, seem reversed. Now only the limiting case of the world of high life is retained in the later novels: the schematic tendencies of Egan's work prefigure a still more abstract model of the city.

The exotic is also allied to early figures for urban exploration. The classic directive appears in *Coningsby*, where Sidonia, meeting Coningsby by chance in a forest, recommends that the young man travel to see the wonders of the world not to Athens, but to Manchester. The inversion is striking in the image of the factory as Egyptian palace, now a sign for the marvels of an urban industrial civilization. The motif of Eastern adventure, so attractive in early nineteenth-century literature, courts alterity.[15] Bakhtin's comment that exoticism "presupposes

---

14. Benjamin Disraeli, *Lothair* (London: Oxford University Press, 1975), 30. Disraeli notes that Venetian splendor was at that time rare in the metropolis. After 1857, however, the Italian influence was more apparent in London's architecture. See John Summerson, "London, The Artifact," in *The Victorian City: Images and Realities*, ed: H. J. Dyos and Michael Wolff, 2 vols. (London: Routledge and Kegan Paul, 1973), 1:312. The St. James family lives, of course, in St. James's Square: "a great patrician residing there dwells in the heart of the free and noble life of which he ought to be a part." The hyperbolic terms suppress the sordid and ugly parts of life in London.

15. In addition to such Romantic works as Byron's Oriental Tales, which have their own political overtones, a number of Disraeli's novels, among them *Contarini Fleming* and *Tancred*, represent the quest to the East as a preparation for an appropriate, often political metropolitan life. Rome, so important a place in *Lothair*, stands on the threshold of the exotic.

a deliberate opposition of what is alien to what is one's own, what is ordinary and familiar," resonates here.[16] The exotic within the city does not simply extend the scope of the known; paradoxically it also attests to the limits of that knowledge, to the possibility that this region of urban life, at least, will never totally surrender to demystification. There will always be quasi-sacred spaces within urban topography. Such spaces prefigure some Paterian valorizing of an art dedicated to the moment and to the senses. That they are also sybaritic, or that they mark a hyperbolic straining for experience beyond the conventional, need not cancel their significance on another level, where an urbane, self-aware, even self-mocking fantasy remains a constituent of city life. If the exotic is present to the senses, it also appears as a present absence, something potentially recoverable to the senses were it not, almost by definition, just beyond the limits in some Regent's Park of the mind. Hyperbole at its limits, open to irony: such parabolas are not entirely unrelated to the horizontal or limited metaphors of other urban fictions. Hyperbole realized as a fantasy of the exotic may, then, appear not as self-enclosed description but rather as description designed to get beyond the repetition of convention, as a sign of the narrative imagination. The apparent superfluity observed earlier is now justified within a narrative economy of excess.

Despite all this justification, one may be left with the nagging suspicion that the proper label for all this exotica is the problematic of the trivial. At some point in this scenario, the argument might run, the continual recirculation of the senses, however ingeniously effected by the mechanical devices, the perfumes, the orchestras, the dancing, should give way to the more elevated experience to which hyperbole itself gestures. Instead, the light of sense may be said to go out only when the sun, that greatest of all lights for the senses, rises. In the place of nocturnal spirits or daemons, there is only Canova's Venus presiding over a secularized temple. The retreat from public space (in a referential as well as a textual sense), the privatization of experience: while these appear to be narrative gestures, they may only substitute the veneer of art for the passional drama proper to narrative. These elegant surfaces seem to foreclose genuine passion, to confirm the gap between the narratable and a world dedicated to the visual or representational arts. The emblem of this situation is the fashionable

16. Mikhail Bakhtin, *The Dialogic Imagination*, ed. and trans. Michael Holquist and Caryl Emerson (Austin: University of Texas Press, 1982), 101.

demystification of the word "sublime." The word appears in its cus-
tomary contexts in Disraeli's novels; for instance, Jerusalem is the
sublime city in *Coningsby, Lothair* and *Contarini Fleming*, as the Alps
are the properly sublime mountains in *Contarini Fleming*. One may
then ask why there are sublime coxcombs in *The Young Duke*, or the
urbanization of the sublime "biblical moment" in *Cecil, A Peer*, whose
narrator learns the most difficult of London lessons, " 'to subside into
a fraction of the multitude, and satisfy yourself with being a mere link
in the chain of society. . . . You have no right, at present, to indivi-
dualize; but must live and move and have your being, in the life,
movement and sensibility of the mass' " (1:108). The stamped sov-
ereignty of the Young Duke and the linked selfhood of Cecil bespeak
men of the same mettle. Instead of separation from the crowd, immersion in it; instead of the sensory blanking out before the realm of
infinity where man lives and moves and has his true being, the glor-
ification of the social. It seems that the true blanking out occurs in
the signification of "sublime" itself, which passes for common cur-
rency in the dandy world, a token of approval that no longer entails
mystery or fear or passion but instead signifies a purchase on the
known good. The sublime domesticated into the beautiful? The small-
ness that Burke associated with the beautiful seems to have returned
as the petty.

It is with a discussion of the sublime, apparently drained of its
constituent emotions of fear, awe, and terror, deprived of its mysteriousness, and circulated as a sign of urbane approval in the fashionable world, as a privileged word in the lexicon of high life, that we
may sum up the contradictions to which the fashionable novels give
rise. Description frequently turns to the exotic, and by its details of
wealth reveals the traces of a life that can lay no claim to sublimity
in its original sense. (The other kind of scene to evoke a reasonably
full description is the scene of low life—the crowd outside the gin
shop in Holborn or St. Giles in *Pelham*, for example.[17] But this scene,
too, exerts a claim because of its difference. The fascination with
otherness and mystery in urban life lures not only the dandies but the
urban novelist.) One aim of that description, which accords with the
advice given to Cecil, is that of the loss of self in one's surroundings,
whether they be defined as the social mass, or as objects, or as conventions In this respect, the loss of self is a tame counterpart to that

17. See *Pelham*, 198–99.

early stage of the authentic sublime experience in which the self is overwhelmed by the grand phenomena of the scene. Self-recovery may be equally facile but, as in the genuine sublime, daringly arbitrary. The dominance of the exotic in particular, however, testifies as well to the aestheticizing of existence. What all those elaborate interiors represent is the farthest point of withdrawal from public life, or any public life other than display. Yet the appeal to the absolute and the incomparable turns away from description to a set of urban deictics or allusions. If no word or figure is adequate to the object or experience described, how can one be sure of the nature of that object? The fade-out of the sensory in the dandy novels, even in light of the richness of the experience, of one's status in life, or of the material world, might contribute to the experience of the sublime in an urban context. Yet the series of incommensurabilities between object and word, object and self, even word and self, makes the experience of the sublime problematic even as it makes it possible. The mysteriousness of the city, which must be incorporated in its representation at the same time that it makes representation so difficult, now reappears as a sensory fade-out, as an evocation of the sublime, and as a form of hyperbole that is continually open to irony. The sublime is, then, more conditional, an ideal occasionally realized but more often only glimpsed. Similarly, Jerusalem, the sublime city, qualifies the worldly marvels of London. "Sublime," that sign of supreme approval in the fashionable lexicon, reveals its obverse, where corruption resides in the term itself but where, in a further ironic twist, the fullness of authentic sublimity is deferred to those moments of self-perfection more often desired than achieved.

Hyperbole in the city, with its attractions to all forms of excess save those of "reality" (Paris is full to excess, Pelham complains—and ennui lurks just beyond excess) cancels the sensory to appear as the sublime or as the desire for the sublime. It appears in grammar as the superlative; in spatial exploration as the exotic; in ideology as the polarizing of low life and high life, and of art and reality. (The bourgeois, however, alter the poles: in this symbolic economy they constitute a more absolute other.) Hyperbole appears also in convention, as the contrast of the conventional with the scandalous, and in narrative, as melodrama. But the hyperbolic mode, characteristically infused with irony, is also the medium of the contradictions that play across the surface of the fashionable world: the beautiful versus the sublime, the political versus the private, the familiar versus the exotic, convention versus passion, the quotidian versus the melodramatic, selfhood versus coxcombry or role-playing, individuality versus immersion in the mass. Hyperbole becomes the term for this series, whose inclusiveness is apparent insofar as it is the medium that expresses the perfected surfaces of the fashionable world at the same time that it conveys the scandals and melodramas, the passions and deception that complicate the art of the fashionable.

IV

This attempt to identify the guiding figures of the fashionable novel has not yet, however, addressed the problem of narration, to which the spatiality (however metaphorical), the antitheses, and the conventions of the fashionable world seemed so inimical when we examined them in connection with *Life in London*. In the later novels, too, high life seems to be predicated upon sheer repetition:

> Sir Carte [an interior decorator; his full name is Carte Blanche] and his tribe filled up the morning. Then there were endless visits to endless visitors; dressing; riding, chiefly with Lady Caroline; luncheons, and the bow window at White's. Then came the evening with all its crash and glare; the banquet, the opera, and the ball. (*The Young Duke*, 26)

The verbs recede before the categories of activities, all of which demarcate the day, but which also become, in the telling, static and patterned. Such activities exist in forms of reification. The subject, or the agent, of these activities is excluded from the written sequence, so that convention displaces authentic human action.

Disraeli himself was aware of the narrative potentialities of the world of fashion. Life in society is like a pantomime, he remarks, which, played too often, becomes monotonous.

> Who can see a pantomime more than once? Who could survive a pantomime the twentieth time? All the shifting scenes, and fitting splendour; all the motley crowds of sparkling characters; all the quick changes, and full variety, are, once, enchantment.

But when the splendour is discovered to be monotony; the change, order, and the caprice a system; when the characters play ever the same part and the variety never varies, how dull, how weary, how infinitely flat, is such a world to that man who requires from its converse, not occasional relation, but constant excitement! (301)

It is said that the conduct of refined society, in a literary point of view, is, on the whole, productive but of slight interest; that all we can aspire to is, to trace a brilliant picture of brilliant manners; add that when the dance and the festival have been duly inspired by the repartee and the sarcasm, and the gem, the robe, and the plume adroitly lighted up by the lamp and the lustre, our cunning is exhausted. And so your novelist generally twists this golden thread with some substantial silken cord, for use, and works up, with the light dance, and with the heavy dinner, some secret marriage, and some shrouded murder. And thus, by English plots and German mysteries, the page trots on, or jolts, till, in the end, Justice will have her way, and the three volumes are completed. (*The Young Duke*, 307)

Disraeli rejects these Gothic formulas and prefers "trusting to the slender incidents which spring from out our common intercourse" Although "that great pumice-stone, Society, smooths down the edges of your thoughts and manners," and people resemble each other so that "the life of the majority must ever be imitation" (307, 308), this comments as much on general human nature as on society. It also remarks dourly upon the dandy project of immersing oneself in society. Disraeli couples the conventions of conduct with the limited capacities of the majority for "thought": "The great majority of human beings in a country like England glides through existence in perfect ignorance of their natures, so complicated and so controlling is the machinery of our social life!" (308). It might seem, then, that the constraints of high life would delimit a situation that, in the celebration of the conventional, would allow no hint of man's real passional nature, no opportunity for self-knowledge. What could be more obfuscating than the social machine? Yet this apparently Wordsworthian position, that only in nature, rather than the city, can one attain true self-knowledge, is no more acceptable to Disraeli than the Gothic solution. Although he depends less upon "the slender incidents of our common intercourse"

ᶜᶜ than he claims, he casts the brilliant appearances of fashionable life
into a bifurcated structure:

> | A mode of life which encloses in its circle all the dark and
> deep results of unbounded indulgence, however it may appear
> to some who glance over the sparkling surface, does not exactly
> seem to us one either insipid or uninteresting to the moral
> speculator; and, indeed, we have long been induced to suspect
> that the seeds of true sublimity lurk in a life which, like this
> book is half fashion and half passion. (*The Young Duke*, 308) |

The repeated pantomime of the brilliant life need not serve a negative
urban aesthetics if one sets aside its claims to exclusiveness and
instead views it as one part of an antithesis. The effective contrast is
between Apollonian surfaces and Dionysian depths.[18] On the surface,
the reliance upon convention, upon the repeated and repeatable acts
of social life entails no questioning of their brilliant display. If this
were all that fashionable life afforded, then all it could do would be
to go on representing itself, as if one afternoon ride in Hyde Park, one
soiree, one ball, were virtually identical with its predecessors. The
writing of a fashionable novel would then be, after the first one, an
act of sheer repetition, and representation—Disraeli's pantomime—
would be unproblematic. But repetition must go beyond the formulaic.
What makes the fashionable world narratable is its relation to the
Dionysian depths of passion that lie concealed beneath those spar-
kling surfaces and that contain the "seeds of true sublimity." That
passion would then manifest itself in various narrative modes. Some
of them play upon melodrama, in episodes of gambling, duels, even
murder, but then seek to contain that violence by an accommodation
to normal life in society. At the same time, the Dionysian element is
closely connected to the suppressed representation of low life in the
city, which now emerges as part of the intimate process of self-
discovery, or as the equivalent of the exotic, which in this case is
easier to glimpse as something so totally other that it need not solicit
one's moral speculation. We will return later to the political ramifi-
cations of this narrative strategy. What concerns us here is the more
narrowly aesthetic justification whereby the visible and sensory ap-

18. See Friedrich Nietzsche, *The Birth of Tragedy*, trans. Walter Kaufmann (New York:
Vintage Press, 1966).

paratus of the fashionable world, including its patterns and artificial way of life, is made to signify only in relation to the very otherness of concealed depths. Disraeli makes higher claims than the more superficial formula that Thackeray scornfully sets forth in the Preface to *Pendennis*:

> What more exciting than a ruffian (with many admirable virtues) in St. Giles's visited constantly by a young lady from Belgravia? What more stirring than the contrasts of society? the mixture of slang and fashionable language? the escapes, the battles, the murders?[19]

The novelistic formula, which Thackeray rejects, presents one development out of *Life in London*'s structure; Disraeli, on the other hand, interiorizes. Lest this should seem too solemn an evocation of the Apollonian–Dionysian structure, one may observe not only that the artificial lights of the fashionable world have already eclipsed the Apollonian daylight, but also that Apollo appears in the dandy novels in ambiguous avatars. In *The Young Duke*, Prince Charles de Whiskerburg, "a young man, tall, with a fine figure, and fine features," is a sort of "Hungarian Apollo" whose catalogued features—beard, mustachios, whiskers, *favoris*, *padishas*, sultanas, mignonettas, dulcibellas—do nothing to enhance his Apollonian position (288). He is, instead, "an apter representation of the Hungarian Hercules" (288).

On the other hand, to take seriously this bifurcated structure in urban society entails the recognition of (1) the way in which the narrative voice plays over its materials and (2) the way in which the city loses some of its spatial determinacy in its fictional representations. Each of these factors is a precondition for narrative.

To start with, one may question whether Disraeli's comments constitute anything more than a program for a single novel, as they are, after all, the words of a fictive narrator. Yet it is precisely his fictional status that allows us to mine those passages and find in them metaphorical and even proto-Nietzschean significances. The recognition of narratorial instability opens the way to aligning this third-person narrator with the clearly fictional first-person narrators of *Pelham* and the two Cecil novels. Cecil in particular, by his virtually parodic stance,

---

19. William Makepeace Thackeray, Preface to *Pendennis* (Baltimore: Penguin, 1972), 33.

demonstrates the perspectival and generic indeterminacy of the dandy novels. The narrators of the dandy novels, like the narrators of Dickens and Gissing, perform the fictive moves of entering urban spaces, in order to represent the city and to realize its full textual possibilities. Whereas the narrator of *Life in London* accomplishes this by the more limited means of spatial gestures, and by making Tom into a guide, the later novels employ more complex strategies. The immersion and even self-surrender that appeared in the urban sketches swerve to the order of self-representation as well, even when it involves the kind of betrayal, however inadvertent, associated with parody. The rituals and conventions of urban life demand a surrender of narrative perspective, even something like narrative confusion, insofar as the narrators, those endless fountains of maxims and bons mots, of trivialities and insights, at once validate their pretensions to wisdom and reveal their cox-combry. Here, for example, are some of Pelham's maxims:

> Keep your mind free from all violent affections at the hour of the toilet. A philosophical serenity is perfectly necessary to success. Helvetius says justly, that our errors arise from our passions.

> A fool may dress gaudily, but a fool cannot dress well—for to dress well requires judgment.

> There may be more pathos in the fall of a collar, or the curl of a lock, than the shallow think for. Should we be so apt as we are now to compassionate the misfortunes, and to forgive the insincerity of Charles I., if his pictures had portrayed him in a bob wig and a pigtail? Vandyke was a greater sophist than Hume. (177, 178)

No Hamlet, Pelham reweaves the princely aphorism into a maxim that puts both the shallow and the regal in their places. Shakespeare's text is all texture for the dandy. Yet the philosopher of dress is also capable of self-irony:

> It is by no means an unpleasant thing to turn one's back upon the great city, in the height of its festivities. Misanthropy is a charming feeling for a short time, and one inhales the country, and animadverts on the town, with the most melancholy sat-isfaction in the world. (320)

And he is also given to straightforward reflection:

> | How different is the human mind, according to the difference
> of place. In our passions, as in our creeds, we are the mere
> dependents of geographical situation. . . . The man who is
> meek, generous, benevolent and kind in the country, enters
> the scene of contest, and becomes forthwith fiery or mean,
> selfish or stern, just as if the virtues were only for solitude, and
> the vices for the city. (331) |

We may return to the topography of London and recall that beyond
the perimeters of the fashionable world, beyond the dandy quadrant
formed by Piccadilly, Regent Street, Pall Mall and St. James's Street,
and beyond the familiar streets of Mayfair and the West End lies the
labyrinthine city, with its slums and criminal lairs. The plan of the city
retains its clarity in fashionable novels only at a price: the exclusion
of a significant part of London. Instead the world of high life enters
the grid of a moral and psychological labyrinth: the bright lights of
the dandy world form part of an ambiguously textured city. Disraeli's
program for the fashionable novel entails a redefinition of urban surfaces, where the great metaphors for the city, the labyrinth and even
the wilderness, for example, are engendered not so much on the experiential or sociological levels as they are at the level of narrative
itself.

The intangible dimensions of the fashionable world exist, as Burton
Pike points out, in the spaces between the visible urban monuments.[20]
What this presupposes is that the behaviors, postures, conventions—
the stuff of repetition—will appear to be familiar when perceived from
within. If the dandy narrator were situated entirely within this world,
his enterprise would be primarily mimetic, that of communicating but
not really interpreting the fashionable social codes; it would be as if
the dandy were to have only the voice of the philosopher of clothes,
of the first set of maxims. To represent the fashionable world would
be to present its codes, its special languages, without interpretation.
Thus *Coningsby*, which Thackeray enthusiastically called a dandy-
social, a dandy-political, a dandy-religious novel, contains so much

---

20. See Burton Pike, *The Image of the City in Modern Literature* (Princeton: Princeton
University Press, 1981), 41.

localized language, so many unexplained allusions, that today the outsider needs a key to read it.[21]

But these allusions are also dramatic self-representations. Cecil, a Peer (the titular figure of Mrs. Gore's second novel) need not explain himself to his peers. Rather, he leaves in his language the equivalent of the physical objects such as bijouterie that "trace" Mrs. Darlington Vere in *The Young Duke*: an abstract form of what Walter Benjamin calls "traces":

> The interior was not only the private citizen's universe, it was also his casing. Living means leaving traces. In the interior, these were stressed. Coverings and antimacassars, boxes and casings, were devised in abundance, in which the traces of everyday objects were moulded.[22]

The traces that appear in material objects have their counterpart in the specialized language of the narrator, which now becomes the sign of the narrator's position, the image, as it were, of his voice. If, however, the narrator were to incorporate in his discourse more than one specialized language or sociolect, he would then appear to be equivocal.[23] The three kinds of maxims that Pelham proffers contain the traces of more than one world of discourse and suggest surprising affinities among them.

It is the extension of this equivocality to include low life that affects the rewriting of urban spaces. The dandy narrator's familiarity with low life, its flash terms, its moral indeterminacies, and its physical locales reveals his liminality. Far from subscribing to the language of exclusion, to the clearly demarcated spaces of the aristocracy, he stands both within and between different urban spaces. Egan sup-

21. See Thackeray's review of *Coningsby* in *Contributions to the Morning Chronicle*, 40.

22. Walter Benjamin, *Charles Baudelaire: A Lyric Poet in the Era of High Capitalism*, trans. Harry Zohn (London: New Left Books, 1973), 168–69. Benjamin notes the fancier's value, "in which things were free from the bondage of being useful," that was conferred upon commodities. "Traces" are, for Benjamin, the residue of living, left by objects and by residents on interiors. William Greenslade calls attention to the significance of "tracings" in James's *The Ambassadors*. See "The Power of Advertising: Chad Newsome and the Meaning of Paris in *The Ambassadors*," *ELH*, 49 (1982): 104–5.

23. This comes close to Bakhtin's conception of heteroglossia, though not necessarily with the concealment or the absence of "*formal* markers." The dandies' love of display makes them more open in this respect, with some exceptions. See M. M. Bakhtin, "Discourse in the Novel," in *The Dialogic Imagination*, 301–21.

plants the Asmodeus figure of the narrator—the devil on stilts who peers through rooftops—with that of the narrator-as-spectator who moves through the city. By these moves, the gradual metaphorization of the city revolves and returns to the concrete, this time to incorporate the excluded world of low life. An important example of this process appears in the low life episode near the end of *Pelham*.

The conventional clarity of an antithetical relationship (every West End implies an East End, as Jerome McGann notes[24]) raises the image of the mean streets and labyrinthine passageways of the East End. Pelham goes there to obtain a criminal confession that will resolve a murder mystery. In addition to its role in the plot sequence,[25] however, the episode attests to the narrator's liminality. While it at first maintains the antithetical, high-low structure of the city, that structure soon becomes more dubious. A hitherto unknown or ignored part of the city is recovered into the text, through false and authentic self-representations, through the motif of the double. Through the recognitions of that episode, the East End is appropriated into the text.

On his quest for a witness to the murder, Pelham goes to Brimstone Bess's "asylum" for hunted or untrustworthy criminals (the latter are incarcerated there lest they betray their associates). With its labyrinthine interior, the asylum is the innermost haunt of low-life society, guarded by a "club" the strictness of whose code can be matched only by that of the fashionable world. It is also the antithesis of both the isolated madhouse that figures earlier in the novel, and the boudoirs or salons of several female characters. In the asylum, Job Jonson, the intellectual thief of many disguises, displays an honor to which fashionable and publicly prominent figures are not always equal. Even more important, language itself rises up to question the moral and social codes that utilize it. In order to hear the confession, Pelham must go in a double disguise: to Dawson, the accessory to the crime, he must appear to be a parson; to the other denizens of the asylum, he must appear to be a fledgling criminal disguised as a parson. He must learn not only the rigorously prescribed behavior but also the flash language that will make him appear to be a convincing neophyte. Language is now not simply a code, or a repository of social wisdom and knowledge; it is also an instrument of such power that its proper use will effect an entry into the underworld but its improper use will

24. See Jerome McGann, Introduction to *Pelham*, xxiv.
25. See Roland Barthes, *S/Z*, trans. Richard Miller (New York: Hill and Wang, 1974).

threaten him with death. Language thus is both a matter of survival and the corollary of total self-effacement. Pelham is never closer than he is at this moment to being most absent when he is most present. It is this very scene, in which the element of danger is so significant, that calls into question both the clarity and the signifying function of the code. Dawson tells Pelham that Thornton, a figure who becomes increasingly sinister,

> " . . . introduced me to three or four *gentlemen*, as he called them, but whom I have since found to be markers, sharpers, and black-legs; and this set soon dissipated the little honesty my own habits of life had left me. They never spoke of things by their right names; and, therefore, those things never seemed so bad as they really were—to swindle a gentleman did not sound a crime when it was called 'macing a swell'—nor transportation a punishment, when it was termed, with a laugh, 'lagging a cove.' Thus, insensibly, my ideas of right and wrong, always obscure, became perfectly confused; and the habit of treating all crimes as subjects of jest in familiar conversation, soon made me regard them as matters of very trifling importance." (*Pelham*, 422–23)

The reformulations and confusions of the criminal world bespeak a form of catachresis, which has its correspondences in the public world. Pelham's own experience with the broken promises of the party leader he has served (whose name, Dawton, is markedly close to that of the minor criminal Dawson) also attests to the corruption of language. Pelham's descent into the underworld represents, then, a moment of recognition in which the strict repetitions, codes, and conventions of high life are perceived as inadequate either as representations or as determining factors of that fashionable life.

At this point too, simple antithesis no longer seems to be a proper figure even for the spatial structure of London. At the very least, it would have to be reformulated as a phenomenon not confined to the surface but rather representative of the interplay between perceivable surfaces and the confusions and passions beneath. The distinction between high life and low life, the world of fashion and the world of crime, initially understood in precise spatial terms as the difference between the West End and the East End, tends to disintegrate under the pressures of a language that not only figures the secret ties between high and low, but that reveals its own evasive nature. The passage above not only desacralizes moral codes, it hints paradoxically at the worldliness of a language that ironically both validates and qualifies the planetary metaphors of a Cecil Danby.

The novel of high life seeks to enable authentic narrative by a series of strategies: these include suppression, to the point of subordination if not effacement, of low life and its reincorporation where the central urban metaphor of high and low is rewritten to convey the opposition between surfaces and depths, convention and passion, Apollonian and Dionysian, so that there is a redistribution of the terms of urban representation. The city's topography is also suppressed to the point where place names supplant description. Except for brief notation, or for passages on the exotic extremes of high and low life, physical description is frequently displaced by forms of dialogue, or occasionally by lexical catalogue. Within the narrative, the narrator retains the position of privileged observer to a degree but also stands on the threshold of action. Finally, the code of fashion is represented as an integral part of urban life, some kind of normative text. All this rewriting now permits high and low to stand conjoined against a new oppositional term, that of the middle, or the bourgeois, as an undistinguished, even indistinct entity that lacks both passion and panache.

V

Even to approach the threshold of narrative, the fashionable novels have had to break the domination of the visible, the figure for which is the appearance in the bow-window of White's. The turn to the hyperbolic in description anticipates the hyperbolic in narrative: perhaps the simplest form appears in melodrama or mystery. Instead of the grand fete, the duel before dawn in a deserted park, the murder on a lonely wasteland, the desperation of the gambler in a crowded "hell" in which his passion nearly overwhelms consciousness of his surroundings. If duels and gambling are threshold activities, socially permissible as acts but ruinous and scandalous in their consequences, they also initiate narrative violence. (In this context, the murder mystery in *Mary Barton* may be understood as the social obverse. It marks not the abandonment of social concerns for romance and melodrama, of which the novel has been accused, but rather the violent break from the sheer repetition of the life of the poor.) It is more difficult to explain the appearance of a popular form, even if it is a mere shadow of the Gothic elements that Disraeli wished to bar, in theory at least, from his novels. If we recall, however, that high life encounters its double or supplement in low life, and that the conventions of the fashionable world enclose forms of excess, then the alliance of a popular mode with more "aristocratic" forms of repetition and vocabulary within an antithetical fiction may be comprehensible. Melodrama as a form of excess is then a necessary component of the fashionable novel.

Within this context, gambling carries the traces of its aristocratic origins as an activity that in effect replaces work. But it is also, as Northrop Frye and Donald Fanger have remarked, a worldly activity in which the older, vertically structured myths of heaven and hell are secularized, compressed within the urban domain and restructured horizontally: now all depends upon the turn of a card, the turn of the wheel.[26] Yet any passage on a gambling club or den, popularly termed a "hell," is likely to evoke in the description of its dimness and enclosure (to say nothing of its atmosphere of desperation), the cosmology it reduces or parodies. It is these scenes to which the fashionable spas and resorts with their gambling ultimately lead. (It would be enlightening to read the episodes of Gwendolen Harleth at Leuven in *Daniel Deronda* and Becky Sharp at Pumpernickel in *Vanity Fair* as embedding traces of their narrative origins.) That fortunes are sometimes made but more often lost will signify not only the high, quasi-cosmic stakes, but also the decline of the fashionable world, thus more than a seasonal or a meteoric affair. Here, too, repetition leads to excess, as the mornings with Sir Carte Blanche pile up expenditures and finally drive the Young Duke to gambling in a desperate attempt to recoup his fortunes. As a narrative hyperbole, gambling projects a desire that appears in the subjunctive mode. In *Pelham*, gambling is instrumental in a plot by which Glanville seeks to ruin the seducer of his mistress. In both novels, gambling entails the association with characters who live in the margins of the fashionable world: excess, whether in the form of seduction or expenditure or desire, occupies the modes of aristocratic life but erupts in the scenes of gambling.

26. See Donald Fanger, *Dostoevsky and Romantic Realism* (Cambridge: Harvard University Press, 1965) and Northrop Frye, *Anatomy of Criticism* (Princeton: Princeton University Press, 1965).

The later, bourgeois forms of gambling, upon which Benjamin has commented so astutely, then appear to be doubly ironic: the bourgeois subjects imitate the interplay of excess and emptiness in the fashionable urban hells.[27]

But gambling may not be violent or melodramatic enough. In *Pelham*, it is only one stage in a subplot, a pattern of mysterious plots and passions sketched out against the brilliance of Parisian fashionable life, in which Pelham himself plays the role of a mystified spectator. The failure of gambling as a means of revenge is the catalyst for the murder that ensues. That murder, committed on a bleak rural landscape but resolved and explained in the two polar areas of the city, offers the final comment on excess and the meaning of urban spaces.

Duels, gambling, and murder, then, are not only thematically scandalous: they are the occasions of the formal scandals that enable the novel of high life to break away from the patterns, repetitions, and fantasies that would otherwise constrain it. But while all three of these actions are associated with interiorization, seclusion, and isolation, they are in other ways still exterior, their actors emblematic.[28] It is in Glanville, whose dandy apartment we noticed earlier, and who represents the Byronic strain of dandy, that we perceive a more authentic interiorization. Here the dandaical surfaces are separated from the passion which rages beneath. (It is symbolized, however, in the disease that wastes Glanville.) By this separation, the dandy is rescued from spectacle or tableau and distinguished from the order of imitation dandies. Passion not only explains the elegant furnishings (not an end in themselves so much as a distraction from the storm within), but refigures that elegance as excess. The ultimate scandal in the dandy apartment may now be seen to proceed unnaturally from passion and to represent a form of reification. (The Romantic ruin, insofar as it, too, is a piece of reified landscape, appears ironically as its rural counterpart. Both threaten to suspend narrative.)

Those moments of suspension reveal how inadequate melodrama is as a narrative solution. It is at best a first step. Even if one recognizes

27. See Walter Benjamin, *Charles Baudelaire: A Lyric Poet in the Era of High Capitalism*, 135–38.

28. For an illuminating linkage of melodrama, hyperbole, excess, and allegory, see Peter Brooks, *The Melodramatic Imagination: Balzac, Henry James, Melodrama, and the Mode of Excess* (New Haven: Yale University Press, 1976), whose subtitle is echoed in the title of this chapter.

the pervasiveness of melodrama in Victorian fiction, the problem is not simply one of normalizing the novel of high life within the main traditions of the novel. Although the excess that melodrama exposes in the dandy novels involves action rather than emotion, it is more a signifying action than a constitutive one.

This is no less true of parody, which also opens up the possibilities of action, and which often severely qualifies the fashionable world, but which we may still characterize as an enabling gesture toward narrative. Mrs. Gore's two Cecil novels are prime exhibits. Cecil's coxcombry is marvelously ingratiating as he makes his way through the worlds of London and Paris, through Parliamentary maneuverings and love affairs. His coxcombry is the source of both his social success and his social ruin. Yet parody may foreground what is crucial to a fictional enterprise: central motifs and definitive aspects of style. Here are four exemplary passages from the Cecil novels:

> Now and then, I glanced meteor-wise across the surface of London Society; and as the brilliancy of a shooting star attracts fifty million of times more attention than your matter of fact planet, whose phenomena are duly set down in the ephemeris, I gained much by the rapidity of my transit. (*Cecil, A Peer*, 1:11– 12)

> After all, philosophy may do its best to refine our minds, or utilitarianism to vulgarize them, but there is nothing more joyous, so long as the pulse beats high and the nerves remain firmly strung, than the existence whose sunshine is candlelight,—whose nightingales are opera singers,—whose nectar, Sillery,—whose ambrosia, bastions de volaille! All the poetry of civilized life condenses itself into such a destiny as I was then enjoying. (1:29–30)

> For there really was a good deal to talk about in London, just then, for those great enough to delight in small talk. There were two or three young fellows of fortune come of age, who were pelting people with their guineas; and two or three of the prettiest creatures brightening the ball rooms, that ever played the Houri to Christian Turks. It was the very meridian hour of fashion,—and gorgeous enough for a *coup de soleil*. (1:33)

> In the way of difficulties to be overcome, every next street con-
> tains the embryo of a Conquest of Persia; while almost every
> park paling surrounds the germ of a romance. (1:64)

The narrative voice of the four passages conveys the mode of hyperbole (which even separates rapid transit from the ephemeral), the
inversion of the natural that is the hallmark of urban life, the mode
of romance that includes the exotic in the space of everyday life, the
dominance of convention in both manners and narrative. Cecil offers
other distinguishing features: the importance of small talk, of costume
and carriages, of clubs no less than town houses as markers of the
urban scene, of the antithesis of urban and pastoral, and the intrusion
of political issues into the beau monde with force and insistence.
Thus the divisive Catholic question: "The whole frame of the beau
monde was broken up.—No more large parties! The solution of the
Catholic Question served at least to relieve society from the curse of
crammed assemblies, for half the world no longer chose to meet the
other half" (1:191). Parody, which strikes home by evoking what its
subjects cannot admit, here reveals the pressure of the political upon
the fashionable world.

The irony of such a remark as Cecil's is underlined by Disraeli's
differing narrative solutions: the sympathetic championship of the
Catholic cause by the Young Duke (his maiden speech in the House
of Lords, on this issue, is a rhetorical triumph); and the more sinister
plotting of the Catholics (in what comes close to being an international
conspiracy) in the later novel, _Lothair_. What Mrs. Gore and Disraeli
convey, the one parodically and the other more straightforwardly, is
the complex relation between the beau monde and the political world.
There is, of course, open traffic between the two, for which there is
the most fundamental justification in the position of the aristocracy.
But this by no means solves the narrative problem. On the one side,
there are fashion, being seen, the tableau, the mot juste, the melodramatic gesture: even collectively, these project little more than an
episodic narrative. Politics complicates and to an extent replicates the
series: in the conventions of appearance at Parliament as well as at
the proper clubs, in the proper speeches as well as in the equivocating
promises,[29] in the dramatic meetings between sovereign and minister
to form a cabinet or dissolve a parliament (always reported and thus

---

29. Equivocation displays its most serious side in Disraeli's _Sybil_.

clear gestures). At times a boundary emerges, where to be fashionable means to be politically perfunctory, and to be political means to be indifferent to the cut of one's coat or the taste of one's beef. It is this difference that allows a sustained narrative to be projected, one that is not predicated upon melodrama but that instead converts the arts of talk and display into the art of being in the public world. Such transformations inform narrative both in *Pelham* (one of Pelham's most arduous efforts is to enlist the epicure Guloseton into political action) and in *Coningsby* (although Thackeray's appellation, a "dandy-political" novel, admits its generic ambiguity).

In the end, what matters is not political affairs—the Reform Bill, the Corn Laws, the Catholic Issue—or even party maneuvers, all of which contribute to the manifest content of the novels but which may be understood through simple keys or footnotes. What is more important is the underlying, total political significance, which can be understood only in a double sense. First, there is the commitment of the self to a responsible political role: an ending that confers continuity in retrospect to the episodes of the novel (which can now be seen as steps toward this ending) and that also projects an optimistic narrative. It is precisely one's role as a political being that will allow one to abandon the nullifying modes of repetition and display and to undertake meaningful action, that will allow one to enter the mode of narration. But this is a projection from within. The second way of construing the political significance of the fashionable novels comes from without. It is here that we may recall two theses of Baudelaire: first, that the dandy is somehow connected with the heroism of modern life, and, second, that the heroism of modern life resides in the connection between elegant life and "subterranean" existence:

> En relisant le livre *du Dandysme*, par M. Jules Barbey d'Aurevilly, le lecteur verra clairement que le dandysme est une chose moderne et qui tient à des causes tout à fait nouvelles.
>
> Pour rentrer dans la question principale et essentielle, qui est de savoir si nous possedons une beauté particulière, inhérente à des passions nouvelles, je remarque que la plupart des artistes qui ont abordé les sujets modernes se sont contentés des sujets publics et officiels, de nos victoires et de notre heroïsme politique. Encore les font-ils en rechignant, et parce qu'ils sont commandés par le gouvernement qui les paye. Ce-

ti c

pendant il y a des sujets privés, qui sont bien autrement hér-
oïques.

Le spectacle de la vie élégante et des milliers d'existences
flottantes qui circulent dans les souterrains d'une grande
ville,—criminels et filles entretenues,—la *Gazette des Tribu-
naux* et le *Moniteur* nous prouvent que nous n'avons qu'à ouvrir
les yeux pour connaître notre héroïsme.[30]

Baudelaire's brief sketch of the dandy in the essay on dandyism offers
the most compelling reasons for taking that figure seriously, among
them the aspiration not only to material elegance, but to the "aristocratic superiority of the spirit" of which material elegance is the
symbol. If the sphere of his heroism is private, it will be related to the
double spectacle of high and low. The dandy has his political moment,
which Baudelaire identifies as that of the waning of the aristocracy,
before the rising tide of democracy has gained full ascendancy. Modern heroism, then, must appear to be ambiguous: on the one hand,
the shift from public to private spheres is justified by the very circumstances of modern life; on the other hand, insofar as we can accept
the dandy as a valid political symbol, he appears at a moment of
decline, rather than the moment of revitalization that Bulwer and Disraeli project from within. If we add to this the images of decline, as
well as the hyperbolic mode of the fashionable novels, then their
political significance seems far more problematic, their narrative pos-
sibilities at once more open and more equivocal.|

VI

In the novels of high life, the melodramatic plots of duels, gambling,
and murder, as well as their more inert counterpart of the fatal illness,[31]
have their psychological components of desperation and guilt, but
these tend to be exteriorized, allegorized, or textualized in the passages of interplay with the Gothic, the Byronic, or the various Romantic

30. Charles Baudelaire, "De l'héroïsme de la vie moderne," in *Salon de 1846, Oeuvres
complètes*, 951.
31. In addition to *Pelham*, note the illness in *Cecil, or the Adventures of a Coxcomb*.

landscape topoi of picturesque ruins, forests, and the like. The actors in these little dramas play out the abstract forms of desire, without doing more than raising the problematic of selfhood that the dandy novels always seem to circle around. Even Reginald Glanville follows the conventions so closely, if ingeniously, that he seems to have wandered into the novel arbitrarily; his dark brooding anguish, however, motivates a plot in *Pelham* so significant that it seems to relegate Pelham himself to the role of observer. His narrative of guilt and despair is insulated from a genuine dialectic: his wasting disease, although not understood, is the emblem of his despair. It is only when Glanville's desperate situation becomes the occasion for Pelham to test his principles and his loyalties—to act—that the narrative achieves its greatest cohesion. As a consequence, Pelham's urbanity undergoes a transformation, as the scheme of the city itself changes. In addition, that urbanity, so closely implicated in the art of self-presentation, evolves into a form of political responsibility.

A similar scenario appears as a subtext in *Coningsby*, a novel that subsumes rather than explores the mingling of fashion and politics. One negative episode is particularly telling. Lord Monmouth assembles a house party at Coningsby, his estate. Because he has lived abroad for several years, the great house has none of the traces that a house which has been continuously lived in possesses; it seems, rather, as if the artificial world of London fashion has simply been transplanted there—with the ironic result that the apparent fullness of London life now seems, to one who is aware, curiously empty. Yet it is the landed estate that has hitherto been the source, or the center, of political representation. The doubled artifice in the situation is only underlined by the debut of a young actress as part of the theatrical entertainment at Coningsby: her affecting performance is the result of real passion unrelated to and thus displaced onto her role. This doubled critical perspective upon fashionable life is intensified still further by the appearance of Sidonia, the financier (modeled upon one of the Rothschilds) of Spanish Jewish origins whose family has preserved its integrity and authenticity, and increased its fortunes, through centuries of political and religious persecution. The house party, then, for all its attention to a brand of high life imported from London, signifies a political crisis that Coningsby will resolve as he learns political responsibility (the interior theme) and turns to the manufacturing cities of the North (the spatial or external motif) for new energy.

In *Coningsby* the optimistic narrative prevails, despite the signs of

aristocratic emptiness and the fact that Coningsby wins his first political contest because his future father-in-law, a northern manufacturer, steps in as a deus ex machina. Nevertheless, the wit and eloquence of the dinner table, the bon mots and anecdotes of high life,
emerge as the underside of a sustained political eloquence. The art
of the self passes its most important tests not in the private but in the
public sphere.

This easy transformation of wit into eloquence has been achieved
by revitalizing the metaphoric aspects of aristocracy and sloughing off
the literal aristocracy, or at least those of its members who have become so much inert matter. In the end, the "natural" liaison between
politics and high life seems to be self-contradictory. Cecil remarks on
the indifference of high life to all sorts of constitutional crises: "the
politenesses of London proceed unmolested.—Like a passing breath
on any other surface of polished steel, society shines the brighter for
that momentary obscurement" (*Cecil, A Peer*, 1: 254). Here is the description of the Brettinghams' house: "a pale imitation of Parisian
society. Luxury and grace employed as arabesques and gilding to
disguise the unsightliness of political and official life, constituted its
charm" (1:303).

Why, then, is political life eventually valorized, the world of luxury
reduced to a setting for motifs of political responsiblity, spiritual commitment and noblesse oblige? Political life is a necessary supplement
to the dandified world; at the same time, it is no more than "a passing
breath" on a "surface of polished steel." Disraeli's passage on the
conjunction of elegance and passion—a more abstract counterpart
to Baudelaire's linkage of high and low life—affords one answer. If
we take Baudelaire seriously, the descent into passion and the
underworld demands some private but nevertheless heroic self-
recognition. But after that clandestine recognition, there is the re-
binding to the surface, not only to high life but to a city that offers
coherence.

Another answer is related to hyperbole itself. As hyperbole leads
beyond the mere gratification of the senses to an ultimate epicureanism, high life is written as a form of romance. But it is the forms of
romance that can make the representation of the city so problematic.
Lothair's phantasmagoric experience of Rome as he recovers from his
battle wounds, an experience carefully monitored by the Catholics to
exclude anything antipathetic to their cause, is exemplary. The ex-
cursions that the Catholic figures take with Lothair, like the ritual of

affirmation they arrange of whose meaning Lothair is unaware, are ideationally empty: they are sensuous and exotic, but they can be read only as experiences of dislocation. The melodramatic Catholic plot in *Lothair* plays out all the sinister implications and contradictions of high life, including the repression of low life and passion, but now also the repression of meaning. Since the suppression of political life and ideology in *Lothair* is also associated with the suppression of meaning, the connections are unavoidable. What earlier was dandyism or epicureanism extends, in this later novel, to Disraeli's mystification of Catholicism: all involve a retreat from signification. The growth of an underlying skepticism vis-à-vis the fashionable world then requires a centripetal movement back to London as the symbolic center of political life, back to authentic urbanity now understood to be public-spirited and ethical.

It may be objected, however, that a new narrative paradigm whereby the dandy learns political responsibility is simply a new form of hyperbole, either because two excellences are combined, or because dandyism, already hyperbolic, is subordinated to more serious public matters or else revealed as superficial. Either way, it might seem that the text requires more hyperbole to surpass what already exists. (Bulwer's Godolphin, in the novel of that name, serves as a negative instance insofar as he suffers because he refuses political responsibility.) |In the case of superficiality, the luxurious furnishings, the perfumes, the fine paintings and elegant meals may represent an abstract ideal of refinement; but unless that excellence includes political responsibility,[32] it cannot be completely indicative of the inner self.| The tokens of elegance may then appear to be diversionary in relation to the real Pelham or the real Glanville. When the epicure Guloseton cancels—in writing—his political indifference to espouse Pelham's cause,|this seems tantamount to making the obvious moral judgment that fashion needs politics in order to be rescued into substantiality.| Russelton, the fictional representative of Beau Brummell, confirms the inadequacy of what now appears as mere dandyism.|It is not enough to be the supreme embodiment of style and refinement, unless style is inspirited by evidence of the life of the mind.|A hyperbolic mode whose meaning by itself is suspect is now restored to significance by the supplement of a broadly defined political life.

The scenario in Baudelaire's "Le Dandy" is different, however. Dan-

---

32. Cf. Jerome McGann's comments on the dandy's ideal of selfhood, which combines the moral with the political, in the Introduction to *Pelham*, xvii–xviii.

dyism is not, he writes, equivalent to "an immoderate taste for the toilet and for material elegance."|On the contrary, "these things are for the dandy only a symbol of the aristocratic superiority of his spirit."[33] Dandyism cultivates originality within conventions and confines itself to a certain "spirituality" and even "stoicism" within its cult of the self. It has become so prominent during the early nineteenth century because of its refusal to found itself upon a material economy; its valorization of "indestructible" faculties is what has made it so transitory:|

> Dans le trouble de ces époques quelques hommes déclassés, dégoûtés, désoeuvrés, mais tous riches de force native, peuvent concevoir le project de fonder une espèce nouvelle d'aristocratie, d'autant plus difficile à rompre qu'elle sera basée sur les facultés les plus précieuses, les plus indestructibles, et sur les dons célestes que le travail et l'argent ne peuvent conférer. Le dandysme est le dernier éclat d'héroïsme dans les décadences. (1179)

Style and heroism conjoined: the best novels of high life are far more than jeux d'esprit. They resolve, rather, on a symbolic level the very social contradictions and conventions that would relegate the conventional novel of high life to the realm of inconsequence. Not class, but being déclassé as a starting point: Pelham, Godolphin, Coningsby all have something dubious about their family origins or fortunes. These origins allow a space for the cultivation of the self that is conveyed in the combined dandyism and implicitly utopian leanings of the novels. Yet it is Baudelaire who reaffirms the precariousness of dandyism, albeit in a different light: it is "a setting sun"; and "like the falling star, it is superb, without heat and full of melancholy" (1180; my translation).

The narrative closure to which this hyperbolic mode is now seen to be subject, a closure that follows the conventions of popular romance in which the protagonist attains both domestic happiness and public fame, may still leave us with the suspicion that not all dandies are capable of such fictional redemption. The hypothesis hangs badly upon that superannuated dandy of *Bleak House*, Mr. Turveydrop, as

33. Charles Baudelaire, "Le Dandy," *Le Peintre de la Vie Moderne*, in *Oeuvres Complètes*, Bibliothèque de la Pléiade (Paris: Editions Gallimard, 1961), 1178.

well as that dandy afflicted by the fashionable malady of ennui, Eugene Wrayburn of *Our Mutual Friend*, to say nothing of the more cynical dandies of *The Picture of Dorian Gray*. It is possible, of course, to characterize both Turveydrop and Wrayburn as historically superannuated figures whose tarnished dandyism has failed to accommodate to the political moment. Turveydrop, whose main object is to be seen, but who has lost the frame of the bow window at White's, wanders contextlessly in a bourgeois city in which he has no public role. Wrayburn's lassitude is the emblem of his lack of vocation, and, until the end, moral commitment. If his personal dandyism depends less upon the display of costume, what he does display by his very speech and gestures is a self-enclosure that separates him for a good part of the novel from a meaningful community.[34] In this context he comments on the curious lack of personality or individuation in many of the earlier dandies, whose rewriting or literal incorporation of fictional and social conventions nevertheless preserves impersonal ideals of excellence or passion. But whereas Glanville's intense subjectivity may be perceived as passion itself, Wrayburn suppresses all passion and acts as if he had none at all. It is not stoicism, however, that motivates him. The heroic ideal and the political narrative that elsewhere rescue the enterprise of the fashionable novel are destroyed from within, in part by the emptying out of character. Hyperbole by itself cannot sustain the glorious present/presence to which the dandies lay claim.

It is this unsettling inner logic that gives the final twist to the representation of the city in the later dandy novels. Here, for example, is an urban studio in *The Picture of Dorian Gray*:

> The studio was filled with the rich odour of roses, and when the light summer wind stirred amidst the trees of the garden, there came through the open door the heavy scent of the lilac, or the more delicate perfume of the pink-flowering thorn.
>
> From the corner of the divan of Persian saddle-bags on which he was lying, smoking, as was his custom, innumerable cigarettes, Lord Henry Wotton could just catch the gleam of the honey-sweet and honey-coloured blossoms of a laburnum, whose tremulous branches seemed hardly able to bear the burden of a beauty so flame-like as theirs; and now and then the

---

34. Eugene is, in a sense, a figure from another mode who has drifted into *Our Mutual Friend*.

   .·. fantastic shadows of birds in flight flitted across the long <u>tus-sore</u>-silk curtains that were stretched in front of the huge window, producing a kind of momentary Japanese effect, and making him think of those pallid jade-faced painters of Tokio who, through the medium of an art that is necessarily immobile, seek to convey the sense of swiftness and motion. The sullen murmur of the bees shouldering their way through the long unmown grass, or circling with monotonous insistence round the dusty gilt horns of the straggling <u>woodbine,</u> seemed to make the stillness more oppressive. The dim roar of London was like the <u>bourdon</u> note of a distant organ.

   In the centre of the room, clamped to an upright easel, stood the full-length portrait of a young man of extraordinary personal beauty.[35]|

The scent-filled room, the exotic furnishings, the filtering of nature through metaphors of art (the Japanese painting, the organ note), a painting as the focal point (instead of Canova's Venus): all of these recall the dandy theme and at the same time preface its logical end. This passage of word-painting, with its insistent if exquisite alliteration, its foregrounding not only of the senses but of those sensory experiences that are most ephemeral (gleams of blossoms, the "tremulous" branches with their "flame-like beauty," the "fantastic shadows of birds in flight") and that can be arrested only in art, prepares us for the novel's central fantasy in which art will assume the experiences of decay, aging, and corruption in order to allow Dorian Gray to live at least physically unscathed. Wilde's prefatory maxims (which may be compared with the suppressed set of maxims in *Pelham*), by banishing the ethical, apparently restore the purity of the artistic mode, as well as its privacy. "No artist has ethical sympathies," Wilde writes: "An ethical sympathy in an artist is an unpardonable mannerism of style" (5). Yet the ensuing narrative, with its ugly contrasts and choices between life and art, and its ultimate vision of corruption transferred from the portrait to its subject, comments not only upon aesthetic surfaces but upon the very nature of representation. "All art is at once surface and symbol," Wilde notes. That opening passage, by placing art and life on one plane, restores to high life the latent privileging of the surface. Even if we were to disregard the ethical mannerism (which

35. Oscar Wilde, *The Picture of Dorian Gray* (Baltimore: Penguin, 1976), 7.

would relate the corruption here to the corruption of the Young Duke), and refuse to read *The Picture of Dorian Gray* as a moral narrative, we would still be able to read it as an allegory about the representation of high life, or of the beautiful, in the city. Yet as in *Pelham*, the beau monde invokes its antithesis of murder and low life, if more phantasmagorically:

> How quickly it [the murder] had all been done! He felt strangely calm, and, walking over to the window, opened it, and stepped out on the balcony. The wind had blown the fog away, and the sky was like a monstrous peacock's tail, starred with myriads of golden eyes. He looked down, and saw the policeman going his rounds and flashing the long beam of his lantern on the doors of the silent houses. The crimson spot of a prowling hansom gleamed at the corner, and then vanished. A woman in a fluttering shawl was creeping slowly by the railings, staggering as she went. Now and then she stopped, and peered back. Once, she began to sing in a hoarse voice. The policeman strolled over and said something to her. She stumbled away, laughing. A bitter blast swept across the Square. The gas-lamps flickered, and became blue, and the leafless trees shook their black iron branches to and fro. He shivered, and went back, closing the window behind him. (176–77)

The passage presents a series of substitutions: instead of the gleam of a blossom, the gleam of a cab light; a hoarse voice instead of the sullen murmur of the bees; shaking "black iron branches" instead of tremulous ones, and a fluttering shawl instead of birds in flight; instead of a coxcomb (or even a falling star), a peacock's tail in the night sky. Because the ethical has been excluded, however, they occupy the same space of representation, like a bad pun when sensation moves to the sensational.

> The way seemed interminable, and the streets like the black web of some sprawling spider. The monotony became unbearable, and, as the mist thickened, he felt afraid.

> After some time they left the clay road, and rattled again over rough-paven streets. Most of the windows were dark, but now and then fantastic shadows were silhouetted against some

lamplit blind. He watched them curiously. They moved like monstrous marionettes, and made gestures like live things. He hated them. A dull rage was in his heart. As they turned a corner a woman yelled something at them from an open door, and two men ran after the hansom for about a hundred yards. The driver beat them with his whip. (205)

The fashionable cabriolets and landaus have become the plebian hansoms, and the night sky represents not the meteoric career of Cecil Danby but the disordered consciousness of Dorian Gray. The order of the monstrous—in the night sky, behind closed blinds—determines the representation of the city: the exotic has become the monstrous, the ultimate hyperbole. The failed exclusiveness of high life has its counterpart in the failed exclusions of art, whose fashionable coils reveal their underside and whose brilliance invokes darkness. *The Picture of Dorian Gray*, like *Pelham* and *The Young Duke*, restores the concealed terms of low life and passion, but by a strategy that insists upon the primacy of the represented surface, of an image-making process that is virtually inseparable from perception. This may be a variety of impressionism,[36] or of a Paterian attempt to seize the moment. But if we take Wilde's maxims seriously, then we cannot take them literally: we will simply ask different ethical questions about representation. The very suspension that Wilde insists upon may also afford access to the mysterious surfaces and symbols of the city, where hyperbole reappears only to undo itself.

36. Arnold Hauser defines impressionism as an art of the metropolis in *The Social History of Art* (New York: Vintage, 1958) 4:175–76: "At first sight, it may seem surprising that the metropolis, with its herding together and intermingling of people, should produce this intricate art rooted in the feeling of individual singularity and solitude. But it is a familiar fact that nothing seems so isolating as the close proximity of too many people, and nowhere does one feel so lonely and forsaken as in a great crowd of strangers. The two basic feelings which life in such an environment produces, the feeling of being alone and unobserved, on the one hand and the impression of roaring traffic, incessant movement and constant variety, on the other, breed the impressionistic outlook on life in which the most subtle moods are combined with the most rapid alternation of sensations." J. Hillis Miller finds in the opening paragraphs of *Bleak House* a perfect example of impressionism with (in Hauser's words) " 'its nervous rhythm, the sudden sharp but always ephemeral impressions of the city' " (*Charles Dickens, The World of His Novels*. Bloomington: Indiana University Press, 1969), 161. The opening of *The Picture of Dorian Gray*, its studio filled with transitory phenomena, distances the "dim roar of London," which is nevertheless heard. The interiorization in this passage, with the rapid succession of sensations, marks a return to the exclusiveness of dandaical London which, however, bears traces of the more inclusive rhythms of an earlier impressionism.

4

Visual Emptiness and Narrative Dispersion in Gissing's Later Novels

*G*issing's later novels are puzzling not because of their failure to celebrate the city—many nineteenth-century urban celebrations are demonic in character or even displaced saturnalia—but because of their failure to exploit its surfaces. In the earlier novels, using the slum as a privileged object, Gissing tries to confront the phenomenality of the city by breaking free of the social and aesthetic conventions that inform prior urban representations. Those conventions are not so much abandoned as reinserted into narrative and thematized; philanthropy and art cannot finally shape the city, but they are part of the urban experience. The earlier novels are predicated upon a search for the realities of a slum life whose ensuing contradictions foreground the very questions of realism. Urban representation often turns toward voice, a factor which, given its suppression of the visual, hints at Gissing's later concerns. (Voice is a minor but striking motif in the urban sketches and dandy novels as well: a woman's voice crying out in the darkness, for example, bespeaks an excess for which neither description nor classification can account. Often sheer sound, voice gestures toward an economy of the unrepresentable.) The phenomenological fullness and vitality that are the distinguishing marks of so many earlier urban texts—sketches, novels, even Gissing's slum novels—seem virtually to disappear. It is not simply that there is a prevailing sense of "fatigue,"[1] but that the city is "drained of its epistemological excitement."[2] If vision is the privileged sense of realism, and it is manifested in an "epistemophilic passion to *see* or examine human reality,"[3] then it seems as if Gissing is bent on going beyond realism, on redefining the *données* of the city. The spread of poverty is metaphorical: no longer confined to the economic conditions of the nether world, it inhabits the sites and conditions of culture. Vision and imagination are impoverished, occasionally turning in on themselves in casually narcissistic ways.[4] Such a situation should be intolerable for the novelist. How is it, then, that Gissing's novels manage to transform epistemological paucity into narrative plenitude? We should distinguish between the critique of a city dominated by mass culture, by the conditions of secrecy and scandal both social and financial, by the relentless production of texts both tangible and intangible, and the narrative modes of representing that city. From the latter perspective, the totalizing metaphors, the persistent images, the dispersion or instability of character, the continual attempts at reading and interpretation, constitute a rewriting of the city itself.

The model for representation changes dramatically in these later novels. If the earlier ones are not entirely committed to a spatial vision, to descriptive mapping, or to the representation of surfaces, they nevertheless predicate their interpretation of the otherness of the slums upon the phenomenality of that strange and resistant world. The later novels point to the inadequacy of a spatial mode of repre-

1. Cf. Irving Howe, Introduction to George Gissing, *New Grub Street* (Boston: Houghton Mifflin, 1962), xvii.

2. Adrian Poole, *Gissing in Context* (Totowa, N. J.: Rowman and Littlefield, 1975), 45.

3. Jeffrey Mehlman, *Revolution and Repetition* (Berkeley: University of California Press, 1977), 124.

4. In *In the Year of Jubilee*, Nancy Lord stands on the Monument; but "the vision of London's immensity" serves only to feed her "conceit of self-importance." (George Gissing, *In the Year of Jubilee*, [Rutherford, N. J.: Fairleigh Dickinson University Press, 1976], 104.)

sentation, even when that space is in part symbolic. The model that starts with perception gives way to a functional one. Metaphors for the nineteenth-century city often cluster around the idea of the organism[5]; for Gissing, the organic is associated with a totality or a set of functions not immediately available to perception. The problem for the novelist then becomes one of adopting a discourse that will convey the unseen and even the unsaid. Language, which thrives on obliquity in the urban novel, now demands it more than ever. Foucault's terms for the modern "analysis of man's mode of being" have a general relevance for Gissing's novels, insofar as that analysis "does not reside within a theory of representation; its task, on the contrary, is to show how things in general can be given to representation, in what conditions they can appear in a positivity more profound than the various modes of perception."[6] The concern with the world of literary and journalistic communication in New Grub Street represents the shift. In that novel, corruption, bespeaking the fate of the organic metaphor, is almost too facile a term for the state of urban culture. The language of the writer may be inadequate for its task, or it may be the instrument of misrepresentation, as in literary reviews. The ad hoc quality of literary belief, where what is valued serves the interests of expediency, is compatible with the symbolism of blindness. Yet because the contraries may also exist in New Grub Street, the entire literary or communicative network demands redefinition. The vicissitudes of literary culture reveal as much about its subservience to power as about its independent qualities. In this context, the worlds of Gissing's later novels serve as cognate metaphors for each other.

I

Urban literature has long played upon the idea that the city is a repository of secrets. To the exploratory motifs of the urban sketches

5. Cf. Alexander Welsh, *The City of Dickens* (Oxford: Clarendon Press, 1971), 25–26; and Max Byrd, *London Transformed: Images of the City in the Eighteenth Century* (New Haven: Yale University Press, 1978). Cf. also John Goode's distinction between the "experienced" city of Dickens and the "generative" city of Gissing, in *George Gissing: Ideology and Fiction* (New York: Barnes and Noble, 1979), 96. Although the "generative city" has some similarities, insofar as it is a functional one, to the city described here, it does not differentiate between the early and late novels. Nor does it involve the same problematic of representation.

6. Michel Foucault, *The Order of Things* (London: Tavistock, 1970), 337.

we may add the more restricted but more authoritative claim that the secrets and mysteries of London are to be revealed. G. M. Reynolds's popular *The Mysteries of London* (1845–48) demonstrates that a romantic text can signify the real through the detours of fiction. (Eugene Sue's *Mysteries of Paris* [1842–43], a French counterpart, is another urban text for Dickens and Gissing.) Not all urban writing relies on the impulse to reveal secrets; a writer like G. H. A. Sala seems far more intent upon cataloging and writing journalistic taxonomies of London at every hour, in every typical place, as we see in *Twice Round the Clock* and *Gaslight and Daylight* (1859). In Sala's works, the description of surfaces, visible and linguistic, is paramount, with the implicit aim of matching the city's fullness with some form of linguistic plenitude. But such an enterprise stops short of a fictional threshold. An aspect of mystery, rather, whether it lies in the subject to be uncovered or in the figures that uncover the subject, is more likely to be associated with the novel. While the remote or the exotic, the slum or the palace, may contain a secret to be laid bare, nevertheless a major constituent of the late nineteenth-century city is its secrecy.[7] Tensions arise from the precarious balance between secrecy and betrayal, from the circulation of secrets in urban life, from their complicity with the criminal (which may be "real" or itself a metaphor for the existence of secrets) and the resulting necessity for police surveillance and its figural analogues.[8] The condition of secrecy joins knowledge with power. That power seems to circulate almost autonomously, and betrayal may affect the self or others.

> The secret, too, is full of the consciousness that it *can* be betrayed; that one holds the power of surprises, turns of fate, joy, destruction—if only, perhaps, of self-destruction. For this reason, the secret is surrounded by the possibility and temptation of betrayal; and the external danger of being discovered is interwoven with the internal danger, which is like the fascination

7. For one account of the theme of secrecy in the novel, see Richard C. Maxwell, Jr., "G. M. Reynolds, Dickens, and the Mysteries of London," *Nineteenth-Century Fiction*, 32 (1977): 188–213.8.

8. See Michel Foucault, *Discipline and Punish*, trans. Alan Sheridan (New York: Pantheon, 1977), as well as his *Power/Knowledge*, ed. Colin Gordon (New York: Pantheon, 1980). See also Leo Bersani, "The Subject of Power," *Diacritics*, 7 (1977): 2–21; and Mark Seltzer, "*The Princess Casamassima*: Realism and the Fantasy of Surveillance," *Nineteenth-Century Fiction*, 35 (1981): 506–34.

⸫ of an abyss, of giving oneself away. The secret puts a barrier between men but, at the same time, it creates the tempting challenge to break through it, by gossip or confession—and this challenge accompanies its psychology like a constant overtone. . . . Out of the counterplay of these two interests, in concealing and revealing, spring nuances and fates of human interaction that permeate it in its entirety.[9]

The indeterminacies of secrecy, then, open up possibilities for narrative, for forms that evolve from the possible, from knowledge that is half-glimpsed, deferred, or hidden.

Such a view of the city entails a problematic of representation that is the inverse of what Gissing had to face in his slum novels. These later novels question that status of the real, question the possibility of its stasis, so that the object of representation is continually in doubt. Representation becomes re-presentation of a secret; in this city, language is displaced from any referent other than that of the leveling "secret." Narratives represent the structures of the secrets, even as they thematize their presence. The central secret of Gissing's *In the Year of Jubilee* (1894), for example, involves Lionel Tarrant's seduction of Nancy Lord, their marriage, and their child. Nancy's revelation of different parts of her secret to various characters generates the action of a substantial portion of the novel. The secret enters a chain of circulation as one character discloses his partial knowledge to another, who is generally the object of romantic designs. Two of Nancy's rejected suitors, Samuel Barmby and Luckworth Crewe, learn parts of the secret: Barmby about the marriage, from Jessica Morgan; and Crewe about the baby, from Beatrice French. Knowledge is altered by desire, or desire for power, just as the whole truth, split, is modified. Such a network finds its material correlative in the trams and railways that traverse London; errant truth now directs, or is directed by, urban affairs.

The Whirlpool (1897) moves away from the visual and intensifies the role of the secret, which is now linked to scandal. Alma Rolfe's flirtatious behavior, performed in order to get influential supporters

---

9. Georg Simmel, *The Sociology of Georg Simmel*, ed. and trans. Kurt H. Wolff (New York: Free Press, 1950), 333–34. Simmel's conception of the psychology of the secret within a power network anticipates certain theses of Foucault. See especially Foucault's *The History of Sexuality, vol. I: An Introduction*, trans. Robert Hurley (New York: Vintage: 1980).

for her concert debut, puts her on the edge of a distinctively Victorian abyss. To pursue the novel's generative metaphor, she cannot stay away from the social whirlpool. But the metaphor is also economic and, in accord with the financial activity characteristic of the city, predicated on secrecy.

> Ever since traffic in economic values has been carried on by means of money alone, an otherwise inattainable secrecy has become possible. Three characteristics of the monetary form of value are relevant here: its compressibility, which permits one to make somebody rich by slipping a check into his hand without anybody's noticing it; its abstractness and qualityless-ness, through which transactions, acquisitions, and changes in ownership can be rendered hidden and unrecognizable in a way impossible where values are owned only in the form of extensive, unambiguously tangible objects; and finally, its effect-at-a-distance, which allows its investment in very remote and ever-changing values, and thus its complete withdrawal from the eyes of the immediate environment. (Simmel, *The Sociology of Georg Simmel*, 335)

Although the visible material economy of the city makes itself felt in Hugh Carnaby's involvement in bicycle manufacturing as well as in Harvey Rolfe's concern with the photography business (both symbolic of modernity), the investment in intangibles, in stocks and bonds, is if anything more central to the economic life of the city. Thus Bennet Frothingham can bring his financial empire to ruin without being de-tected; conversely, one's ability to stay afloat in the whirlpool depends on living within one's income from investments. The novel has obvious similarities to Trollope's *The Way We Live Now* (1874–75), as John Goode points out.[10] But whereas Melmotte's scandalous financial pro-cedures, the very processes of the City, are central to both the structure and the empty present of *The Way We Live Now*, financial fraud is the initiating action of *The Whirlpool*. The scandal of Frothingham's

10. See John Goode, *George Gissing: Ideology and Fiction*, 184. Augustus Mayhew's *Paved with Gold, or the Romance and Reality of the London Streets* (London: Chapman and Hall, 1858; repr. London: Frank Cass, 1971) offers an earlier version of urban financial scheming; the three novels exemplify a mode of urban fiction where misrepresentation, or referential emptiness, is thematized.

financial manipulations and suicide hangs over his daughter Alma, makes her not quite respectable, brings her close to <u>London's demi-monde</u>. <u>That world subsists on, indeed, nearly consists of, gossip and blackmail, on unstated affairs that skirt respectability.</u>|Mrs. Strange-ways, its exemplar, supports herself by circulating gossip and with-holding it for a price: she is the blackmailer who plays it both ways.| The circulation of money and the circulation of gossip, each scan-dalous in itself, form an additionally scandalous connection. But the scandal also extends to representation, insofar as it arises from the intangibility of its "objects" or components. The constitutive elements of the city can be represented only by allusion, by linguistic displace-ment. The decisions of Rolfe and Carnaby, each in his way estranged from the world of investment and speculation, to turn to material busi-ness for support serve in the end to bring home the city's immateriality. Carnaby's business is in Coventry, and Rolfe is engaged with photog-raphy, with images of the visible: reality is elusive in the metropolis.[11] Neither Rolfe nor his associate, Cecil Morphew (who has devoted himself to—or fixated upon—a suspended romance for years), is much given to noticing change; their devotion to modernism fixes the images and is therefore inadequate in a dynamic urban milieu.

The narrative structures of the novels also work to this end. While Nancy Lord's story is refracted through the versions that circulate through London, the true story of Sybil Carnaby's involvement with Cyrus Redgrave (a millionaire whose economic base is never really clarified) is withheld and revealed only through the indirection of gossip and the allusions of interior monologue. The surfaces of the city are deceptive, as a recurring metaphor suggests. At a musical evening at the Frothinghams, Harvey Rolfe muses about the mysterious financier: "What monstrous cruelties and mendacities might underlie the surface of this gay and melodious existence!"[12] Such mysterious concealments are endemic in social life, where characters like Sybil Carnaby are distinguished by their elegant veneers. What Disraeli dis-

---

11. Walter Benjamin's comment on the inadequacies of photography is relevant here. Berlin at the time he writes is, he tells us, not "receptive to photography. For the closer we come to its present-day, fluid, functional existence, the narrower draws the circle of what can be photographed." See Walter Benjamin, "A Berlin Chronicle," in *Reflections*, trans. Edmund Jephcott (New York: Harcourt Brace Jovanovich, 1978), 8.

12. George Gissing, *The Whirlpool* (London: Lawrence and Bullen, 1897), 39.

cerned in the world of high fashion, Gissing situates in the world of finance and its parvenus. As in Trollope and Dickens, the shift to a milieu predicated upon intangibility makes the contradictions all the more sinister. At a Carnaby dinner party, the envious Alma "longed to expose the things unspeakable that lay beneath this surface of social brilliancy" (*The Whirlpool*, 275). One cannot, therefore, trust in the visible because the surface is meant to conceal. To privilege the visible is tantamount to deferring interpretation. The brilliancy of the dinner and the polished manners of a Sybil Carnaby belong to the category of what Simmel would call adornment, though there is a twist. Here adornment is not innocent; it serves to conceal a secret and to express a power relationship. What is adorned or concealed is both unnatural ("monstrous") and "unspeakable." The mode of the "unspeakable," formerly the property of the slum, is now transposed to the world of the middle class. In effect, Gissing is asserting the synecdochic power, or the metonymic spread, of the slum, whose contradictory linguistic registers characterize a general urban condition. Dickens's later novels also suggest that such a condition has spread throughout the city.[13] Inhabiting both private and public life, it draws upon a metaphorical economy in which the exchange of public and private, display and concealment, destabilizes both domains. The bifurcated structure of the middle class world of concealment and secrecy duplicates the divided structure of middle- and lower-class London. The problematic for the urban novelist is no longer confined either to the slums or to the fashionable world. He must now find a mode of representing that which refuses to yield itself to direct description. The scandals of finance, of infidelity, of criminality—or, in *In the Year of Jubilee*, of fidelity and relationship—now become linked to the scandals of referentiality.

II

If secrecy and scandal are modes, part thematic and part narrative, of unseating the real, of underprivileging the visible by a tacit appeal to the hidden and the half-said, their complementary mode, which plays

13. See Lionel Trilling, "Manners, Morals, and the Novel," in *The Liberal Imagination* (Garden City, N.Y.: Doubleday, 1953), 200–215.

upon the visible, is that of advertising. That enterprise plays an exemplary role in *In the Year of Jubilee*. The year is, of course, 1887, which marks fifty years of Victoria's reign; the Jubilee celebrates both the past half-century and the present state of England. The novel's title, however, is ironic, and not the least important part of that irony has to do with contemporary society's indifference toward the past. At a time of national celebration and self-satisfaction, English society is undergoing an inner corrosion, evidenced in strained family relations, false presentations of self, and fraudulent representations of society's products, both animate and inanimate (thus the fraudulent disinfectant that Arthur Peachey's firm produces, balanced against the false claims to social status that are the mark of the demimonde). In addition, an outer blight is attacking society, to be seen in the badly built suburban estates, in the spread of the railways, and in advertising.[14] The source of the corrosion and blight can only be London itself. Even the Jubilee celebrations, an apparently innocent carnivalesque eruption from the sober surfaces of the city, have their diminished but more sinister echoes in the mob attack upon the kiosks at a stadium where a sporting event has been cancelled and in the violence that periodically tears through the Peachey household in Camberwell. Advertising, the art not just of the present but of the future, is the most characteristic urban art and means of communication, and is most symbolic of the denaturing of the city. Word and image, perpetually at a remove from that which they represent, do more than proclaim their semiotic dominance; their function is not only to represent but to misrepresent, to distort their referents in the interests of

---

14. The suburban "Park" where the Morgan family lives is representative: "It was one of a row of new houses in a new quarter. A year or two ago the site had been an enclosed meadow, portion of the land attached to what was once a country mansion; London, devourer of rural limits, of a sudden made hideous encroachment upon the old estate, now held by a speculative builder; of many streets to be constructed, three or four had already come into being, and others were mapped out, in mud and inchoate masonry, athwart the ravaged field. Great elms, the pride of generations passed away, fell before the speculative axe, or were left standing in mournful isolation to please a speculative architect; bits of wayside hedge still shivered in fog and wind, amid hoardings variegated with placards and scaffolding black against the sky. The very earth had lost its wholesome odour; trampled into mire, fouled with builders' refuse and the noisome drift from adjacent streets, it sent forth, under the sooty rain, a smell of corruption, of all the town's uncleanliness. On this rising locality had been bestowed the title of 'Park' " (*In the Year of Jubilee*, 218). The language of this suburban antipastoral links it to Gissing's thematics of speculation and cultural corruption. If the suburb represents the pastoral dream of the city-dweller, this passage projects it as nightmare.

persuasion. Not only do advertisements gull the public through their invitations to misread, but they invite the reader of the novel to view the city as a peculiarly physical text. Gissing is once more redefining the task of the artist of the city. If reading the city (from the novelist's viewpoint) has in the past entailed reading its signs, immersing oneself in its mysteries, uncovering its secrets, one must now take account of a new intermediary, an oblique and errant sign of a sign. Because of the physical presence of advertising, the city is more immediately than before a palimpsest. To read the signs, one must view them as instruments of power and persuasion, as well as representations of urban or consumable products. What Gissing is most concerned with is not the interpretation of advertising, but rather the representation of a city that is engaged in misrepresenting itself, in covering its cultural origins and presences, and in creating a new culture predicated on inauthenticity. The figure par excellence of this urban enterprise is Luckworth Crewe, himself an orphan, a foundling, whose name is not his own but rather a composite of those of two of his benefactors, who is skilled in using advertising as a mode of urban empire-building, and whose vision is always oriented toward the future. Time is all he needs to make his fortune, he assures Nancy Lord.

If advertising changes the urban landscape—travelers in the city are frequently aware of it—it also spreads to the resorts, which represent the pastoral dreams of city-dwellers.[15] Crewe envisions the development of Whitsand as a resort:

> He unrolled a large design, a coloured picture of Whitsand pier as it already existed in his imagination. Not content with having the mere structure exhibited, Crewe had persuaded the draughtsman to add embellishments of a kind which, in days to come, would be his own peculiar care; from end to end, the pier glowed with the placards of advertisers. Below, on the sands, appeared bathing-machines, and these also were covered with manifold advertisements. Nay, the very pleasure-boats on the sunny waves declared the glory of somebody's soap, of somebody's purgatives.

15. Cf. John Goode's comment in *George Gissing: Ideology and Fiction*: "Holidays are specific forms of pastoral; you go to *resorts* to have holidays—it is a very urban concept, the holiday, requiring a far flung suburb which takes to an extreme the enclosed spaces of the urban park" (171).

> "I'll make that place one of the biggest advertising stations
> in England—see if I don't! You remember the caves? I'm going
> to have them lighted with electricity, and painted all round with
> advertisements of the most artistic kind." (424)

Nature itself is not free from the spread of urban blight. The dream of
development is one of appropriation and undifferentiation, of making
the resort—nature—like the city. It is a dream of cultural uniformity
and debasement, where the latter is understood as transposition
through concealment. Nor can pleasure be its own end or holiday
conceived of as a bracketing of urban affairs. The network of power
extends to the resort as, earlier in the novel, the railway defaces the
resort town of Teignmouth. (The word "stations" has a double resonance in this context.)

The image of the city's surfaces covered with advertisements an-
nounces a cultural crisis. In an episode near the beginning of *In the
Year of Jubilee*, Nancy Lord is on her way to the Jubilee celebration
in central London:

> A throng of far more resolute and more sinewy people swept
> them aside, and seized every vacant place on the top of the
> vehicle. Only with much struggle did they obtain places within.
> In an ordinary mood, Nancy would have resented this hustling
> of her person by the profane public; as it was, she half enjoyed
> the tumult, and looked forward to get more of it along the
> packed streets, with a sense that she might as well amuse her-
> self in vulgar ways, since nothing better was attainable. . . .
>
> Sitting opposite to Samuel, she avoided his persistent
> glances by reading the rows of advertisements above his head.
> Somebody's 'Blue;' somebody's 'Soap;' somebody's 'High-class
> Jams;' and behold, inserted between the Soap and the Jam—
> 'God so loved the world, that He gave His only-begotten Son,
> that whoso believeth in Him should not perish, but have ev-
> erlasting life.' Nancy perused the passage without perception
> of incongruity, without emotion of any kind. Her religion had
> long since fallen to pieces, and universal defilement of Scrip-
> tural phrase by the associations of the market-place had in this
> respect blunted her sensibilities. (60–61)

The city sanctions by incongruity, by visual oxymoron, the advertisements for soaps by the advertisements for Christianity. And the reverse, as clearly cleanliness is next to Godliness. (There is a related ironic episode in *The Emancipated*, where Miriam Baske decides that instead of building the chapel she had promised for a dissenting sect whose beliefs she no longer holds, she will fulfill her commitment by providing public baths.)[16]

The speech of the crowd on the tram is distortive and interpretive; even accent is implicated, as when one woman speaks of the " 'Prince of Wiles' " (*In the Year of Jubilee*, 61). But the sounds of the city, from chance phrases to the roar of the mob, are at this nodal point displaced by the silent images, the silent speech of advertising. It is here that advertising begins to have deeper political implications, as, in its public presence, it absorbs the crowd. The significance of the metonymic shifting from crowd to advertisements emerges during the course of the narrative: as advertisements cover the pier of Whitsand as well as its bathing machines and its caves, they take on the characteristics of the crowd, but a crowd that is manipulated and displaced. One form of vulgarity is substituted for another; still more significantly, the crowd is deprived of its will and is silenced. One reading might place *In the Year of Jubilee* in that series of novels, to which I have already referred, which express a middle-class fear of revolution and mob violence and suppress that possibility by narrative means.[17] The mob and the marketplace become, in this late version, the Scylla and Charybdis of urban "culture": one can choose one's vulgarity, voiced or silent. That Nancy loses sight of her individuality—the 'culture' to which she laid claim, evanesced in this atmosphere of exhalations" (68–69)—confirms the negativity, whatever the choice. Either the carnival of signs or the vulgarity of the crowd would deny the autonomy of the individual will, merely through an overwhelming plurality of signifiers. But as soon as the crowd is overcome, however metaphorically, the threatening placed in the position of the threatened, then the very humanity, the urbaneness, of the city is placed in double jeopardy. The metonymic slide from the assertion of individual personality to the vulgar expressions of the crowd to the silent persuasions of advertisements constitutes the figural or narrative form of the dehumanization of the

16. See George Gissing, *The Emancipated* (Rutherford, N. J.: Fairleigh Dickinson University Press, 1977), 436–37.
17. See Raymond Williams, *Culture and Society, 1780–1950* (New York: Columbia University Press, 1958).

city. The crowd, notes Walter Benjamin, is the great nineteenth-century subject for the writer.[18] But the particular form of intoxication (Nancy's exhiliration) that it induces is associated with an abandonment within the crowd, with an empathy that entails a loss of self. Benjamin's further correlation of the crowd of people with the "crowd" of commodities (they, too, are lost or abandoned in the crowd) is then exemplified in Gissing's images of advertising. The perspectives on incongruity that accompany urban mobility (travel in a tram, circulation in the crowd) end by asserting not simply an empathy with the inorganic but a dominance of the inorganic, not as material objects but as signs for those objects. If "epistemophilia" is involved here, it can only be a special case, for what the eye sees are the loss of the real, displacements—an errant city figured in errant narratives. An original plenitude is replaced by the epistemologically drained city: the direction of drainage can be only into signs and language, and into the circulation of narratives that feed on secrecy and concealment.

As the sign of mass culture, and as the purveyor of its myths, advertising operates through the modes of concealment and, as the casual juxtaposition of different signs for soap, jam, and religion suggests, dispersion. One may distinguish here between the more justifiable aims of mass culture to disseminate—late Victorian London becomes, as Adrian Poole points out, the heart of an international communications network[19]—and its attempts to manipulate. Literature, as in *New Grub Street*, enters a mode of production directed toward consumer society; but to do so, it must change its nature. It is not surprising that the very instruments of culture should provoke a cultural crisis. Whelpdale's journal in *New Grub Street*, entitled *Chit-Chat*, is the limiting term of this crisis, where words and sentences, indeed, language itself, are reduced to their lowest common denominators. Newspapers, too, with their columnar structures, reinforce visually the compartmentalized forms that communication now assumes, where unrelated items of information appear side by side and symbolize the disjunctions of modern life.[20] Samuel Barmby, in *In the Year of Jubilee*, culls random facts from the newspapers, more than enough to justify, in his eyes, his authoritative manner. Authority, or

18. See Benjamin's *Charles Baudelaire: A Lyric Poet in the Era of High Capitalism*, trans. Harry Zohn (London: New Left Books, 1973), 122.

19. *Gissing in Context*, 139.

20. See Walter Benjamin, "The Storyteller," in *Illuminations* (New York: Schocken Books, 1969).

authorship, is then a function of dispersal. Similarly, Jessica Morgan tries to cram facts for her university entrance exams, while Arthur Peachey is alarmed by half-digested, popularized theories about heredity as he contemplates his vulgar wife and tries to isolate his son from her. In effect, the London of Gissing's later novels is strewn with cultural debris. If one image for cultural dismemberment is the newspaper, another is architectural:

> At that corner of Battersea Park which is near Albert Bridge there has lain for more than twenty years a curious collection of architectural fragments, chiefly dismembered columns, spread in order upon the ground, and looking like portions of a razed temple. It is the colonnade of old Burlington House, conveyed hither from Piccadilly who knows why, and likely to rest here, the sporting ground for adventurous infants, until its origin is lost in the abyss of time.[21]

The odd perspective and the odd de-construction constitute dominant visual aspects of the city. Even the British Museum Reading Room, which might have seemed an impregnable center of culture, is not entirely safe. The problem is not simply the depredations of the hacks who form so significant a part of its population. Its domed structure, apparently classical and noble in its associations, evokes the image of that other characteristic nineteenth-century dome, the Panopticon.[22] Bentham's structure, suitable for prison, hospital, school, factory, is, as Foucault points out, the instrument for surveillance, for the exercise of power, discipline, and social coercion. One finds, in the Reading Room, the Panopticon superimposed upon the classical dome: culture reduced to hackwork has its own discipline, its own formulas, its own constraining norms. Foucault argues for the pervasiveness of the Panopticon as a social symbol; even the literary world of New Grub Street seems to be affected by it. New Grub Street presents us with the unstable interplay between cultural dispersion via the journalistic media and cultural concentration into a complementary "obscurity" within the "trackless desert of print," the Reading Room.[23] Either one will baffle the sense of vision.

21. George Gissing, *The Odd Women* (New York: Norton, 1971), 38.
22. John Goode notes the similarity to the Panopticon (*George Gissing: Ideology and Fiction*, 120) without, however, drawing Foucauldian inferences.
23. *New Grub Street*, 89, 90.

|Literary culture, then, gives rise to a system of reading that is both limited and fragmented despite its goal of uniformity. Culture is separated from its origins and its meanings; thus the debris, which is unobserved or misinterpreted.|The insistence of the new in the city, from typing machines (*The Odd Women*) to advertising to pulp literature, disallows any nostalgia, any of the *ubi sunt* themes (Vauxhall Gardens, May Day, even certain kinds of omnibuses), implicitly cultural, that wander through the *Sketches by Boz.*| The romance of the past that caught the imagination of the writers of urban sketches finds little tolerance in Gissing's London. (It is, however, a pastoral dream for Harvey Rolfe in *The Whirlpool*, and a sign of Reardon's defeat in *New Grub Street*.) The vocabulary of romance assumes new meanings for Luckworth Crewe:

> So they rambled aimlessly by the great thoroughfares, and by hidden streets of which Nancy had never heard, talking or silent as the mood dictated. Crewe had stories to tell of this and that thriving firm, of others struggling in obscurity or falling from high estate; to him the streets of London were so many chapters of romance, but a romance always of to-day, for he neither knew nor cared about historic associations. Vast sums sounded perpetually on his lips, he glowed with envious delight in telling of speculations that had built up great fortunes. He knew the fabulous rents that were paid for sites that looked insignificant; he repeated anecdotes of calls made from Somerset House upon men of business, who had been too modest in returning the statement of their income; he revived legends of dire financial disaster, and of catastrophe barely averted by strange expedients. (*In the Year of Jubilee*, 106)

The vast and the fabulous, disaster and catastrophe—the vocabulary of the extraordinary—glorify the quotidian, the material of the "journal." (The proneness to hyperbole of today's financial pages continues such linguistic practices.) The counterpart to indifference to the past is a narcissistic self-awareness. Barmby's vainglorious intellectual struttings are the self-display of a newspaper consumer. Similarly, Nancy Lord's visit to the Monument, the commemoration of the Great Fire of London, excites not historical speculation about the city, not awe at "the vision of London's immensity," but rather a "conceit of self-importance."

> [S]he stood there, above the battling millions of men, proof
> against mystery and dread, untouched by the voices of the past,
> and in the present seeing only common things, though from
> an odd point of view. Here her senses seemed to make literal
> the assumption by which her mind had always been directed:
> that she—Nancy Lord—was the mid point of the universe.
> (104)

This city has no aura for Nancy. I use the term in both ordinary and
special senses: in the latter, in Benjamin's sense, the aura is a simultaneously perceptual and memorial phenomenon, in which associations from the _mémoire involuntaire_ "tend to cluster around the
object of a perception." The ensuing mutual gaze between perceiver
and object realizes the object's quasi-sacred status.[24] In contrast, the
language of vision has no object for Nancy, and her gaze, her position
on top of the Monument, forecloses the possibility of any transaction
between her and the city. The Monument is more a crypt than it is a
vantage point for her. Later, we learn that Nancy's reading is a form
of adornment: she takes books from the library not to read but to
impress people with their intellectual titles. Thus reading—an openness to the "voices of the past" (and of the present)—is an empty
process, a denial of the personal and historical memory that does so
much to direct and shape one's awareness of an intermingled self and
city. The city, Benjamin observes, is the literal site of the encounters
that vivify memory and lead to self-understanding.[25] In Gissing's novels, the suppressed returns only as cultural debris, as random signifiers
without a point of entry into the consciousness of the city-dwellers.
The result is self-limitation on the one hand, self-dispersal on the
other.

Narcissism, or the "conceit of self-importance," is thus a limitation
to the present or to the literal. That this is one version of urban fantasies
about the self is suggested by the instability of other urban characters:
by Samuel Barmby who is the product of newspapers, a site traversed

24. Walter Benjamin, "On Some Motifs in Baudelaire," in _Illuminations_, 186–88, and
"The Work of Art in the Age of Mechanical Reproduction," in _Illuminations_, 221–23. Benjamin's discussion of aura and the changing modes of sense perception through history
would allow us to interpret Nancy's literal vision from the Monument as affected precisely
by that loss of aura. Her subsequent walk with Crewe, whose complementary reading of
the city rejects London's traditional associations, confirms the cultural implications of her
perceptions.
25. "A Berlin Chronicle," in _Reflections_, 30–32.

by urban texts; by Jessica Morgan, whose empty drift from academic cramming to the Salvation Army is the sign of futile dreams of power; by Lionel Tarrant, who is a rather specious gentleman. To these we may add all those who displace themselves into their anonymous writings: Godwin Peak of *Born in Exile*, and Marian Yule (among others) of *New Grub Street*. In the phantasmic financial world of *The Whirlpool*, one's occupation cannot ensure one's identity. The invisible nature of stocks and bonds drives a wedge between the person and his compensation. The structure of the financial world is like that of gambling, where, according to Benjamin, there is a temporal phantasmagoria, in which instant satisfaction or despair succeeds the throw of the dice, the turn of the wheel.[26] By the same token, gambling and financial speculation make the actions of "fate" independent of human action and will. Where scandal negates will in the social sphere, gambling or speculation blocks it in the monetary world. One should distinguish the more conscious wishes, fantasies of self-recovery nonetheless, that direct the gambling of a Becky Sharpe or a Gwendolen Harleth. The phantasmagoria is all the more dehumanized in the financial world by the absence of the wish, of the desire to change one's fate, by a spectral substitution for work.

Despite all the images of production,[27] the concern for forms of work and for issues of vocation, there is a counterimage of the nonproductive city, governed by the adventitious ideal of the gentleman, which may be transformed into something that approaches narcissism. But there is still another turn of the screw; to be free from work is also to be free from bourgeois convention. Nineteenth-century literary explorations of the city often portray its class structure as one in which both the aristocracy and the poor are free of those conventions: thus the voyeuristic interest, from a middle-class perspective, in the exoticism of the higher and lower worlds.[28] The aristocracy, for whom gambling is a major occupation or pastime, is linked with the unpredictable. Practiced by the middle class, however, gambling tends

---

26. See *Charles Baudelaire: A Lyric Poet in the Era of High Capitalism*, 174.

27. Cf. John Goode's characterization of London as a "generative" city whose geography is in part determined by its modes of production in *George Gissing: Ideology and Fiction*, 98–99.

28. Although it antedates Gissing's novels by some fifty years, James Grant's discussion of London's class structure in *The Great Metropolis*, Vol. 2 (London, 1837) provides a relevant nineteenth-century view of class differences. The middle classes are happier and more moral, but the otherness of the upper and lower classes affords more material for the writer.

to become imitative, part of the city's inauthenticity. The unpredictability also appears in the apparent freedom from ethical constraints:
thus Widdowson's middle-class suspicions of Everard Barfoot's "aristocratic" manners (*The Odd Women*, 236). Lionel Tarrant's gentle-
manly manners contrast with his general instability: his illegitimacy,
his unrealized hopes for wealth derived from manufacturing (which
he snobbishly tries to conceal), his callous treatment of Nancy. The
world of the middle-class gentleman in Gissing's novels betrays its
uneasiness, its inauthenticity as it strives to realize borrowed ideals
it can never fully accept. Even its passions are hedged by convention
(Bevis's flirtation with Monica Widdowson ends because he can accept neither the responsibility nor the opprobrium involved in running
off with a married woman), secrecy, and coldness (Redgrave's prop-
osition to Alma Frothingham envisages their future as a matter of business rather than passion). The city is beset by a general social, financial, and sexual attrition, where passion, like vocation, is often
suppressed, and appears through the play of incomplete transgres-
sions.

IV

Gissing's narrative procedures, his ways of encountering the city, transform its phenomenal nature. Communication and circulation (of
words, literature, secrets, but also of metropolitan railways), which
have no small connection with the metaphorical whirlpool, dominate
urban activity. The pleasantly erring omnibuses that traversed the London of *Sketches by Boz* are now translated into the railways, which
not only "honeycomb" the city,[29] but carry urban blight as far as Teignmouth. The railways, however, are only the most material manifes-
tation of a constitutive city life that is less easy to grasp. Gissing encounters in a new form the same problem he faced in the slum novels.
There, simply because the slums are by convention outside the order
of the re-presentable, there seems to be a chance of approaching the
city's true referentiality, as if the unrepresentable were the thing itself.
Using the slum as an ironically privileged object, Gissing confronts
the phenomenality of the city by breaking free of the social and aes-

29. Gillian Tindall notes this in her Introduction to *In the Year of Jubilee*.

thetic conventions that inform urban representation. But the quest to represent the real engages Gissing in a contradiction: just when his novels seem to be most free of the perceptions and relations engendered by convention, their narrative structures question their own referentiality.|Gissing also discovers that the figures of contradiction and distortion are those that most adequately represent the city| His struggle with the referent, with that which would have seemed to ground his claims to be an artist of the city, becomes foregrounded.|The field of discourse of the urban novel consists of a dialogue between the literal and the figural where the novelist plays the role of a mediator.| The figure of the author emerges at those rare moments when he stands on the margins between city and text, as in the scene in *Thyrza* where he inscribes street dancing as the sign of slum culture: the semi-darkness "cancels" the referent, only to allow its appropriation as figure into the text of the novel.[30] Here is a signature-piece of the urban novelist, just as, in other ways, the poverty of the slums is rewritten as voice or sound, and as the relative plenitude of the novel.

|In the later novels, the "real" would consist of the institutionalization of concealment, secrecy, ambiguity, displacement, limitations, literality: of abstractions that inform the most characteristic events or situations.|Otherwise it would have to appear in that which, given the constraints of the surface, of the phenomenological world, is outside the order of language. This latter possibility would indeed make the linguistic order of the real that of the "indescribable," of displacement carried to its limits. Gissing's reference to secrecy cannot help thematizing the issue.|But one may then question the adequacy of the conception of the nineteenth-century novel as revealing the gap between appearance and reality, where, for example, the glittering exteriors of social life are founded on a sordid underworld.|Gissing's practice, though it seems at first to support this conception, does not dismiss surfaces any more than the dandy novels do. Nevertheless, there is a drive to reinvoke the material or "pre-textual" aspects of the city—buildings, crowds, the brutality of Whitechapel, and even that substantial figure for all monuments, the Monument—as figures for solidity.|In other terms, they are metonymies of a desire for the real that has been dispersed by the very forms of discourse that pretend to name it.| This is manifest in an oddly persistent nostalgia for the

30. Cf. George Gissing, *Thyrza* (Rutherford, N.J.: Fairleigh Dickinson University Press, 1974), 111–12.

brutal that appears in the late novels. Michael Collie claims that the
"brute" forms are indicative of a somewhat gauche narratorial inter-
ference with the subject: they are judgmental words that only emphasize the distance between the writer and his materials.[31] But then they
would be strange judgments, crossed by ambivalence and nostalgia.
In the slum novels, brutality is located in the lower depths of the city:
it is associated with the least civilized inhabitants, and it may be verbal
or physical. Even there, however, there is a measure of admiration for
the other, for the pre-moral, as in the treatment of Clem Peckover of
The Nether World. The mob of *In the Year of Jubilee* (1894), unlike
that of *Demos* (1886), has no specified class affiliation. In *The Whirlpool*, brutality is both made international and located in the middle
classes, notably in characters like Hugh Carnaby who are out of place
in urban society and long for the pursuits of hunter and soldier. The
link between the slums and war appears at the end, when Harvey
Rolfe reads Kipling's "Barrack-Room Ballads" in the rural isolation of
Greystone. Kipling is " 'the voice of the reaction. Millions of men,
natural men, revolting against the softness and sweetness of civilisation' " (*The Whirlpool*, 449) But Rolfe adds,

> 'The brute savagery of it! The very lingo—how appropriate it
> is! The tongue of Whitechapel blaring lust of life in the track
> of English guns!—He knows it; the man is a great artist; he
> smiles at the voice of his genius.—It's a long time since the
> end of the Napoleonic Wars. Since then Europe has seen only
> sputterings of temper. Mankind won't stand it much longer, this
> encroachment of the humane spirit.' (449)

Despite—or because of—Rolfe's irony, Kipling is characterized as the
artist of the modern, the negative interpreter of civilization. The thematic of antiwar sentiments in *The Whirlpool* is complicated not only
by the role of the artist, but by the perceived militarism of "mankind."
If war is unacceptable to Rolfe, and the fatal attractions of the whirlpool
equally so from a cultural standpoint, he has in the end diminished
his own role as interpreter. Conversely, the artist who voices White-
chapel, the barrack-room, the music hall (" '[T]he bully of the music
hall shouting 'Jingo' had his special audience. Now comes a man of

---

31. See Collie's *The Alien Art: A Critical Study of George Gissing's Novels* (Hamden,
Conn.: Archon, 1979), 23.

genius, and decent folk don't feel ashamed to listen this time' " [450]),
has his modern subject. The closed spaces of Gissing's novels create
intolerable alternatives from which only the artist, who makes those
antitheses his capital, can extricate himself.

Brutality and war are, then, signs of a bracketed reality that is invoked as an alternative to the secrets and abysses of the urban whirlpool. But they are important in two other distinct ways. First, they
appear as minor but nevertheless significant points of carnival (especially in *In the Year of Jubilee*), which suspend the narratives only
to be thematized and reincorporated into the action.[32] Second, they
give the spectatorial function of the artist a paradoxically political cast.

There is an apparently isolated interchange, which consists of a
recounting of a mob scene, in *In the Year of Jubilee*, that conveys this
dual significance of the brutal. Luckworth Crewe tells Beatrice French
about a match for the Sprinting Championship that fails to take place.
The enraged crowd rushes for the gate-money first, then tears apart
the refreshment place. The " 'bobbies got it pretty warm.' " Crewe is
the amused spectator: " 'I looked on and laughed—laughed till I could
hardly stand! . . . It does one good, a real stirring-up like that; I feel
better to-day than for the last month.' " The violence is verbal as well:
" 'It's a long time since I heard such downright, hearty, solid swear-
ing' " (176). The episode plays no role in the novel's major narrative
sequences. Yet it mediates between the good-natured vulgarity of the
Jubilee crowds, which approaches but does not break out into violence, and the verbal violence that shakes both of Arthur Peachey's
domiciles in Brixton and Camberwell. The West End, the stadium,
Camberwell, Brixton: there is a symbolic, voiced mapping of the urban
landscape. (Its analogue appears in the other mappings: the disfig-
uring spread of the city to the suburbs, of the railways to the coun-
tryside.)|What is still more striking is that Crewe transforms this scene
into a spectacle that evokes not fear or consternation but laughter.|
There is something healthy about such riots: " 'It does one good.' "
From one perspective, the destructive is translated into the ludic. It
is, in Bakhtin's terms, a form of "external" carnivalization. Social hierarchies are temporarily annihilated within carnival's open spaces, and
through its processes of "familiarization."[33] Crewe's laughter is not

32. See Mikhail Bakhtin, *Problems of Dostoevsky's Poetics*, ed. and trans. Caryl Emerson (Minneapolis: University of Minnesota Press, 1984); and Barbara Babcock-Abrahams,
"The Novel and the Carnival World," *MLN*, 89 (1974): 911–37.

33. *Problems of Dostoevsky's Poetics*, pp. 122–28, 157–60.

nihilistic, however. What was symbolically destroyed—an old system of social order—ought in his eyes to have been destroyed. When this passage is linked to the earlier carnival passage on the Jubilee celebrations, we can more easily grasp the incipient leveling in Nancy Lord's tolerance of "vulgarity." But we may also ask whether that earlier celebration of a still earlier crowning does not also carry in it the suggestion of a carnivalistic discrowning, confirmed by the riot at the sports stadium. Crewe, the foundling of dubious origins, will himself displace the old and be a newly crowned king in the safer carnival world of advertising. If meanings rather than people erupt in the world of the text, if incongruity is a property not of human association but of verbal statements, then such antic depositions can be distanced from their consequences.

Crewe's account of the riot marks another transition. It is as if some perverse theater of the world were converted into the normality of theatrical experience, the occasion for some modern form of anticatharsis, of stirring up. There is ample evidence of the theatricality of urban experience, of the motif of spectacle, which informs both nonfictional and fictional writing of the time.[34] To make the exotic, the unusual, the violent, or even the criminal a matter for spectacle is, paradoxically, to appropriate it into normality. Too canny to risk being arrested himself by the police, Crewe exercises the privileges of vision and enjoys without cost to himself the overturning of physical and social order. The counterpart to physical violence, aggressive laughter, is socially permissible if not sanctioned. The scene offers an analogy to the moral conversions of the city, to the reduction into a common text of the city's constituent ideas, which resist classification as much as its population does. But this leveling, this play of incongruities, also recasts Dickens's chains of horizontal metaphors. Gissing's version of the city does reinscribe the earlier recognitions of its textuality that are to be found in Dickens. Gissing's books on Dickens comment explicitly on the textual interplay between the novelists. We can now recognize three prior textual areas for Gissing: the city itself, his own slum novels, and the novels of Dickens. The distinctiveness of Gissing's method lies less in the multiplication of het-

34. See, for example, J. Hillis Miller, "The Fiction of Realism: Sketches by Boz, Oliver Twist, and Cruikshank's Illustrations," in *Dickens Centennial Essays*, ed. Ada Nisbet and Blake Nevius (Berkeley: University of California Press, 1971), 85–153; as well as Mark Seltzer's *"The Princess Casamassima*: Realism and the Fantasy of Surveillance."

erogeneities than in the metaphorical transformations of ideas of het-
erogeneity, which include incongruity and circulation.|

Such transformations anticipate the conversion of the crowd into
advertising, through the medium of sight and through the laughter that
makes it socially acceptable. There is still another image, however,
which we can locate in *New Grub Street*, published three years earlier.
That novel is singularly devoid of crowds, but its cityscape is traversed
by the production of literature for the masses.|If mass publications
occur at a social juncture where what the public wants is what it gets—
the result is a covert form of verbal control—advertising takes the
further step of determining what the public wants, thus exerting an
overt form of power.|¶The figurative odyssey of the crowd has trans-
formed its inherent violence into the socially acceptable, and at the
same time reversed the direction of power. The crowd no longer threatens to dominate: rather it is dominated, in some oddly specular fash-
ion, by its figurative images.|Crewe's fantasy of power, of an implicit
counterrevolution, is part of an underlying political thrust of the novels.
Demos is tamed through a process of verbal reconstitution that has
begun in the slum novels, in part through images of the verbal inef-
fectiveness of slum characters, and in part through narrative structures
of ambivalence and reversal.

In *Born in Exile*, Godwin Peak's overt scorn for the mob marks a
further step in the process of distancing, although the openness of
his scorn places it outside the symbolic transformations that allow for
the coexistence of sympathy and disdain. (One problem of Peak's
misreading of society is the sheer single-mindedness that causes his
duplicity: the adoption of ideologies suitable to the environment, without admitting the possibilities of heterogeneity.) Gissing's more prominent method suggests instead a suspension of judgment. Peak's story
is that of the manipulator who becomes his own narrative subject, the
self-authorized center of action. In *New Grub Street* and *In the Year
of Jubilee*, in contrast, Jasper Milvain and Luckworth Crewe are just
enough to the side of center to play spectatorial roles. They are somewhat shady surrogates for the urban novelist, whose function is both
spectatorial and transformative. Gatherers of secrets and mediators of
the city's energies and brutality, they remove them at least temporarily
from the sphere of direct action. As the urban artist, a more or less
hypothetical figure who confronts the city in order to turn its materials
into narratives, Gissing stands at the end of a chain beginning with
those figures of the interior. Their texts are always partial, fragments

and synecdoches that inscribe the images and metaphors that dominate the life of the city. It is the novelist on the exterior, however,
who rewrites those interior descriptions within larger chains of metaphor. The problematic for him is one of representing that which may
already be a representation of something else, or that which is known
only by indirection. Dominated by a discourse that is always in a
displaced relation to its referents, the city is both open to possibility
and limited. Even urban characters share in this displacement. While
some may belong to the pre-linguistic order of the brutal, others are
products of an urban idiom. Such characters as Alma Rolfe in *The
Whirlpool* are impersonally motivated by the discourse of society.
Where passion was associated in the earlier novels with the emergence of the individual out of the collective urban life, it is now shaped
by the impersonal life of the large city. The price of acculturating is
abstraction, a process that opens the way to later commodification.[35]

Readers of Gissing have noted a central paradox of his novels: although they employ conventional techniques, they raise advanced,
even startling questions about the nature of fiction. It is possible to
read Gissing's novels as narratives of the mainstream, products of
contemporary theories of realism.[36] But to read in this way would be
to overlook Gissing's nearly relentless pursuit of London's emptiness
and his reconstruction of a city over an abyss. What is "real" breaks
out as overadornment, or superfluity, as in Mrs. Luke Widdowson's
flat with its "taste for modern exuberance in domestic adornment"
(*The Odd Women*, 118), or in the more direct carnivalization of the
mob and of advertising. Such eruptions are symptomatic. But if this
is so, then the sensory qualities of the city, or the senses with which
one perceives the city, are askew. If sight is privileged, as it is in
realism, then what it "sees" here is a city emptied out, plastered over,
viewed from odd angles, caught between the extremes of deprivation
and abundance. It may be that the epistemology of realism frequently
hides such covert aberrations, or that it must naturalize them simply
in order to accommodate that which is not natural at all. The fogs and
twilights to which Gissing's London is bound will never permit the

35. See T. J. Clark, *The Painting of Modern Life*, 36, on the "disappearance" of an older
Paris as a prelude to the advent of commodity capitalism. Although the discussion here
antedates my reading of Clark's book, there are affinities with his account.
36. Michael Collie addresses these issues in *The Alien Art*.

absolute elimination of the "real," but they may also signify that which obscures or replaces the real. His London appears at some moment prior to the end of realism, where culture, passion, all that constitutes the substantiality of the city are turned inside out to serve the endless circulation, the endless dispersion of word and image.

5

Urban Figures: Negative Imaginings

*I*n the face of the city's instabilities, of its oblique ways of furthering narrative scenarios, of the swerve in representation away from the visual to the figurative, character at least would seem inviolable. That novelists have recourse to the typical, that they draw upon class hierarchies, that characters sustain narrative continuity: these are arguments for the persistence of urban identity. Yet we have also remarked on the slippage in character in Bill Boorker's proper names or in Pelham's self-doubling; on the virtual exclusion of the subject from "Meditations in Monmouth Street," with its synecdochic dance of the shoes, to *The Young Duke* with its repetitive round of fashionable activities. We have noted the dominance of the already written: newspapers define Samuel Barmby's mind in *In the Year of Jubilee*, while conventional plots assimilate characters with urbane indifference in the dandy novels; energies and passions manifest themselves *through* characters as much as depict them as individuals. The concepts of the typical and of class structure, preceding proper names, occupy a way-station between individuality and narrative replication. Taxonomy is as suspect in theories of character as it is in the city.

| The concept of character is not in fashion these days. The Cinderella of narrative theory, it has been relegated to a corner, to a parenthesis in the critical text. Within that parenthesis we may find actants, functions, semes, symbols: an array of terms that purportedly designate the self but that effectively depersonalize it. Traditionally, the concept of character derives from a referential illusion—or an analogy—that is furthered by many of the metaphors that convey that concept: for example, Forster's round and flat characters, James's ficelle, Harvey's card,[1] all of which place characters in some relation to the fullness of real life. It is now possible to see that these very metaphors, with their implicit antitheses, their secondary figures of distance and difference from the real, their implicit notions of repetition or reduction and their suggestion that character may properly be reformulated as a set of abstract narrative functions, are as easily assimilated into theories of narrative structure as they are compatible with criteria of referential plausibility. It seems, then, that one could conveniently discard referentiality as a standard for character, or at best bracket it, much as Foucault parenthesizes personality as a nineteenth-century idea.[2] If character is a verbal construct, limited to the words in which it appears and often presented as part of a structure that replicates that of grammar or figure, why not approach it as part of a purely linguistic entity, in which figure is nothing but "figure"?[3] |

| No matter how logical such a procedure would be from a theoretical standpoint, however, it elides certain anterior questions. One question has to do with the ways in which novels represent characters or incorporate theories of character. An ancillary issue is that of the coherence, temporal or otherwise, of a character. Fictional discourse plays with this idea, often employing the language of self-division to m

1. See E. M. Forster, *Aspects of the Novel* (New York: Harcourt, Brace, 1927) 69–125; Henry James, Preface to *The Ambassadors* (New York: Charles Scribner's Sons, 1909) 1: xix–xxii; and W. J. Harvey, *Character and the Novel* (Ithaca: Cornell University Press, 1965).

2. Cf. Michel Foucault, *The Order of Things* (London, Tavistock, 1970), 386: "Man had been a figure occurring between two modes of language. . . ."

3. See William Gass, "The Concept of Character in Fiction," in *Fiction and The Figures of Life* (New York: Knopf, 1971); and Tzvetan Todorov, "Narrative-Men," in *The Poetics of Prose*, trans. Richard Howard (Ithaca: Cornell University Press, 1977), 66–79.

⟨⟨ assert the desirability of wholeness. In Meredith's *Diana of the Crossways*, Diana has a "split consciousness" of her private self as opposed to the public image of "the woman Warwick."[4] But theory too often posits coherence as an artistically or socially motivated desideratum for character, notably in the nineteenth-century novel. This is implicit in Barthes's conception of the "lisible" novel, as well as in Bersani's claim that coherence was ideologically or politically desirable in the nineteenth-century novel.[5] A glance at the novels prior to the application of identifying terms may help to resolve issues for which those terms would be inadequate.⟩

Such an approach would naturally revive the questions of representation and referentiality, particularly in relation to the city. Not only does the city exert a claim to be the true referent, as opposed to the pseudoreferentiality of characters, but the theme of alienated man, that archetypal urban being, becomes recast as the problem of character alienated from the very discourse that constitutes his mode of existence. How are these two questions, that of the disalignment of referential claims and that of the disparity between language and the object of description, related? More broadly, how are urban character and the city accommodated within the same text?

A passage from Benjamin's "A Berlin Chronicle" suggests one way in which persons and cities are related:

> The more frequently I return to these memories, the less fortuitous it seems to me how slight a role is played in them by people: I think of an afternoon in Paris to which I owe insights into my life that came in a flash, with the force of an illumination. . . . I tell myself it had to be in Paris, where the walls and quays, the places to pause, the collections and the rubbish, the railings and the squares, the arcades and the kiosks, teach a language so singular that our relations to people attain, in the solitude encompassing us in our immersion in that world of things, the depths of a sleep in which the dream image waits to show the people their true faces. I wish to write of this afternoon because it made so apparent what kind of regimen cities keep over imagination, and why the city . . .

---

4. George Meredith, *Diana of the Crossways* (New York: Norton, 1973), 114.

5. See Roland Barthes, *S/Z*, trans. Richard Miller (New York: Hill and Wang, 1974); and Leo Bersani, *A Future for Astyanax* (Boston: Little, Brown, 1976), 55–56.

indemnifies itself in memory, and why the veil it has covertly woven out of our lives shows the images of people less than those of the sites of our encounters with others or ourselves.[6]

Benjamin's passage projects a complex problematic of urban representation. By keeping a "regimen" over "imagination," the city assumes an active role. By weaving a veil, it is an artist of sorts, or perhaps a *bricoleur* working with the lives he encounters, however adventitiously. The veil, less solid than people's lives or than the city itself, substitutes for the overt phenomena of the city. Through a process of displacement and reshaping, an urban art deprives both city and persons of their materiality. The material presence of the city, a presence so powerful that in Benjamin's lines it usurps personhood by the very figure of personification, retains its power only by transforming itself into figures, or into a veil of textuality. Covertly retaining some primal power, urban sites proffer scenes of recognition. Thus we perceive character by what is not "character." Yet to indemnify is both to secure against loss and to make restitution for a loss. The presence of the city secures against loss, but paradoxically only in memory, after that loss has already occurred as a result of displacement and concealment.

| Nineteenth-century English novels move slowly toward Benjamin's model. City and character, the materiality of the one and the wholeness of the other, recede within individual texts as they do historically.| Initially, descriptions of the city assume this presence as a base line, just as frequent quests for identity take possible presence for a goal. Dickens's descriptions of London and James's Preface to *The Princess Casamassima* incorporate this assumption. Hyacinth Robinson, James writes, "sprang up for me out of the London pavement"; and Hyacinth's characteristic activity, a kind of pre-text for the plot of the novel, is that of observing the " 'London World.' "[7] |Site determines consciousness, imagination, and, eventually, citation. Yet James's citing of site in the Preface suggests that this is only the beginning of a process of transformation. The strategies of representation will themselves become the means of veiling the proper. To Benjamin's displacements—imagination to city, persons to sites, individual lives to

6. Walter Benjamin, "A Berlin Chronicle," in *Reflections*, trans. Edmund Jephcott (New York: Harcourt Brace Jovanovich, 1978), 30.
7. Henry James, *The Princess Casamassima* (New York: Charles Scribner's Sons, 1908), 1:vi, xvi.

urban veil—we may add James's, whereby the city displaces geneal-ogy, and metaphor and myth displace identity.⎸

The language of representation may serve to distance the city. The well-known opening of *Bleak House*, with "Fog everywhere" as the only binding (and obscuring) element amid random objects and gram-matical fragments, emblematizes one way in which the city loses its materiality.[8] The slums, the "lairs" of the poor, are often paradoxical signs of a bedrock reality, as they are for the Princess Casamassima. Or so she claims. James's novel makes openly equivocal that reality with which so many other slum novels fail to come to terms. His aural image, noted before, is the counterpart to Benjamin's veil: "[T]he sea-son was terribly hard; and as in the lower world [of London's poor] one walked with one's ear nearer the ground the deep perpetual groan of London misery seemed to swell and swell and form the whole undertone of life" (*The Princess Casamassima*, 1, 343). The material splendors of urban high life are often lost as well in the brilliant glow of the hyperbolic language that claims to depict them. The recurring terms "brilliant" and "sublime" leave the fashionable world in eclipse. In effect, the signifier deserts the signified. We may relate this to Ben-jamin's process of indemnification by means of an urban veil. The eclipse of the fashionable world finds its counterpart in the city's loss of aura. There is an intimate connection between the loss of sacred presence and the loss of historical associations, as in that episode in *In the Year of Jubilee* where two characters read London's facades as signs of a contemporaneous exchange economy, ignoring whatever intimations those buildings contain of a splendid, romantic past. If the building facades of Dickens and James are metonymies for their inhabitants and their narrative histories, the associations of these fa-cades are sealed by a perceptual diminution.

With this connection between the aura of urban streets and the intimations of the past, which ground awareness of self-continuity, but with aura and intimation now conspicuously absent, we may return to the problematic implied in Benjamin's linkage of city and person. The active hold of the city upon the imagination, in such a way that it usurps the priority and independence of persons, is implicated with the surrender of its material presence either to a mere phenomenality or to a partial and somewhat exclusive figurality. As a metaphor for memory, the city is an urban spot of time; as a personification of the

8. Charles Dickens, *Bleak House* (London: Oxford University Press, 1956), 1.

urban artist, it weaves its veil. But true to the spirit of that fabricator, memory, the resistances it encounters are both private and public. If the city is, as Baudelaire suggests, the site of modern heroism, that heroism may arise in an agon between person and city.[9] By an agonistic logic, characters, displaced by urban encounters, transform cities.

Each of the three novels I turn to now focuses on a certain aspect of this encounter between self and city. In this agon conducted through modes of suspension, negation and denial, coherence is at best contingent. In Dickens's *Little Dorrit*, the self is dislocated into the enigmatic, inevitably labyrinthine text of the city; in *The Princess Casamassima*, selfhood is suspended between antithetical urban metaphors and myths; in *Diana of the Crossways*, urban character is constituted by texts that have the power to make but not to bind.

I

One exemplary moment in *Little Dorrit* occurs on a morning after Arthur Clennam has accidentally spent a night in the Marshalsea prison for debtors. As he is leaving, he sees a group of "go-betweens" waiting outside.

> There was a string of people already straggling in, whom it was not difficult to identify as the nondescript messengers, go-betweens, and errand-bearers of the place. Some of them had been lounging in the rain until the gate should open; others, who had timed their arrival with greater nicety, were coming up now, and passing in with damp whitey-brown paper bags from the grocers, loaves of bread, lumps of butter, eggs, milk, and the like. The shabbiness of these attendants upon shabbiness, the poverty of these insolvent waiters upon insolvency, was a sight to see. Such threadbare coats and trousers, such fusty gowns and shawls, such squashed hats and bonnets, such boots and shoes, such umbrellas and walking-sticks, never were seen in Rag Fair. All of them wore the cast-off clothes of

9. Charles Baudelaire, "De l'héroïsme de la vie moderne," in *Salon de 1846*, in *Oeuvres complètes*, Bibliothèque de la Pléiade (Paris: Editions Gallimard, 1961), 951.

other men and women; were made up of patches and pieces of other people's individuality, and had no sartorial existence of their own proper. Their walk was the walk of a race apart. They had a peculiar way of doggedly slinking round the corner, as if they were eternally going to the pawnbroker's. When they coughed, they coughed like people accustomed to be forgotten on door-steps and in draughty passages, waiting for answers to letters in faded ink, which gave the recipients of those manuscripts great mental disturbance and no satisfaction. As they eyed the stranger in passing, they eyed him with borrowing eyes—hungry, sharp, speculative as to his softness if they were accredited to him, and the likelihood of his standing something handsome. Mendicity on commission stopped in their high shoulders, shambled in their unsteady legs, buttoned and pinned and darned and dragged their clothes, frayed their buttonholes, leaked out of their figures in dirty little ends of tape, and issued from their mouths in alcoholic breathings.[10]

The go-betweens emblematize the relation between prison and city: urban existence is a continuing transaction between inside and outside, although dominance may shift from one to the other. But it is the go-betweens, displaced and beside themselves, who share in this marginal transaction to the extent that their situation becomes a founding condition for urban character: a condition of difference from oneself, from others, from character itself. A glance back at the sketches and at *Life in London* will help to make the point. In Greenwood and Sala, coughs and clothes inhabit catalogues; while they may be signs for general urban conditions, they do not constitute signs for interior narratives. Coughs illustrate the range of urban misery, as the clothes of the poor stand, in Sala's train station, in antithesis to the elegant trappings of the rich. The class contrast extends to *Life in London*, where to be "at home on board the Fleet" is not to be anywhere else in the city. Class into classification, buildings into taxonomy: Dickens breaks such structures by privileging the marginal and the transactional. The hypothetical narratives of "Meditations in Monmouth Street" emerge full-blown, as one would expect, in *Little Dorrit*. But the relative suppression of the subject (coughs are heard, after all, but the coughers are not seen) anticipates the novels, and within their

10. Charles Dickens, *Little Dorrit* (London: Oxford Univeristy Press, 1967), 91.

ampler dimensions the problematic of the subject is explored. It is here that the concept of "flat" characters or even "cards," to which the go-betweens might once have been assigned, reveals its inadequacy. To be relegated to a flat single phrase or even a simple characterization (where singularity implies coherence) is nevertheless to imply everything that has been left out.[11] The dominant mode of the passage above is one of negation: the go-betweens have "no sartorial existence of their own proper"; the clothes they do wear "never were seen in Rag Fair"; they defer their insolvency to wait upon that of others; they live on credit, by borrowing on commission. Their threshold existence is defined by the play of signifiers that assert, defer, and negate their very being in an endless round. The passage presents a model for the double based on self-division or deferral, rather than on the complementarity of a "hidden self" that traditional theories of the double are apt to assert.[12] While the go-betweens seem to represent a register of humanity so low that they are excluded from a properly descriptive lexicon, their typical actions group them with several other characters who are defined by their changing literal and metaphorical relations with interiors and exteriors, prison and city, or city-as-prison and areas outside the city. Little Dorrit's major dramatis personae—Arthur Clennam, Amy Dorrit, her brother, sister and uncle, the turnkeys, the brain-damaged Maggy, even Amy's father, William Dorrit—all share in this transactional or differential mode of existence. Amy is the cohesive force for her family; her sewing, which serves the neurotically ill Mrs. Clennam (Arthur's mother) in more ways than one, provides the means for her father's subsistence, as well as that of her less responsible brother and sister. She is also the emotional mainstay of the family. But more is at stake here than the nature of service, although that is surely implicated thematically. Rather, service itself, to which Amy Dorrit devotes herself in such an apparently noble fashion, now appears in the metonymic shadow of the deferral of identity. (The housekeeping of Esther Summerson, the "Dame Durden" of *Bleak House*, also marginalizes identity in the name of service.)

What prevents one from isolating the go-betweens may be identified as a form of contagion. The analogous actions constitute one part,

11. On the concept of the card, see W. J. Harvey, *Character and the Novel*, 58, 62. On "flat" characters, see E. M. Forster, *Aspects of the Novel*, 103–12.

12. For a survey of theories of the double, as well as texts in which the double is central, see Claire Rosenfeld, "The Shadow Within: The Conscious and Unconscious Use of the 'Double,' " *Daedalus* 92 (Spring 1963): 326–44.

and the financial terms, so tenuously applicable in a literal sense but so horrifyingly appropriate metaphorically, constitute another. Contagion, as we know, is a widespread urban condition for Dickens. In the early sketch, "Gin-Shops," a contagion for decorating, akin to rabies, spreads though various trades and establishments. Contagious disease is, of course, crucial to the narrative in *Bleak House*. In both sketch and novel, contagion is literal and metaphorical, and it spreads horizontally. The equivalence between the spread of metaphor and the spread of contagion often substitutes for, if it does not dominate, the temporality of narrative. In *Little Dorrit*, the image of rags, first perceptible negatively in the go-betweens, spreads through London and even beyond. "Miserable children in rags" (*Little Dorrit*, 166), playing among the arches of Covent Garden, contrast with the district's romantic theater, market, and coffee houses. In Rome, after the Dorrits have become rich, Amy envisions herself as a child with patches on her clothes and dreams of a threadbare dress she wore when she was eight (554). The authenticity of poverty, here displaced into memory, contrasts with the pretensions of wealth. Yet the go-betweens make suspect the possibility of an "honest" poverty, for poverty reveals raggedness and incoherence within identity itself. Nor are lawyers free from a contagion, from a dissemination of the image, that transgresses class and professional lines. " 'We lawyers are . . . always picking up odds and ends for our patchwork minds,' " says Bar proudly at an elegant dinner (564). More is involved in the power of the patch than casting a shadow over present splendor, or arguing for the persistence of memory as a form of juxtaposition or repetition rather than continuity. Even the ironic qualification the image places upon the minds of lawyers does not account for its power. Rather, the metaphor of rags contains a latent but contagious violence and opens up the possibility of a suspension of identity: the social fabric never can be seamless. Toward the end of the narrative, a "blurred circle of yellow haze" that rises in lieu of the sun puts a "patch" upon the wall of Clennam's prison room when he, too, is imprisoned for debt. That patch, an image of something not quite the sun, a displacement of a displacement, is associated with Clennam's fevered mind. Consciousness and site are held in equilibrium here, subject to the veil of a negative transcendence.

The mode of displacement and negation extends to names as well: to Clennam's coy self-cancellation as "Nobody" in his amorous fantasies; to Maggy, who as "Nobody" cannot act as a witness. (Although

Maggy is brain-damaged, her allegiance to Little Dorrit makes her a moral touchstone, so that the situation is doubly ironic.) The demonic obverse appears in Blandois-Rigaud, who is only too assertive, who chooses whatever name suits him in context, and who fictionalizes his past and his present. "Cosmopolitan" by his own account (more accurately, "homeless"), a scoundrel who aspires to the title of "gentleman," he makes mystery into a sinister gesture of self-assertion. To his doubled names, we may add the playful punning by which "Harriet Beadle" slides into "Tattycoram." "When identifical semes traverse the same proper name several times and appear to settle upon it," Barthes writes, "a character is created. . . . The proper name acts as a magnetic field for the semes" (S/Z, 67). But if the proper name is itself unstable, we may find a wavering, not quite a "figure" in Barthes's sense of the term, but nevertheless a fissure in fictions of identity. Suspended between public and private selves—" 'Arthur, Mr. Clennam far more proper, even Doyce and Clennam probably more business-like,' " Flora Finching babbles (269)—displaced from the present into a shadowy past or imagined ends, practitioners of the art of seeming, the characters of Little Dorrit defy representation. Mr. Casby's benign patriarchal appearance belies his professional rack-renting: "Nobody could have said where the wisdom was, or where the virtue was, or where the benignity was; but they all seemed to be somewhere about him" (147). Casby is "a mere Inn signpost without any Inn—an invitation to rest and be thankful, where there was no place to put up at, and nothing whatever to be thankful for" (149). Young John Chivery, the turnkey's son, writes his own epitaphs as he contemplates his death, a kind of personal abyss, as he becomes "[n]ever anything worth mentioning" (220). John's own texts are an exemplary undoing; to imagine the future as already past, to reduce oneself to what amounts to a rhetorical form, is to court negation with a vengeance.

It would seem, then, as if the persistence of negation and denial would also undercut the narrative, which would lack true subjects for its predicative activity. Some of the most decisive actions are those that exert violence upon the text itself. For instance, Amy agrees to suppress the codicil to a will that would have redefined Clennam's identity; in effect, she denies the past and its pressures upon the self. Such a gesture for freedom repudiates the genealogical, legal context for character and moves toward figure in the Barthesian sense, with its accompanying illegality, nearly literal in this novel. The curious lack of closure at the end, when Amy and Arthur merge with the crowd in London's streets, allows then an entrance into the very mode of signification that the novel's negations had hitherto disallowed.

There is one final twist. Amy's actions, like Young John's epitaphs and the financier Merdle's silences, are gestures of undoing insofar as they alter narrative directions or expectations about temporal closure or speech. The quasi-ritual acts of making and unmaking suggest that the margin between narrator and characters has worn thin, been made ragged. Amy first appears as seamstress and spectator, an after-recognition of Arthur's, a shadowy presence dismissed as "nothing," a "whim" of Mrs. Clennam's: "Punctual to the moment, Little Dorrit appeared; punctual to the moment, Little Dorrit vanished. What became of Little Dorrit between the two eights, was a mystery" (40, 53). But her profession (which makes her a dim embodiment of those other fabricators, Penelope and Philomela), as well as the way in which she copes with the city, identifies her as a type of urban *bricoleuse*. One notable strategy of Dickens is to place his narrators at the margins of scenes, frequently in semidarkness or twilight. Their spectatorial presences then take in the scenes, so that the literal aspects recede before the imaginative portrayal. The process occurs, as we have seen, in such an early work as *Sketches by Boz*, where the narrator begins as flâneur and ends as urban artist. Even if Little Dorrit is a less imposing figure, even if the narrative voice is less easily specified in the later novels, there is nevertheless more than a hint of the artist of the city in her. Her marginal presence in certain scenes; her memory, which appears as a palimpsest in the texts of her letters; her espousal of discontinuity: all these show that she emblematizes at these crucial moments an urban poetics. To substitute artist for character would then point to one way out of the abyss of sheer negation. In the process, however, all issues of referentiality, true or simulated, would be cancelled. What would remain is a sign of power embodied in the passive resistance of the artist of the city to the sheer power of the city as agonist. " 'We women are the verbs passive,' " Diana writes (*Diana of the Crossways*, 64): but verbs passive may be part of modern heroism.

II

While it is superficially more unified and less "dialogic" than *Little Dorrit*, *The Princess Casamassima* presents an equally radical perspective upon character. It plays upon mysteries of identity and obscurities of genealogy. Conventional interpretation places its protagonist, Hyacinth Robinson, in a position of indeterminacy. Illegitimate child of an English nobleman and a French seamstress, he divides his loyalties between the aristocracy and the lower classes, between a commitment to the grand achievements of civilization and a vision of revolution and social justice. His small stature, however, symbolizes his status in the eyes of his friends: he is a child, a *naïf*. He is held at a remove from the sources of power, decision, and culture; the rites of passage that ought to enable him to reach these sources are, by and large, blocked for him. Hyacinth frequently finds himself on the outside, in the dark, in the position not of an initiate but of a baffled interpreter. Despite the obscurities, the information withheld from Hyacinth, even the word "strange," which tolls through the novel and qualifies so many of his experiences, despite even the role-playing of the Princess (who is of course not a princess and who eventually lives like the lower middle class so that she can get closer to "the people," to "reality"), *The Princess Casamassima* still presents conventional narrative enigmas. At points, however, the interpretive mysteries that confront Hyacinth are insolvable. One episode is that of Hyacinth's visit to the theater, when he first meets the Princess. Sitting in the balcony with Millicent Henning (a "daughter of London" allegorized as "a nymph of the wilderness of Middlesex, a flower of the clustered parishes, the genius of urban civilization, the muse of cockneyism" [1:61–62]), Hyacinth is summoned to the Princess's box: he goes through a dark passage to reach it. In the box with the Princess and her companion, Hyacinth, the object of the women's gaze, is both spectacle and spectator. The darkened space of the theater, between stage and box, box and balcony, or within the passage leading from balcony to box, marks the simultaneous insistence and indeterminacy of space. Within this space, interpersonal relations cannot be properly constituted; identity is put into question. Similar spatial configurations appear several times in the novel, in various dwellings where dark passages, enclosed spaces, and disputed relationships coincide. One notable place is the Sun and Moon, the tavern where the anarchists to whom Hyacinth pledges himself meet, and where the meeting-room is reached through a dark passage. The very name of the tavern signifies an inverted cosmos, as if inside and outside, large and small, had reversed themselves. The commentary on these perpetually reversible oppositions, between inside and outside, spectator and actor, large and small, sky and room, emerges from another series of images that situates Hyacinth on the outside, excluded from interiors where Millicent and Captain Sholto, the Princess and the anarchist Paul Muniment, are enclosed. A child of the London streets, Hyacinth returns to them; the "impressions" they convey are unreadable, figures for interpretive opacity. The novel's political situation, which projects an anarchist plot, spreads to a possible anarchy of figures as well as identity. To be an anarchist is to be without beginnings. Freedom from sources, or the possibility of alternative sources, amounts to a spatialization more determining than genealogy or temporality. Captain Sholto, that enigmatic hanger-on of the Princess, may be a cat's-paw or a deep-sea fisherman—one metaphor is not more clearly motivated than the other; tout or angler, he is himself fathomless.[13] Hyacinth's own choices are figured spatially: London versus Paris, the slums versus the Boulevard. Place and consciousness are intertwined and inseparable. Where spatial metaphors involve selfhood, then Hyacinth's dilemma arises from the way in which the city-as-text enforces the phenomenal component of its metaphors of identity, while Hyacinth formulates his problem in ideological or familial terms.

One variant of spatial determination arises from context:

> The splendours and suggestions of Captain Sholto's apartment were thrown completely into the shade by the scene before him, and as the Princess didn't scruple to keep him waiting twenty minutes (during which the butler came in and set out on a small table a glittering tea-service) Hyacinth had time to count over the innumerable *bibelots* (most of which he had never dreamed of) involved in the character of a woman of high fashion and to feel that their beauty and oddity revealed not only whole provinces of art, but refinements of choice on the part of their owner, complications of mind and—almost—terrible depths of temperament. (1:284–85)

One may distinguish between the metaphors that define character and the "traces" that also convey it. From the perspective of the novel, whether character is defined by object or figure, context or text, me-

---

13. Paul Muniment remarks that Sholto "throws his nets and hauls in the little fishes— the pretty little shining, wriggling fishes' " (*The Princess Casamassima*, 1:258–60). The narrator adds the definitive comment: "He was nothing whatever in himself and had no character or merit save by tradition, reflection, imitation, superstition" (2:82).

tonymy (even "Princess" is a metonymic borrowing from her now-estranged husband) or metaphor, character is still atemporal: it owes its continuity to word or surroundings, to the veil woven by the city. The merging of city with text becomes evident when we note that the "splendours" of Sholto's apartment, as urbane a domicile as one may imagine, derive from the dandy apartment in *Pelham*, as Hyacinth himself realizes.[14] The *bibelots* of the Princess's apartment, too, find precursors in the less complex exotica of Mrs. Darlington Vere.

Presented with so many texts and contexts, Hyacinth seems suspended in interpretive indecision. Not only is he an interpreter, he is a text as well: the other characters discuss him in terms that are often oblique. How, then, can he be a bookbinder, a binder of texts? Hyacinth, too, is an urban craftsman, who refuses to bind his vocation, as a minor episode demonstrates. After his first visit to the Princess, Hyacinth takes apart a volume of Tennyson's poems and rebinds it. As craftsmanship, the work is superb. But when he brings it to the Princess, he learns she has left her South Street lodgings; he refuses to give the volume to the butler for "transmission" to her. This may be a parable of the fortunes of the text, undone and redone, of a "floating signifier" that starts out as a message or gift but ends up, in his mind, as the reverse:

> Later on it seemed to create a manner of material link between the Princess and himself, and at the end of three months it had almost come to appear not that the exquisite book was an intended present from his own hand, but that it had been placed in that hand by the most remarkable woman in Europe. Rare sensations and impressions, moments of acute happiness, almost always, with our young man, in retrospect, became rather mythic and legendary; and the superior piece of work he had done after seeing her last, in the immediate heat of his emotion, turned to a virtual proof and gage—as if a ghost in vanishing from sight had left a palpable relic. (1:300)

In the absence of the closure that the knowledge of origins would allow, or of the closure that a less mystified interpretive process would reach, Hyacinth creates false closures in an ad hoc manner. The his-

14. For a description of Sholto's apartment, see *The Princess Casamassima*, 1: 263–67.

tory of the book, like his dual familial and social histories, and like the alternative metaphors or literariness of Sholto and the Princess, reaches a narrative closure that is nevertheless incompatible with any totalizing interpretation. The Jamesian reflective consciousness, register of impressions but a text to be interpreted as well, gestures toward effacing the margin between artist and character and cannot thus be bound.

III

Diana of the Crossways comes even closer to presenting an oscillating, reversible, or figural form of character than do the other two novels. Gossiped about and quoted, written in others' diaries, Diana appears first as sheer text. Meredith renders problematic such a mode of being in an early comment on language:

> When a nation has acknowledged that it is as yet but in the fisticuff stage of the art of condensing our purest sense to golden sentences, a readier appreciation will be extended to the gift, which is to strike, not the dazzled eyes, the unanticipating nose, the rib, the sides, and stun us, twirl us, hoodwink, mystify, tickle and twitch, by dexterities of lingual sparring and shuffling, but to strike roots in the mind, the Hesperides of good things. (2)

Whatever role the Hesperides may play as the object of desire, as the symbol of a language that is straightforward and condensed, even premetaphorical, to use language—and to enter London—is to engage in sparring and shuffling. The myth to counter that of the Hesperides is that of Diana herself, a goddess who has descended into time and suffering (not unlike Pater's medieval Dionysian Denys or Keats's Titans).[15] By her very descent into time she undergoes division, so that her mundane, sublunar selves are partial, illegitimate figures, as it were. As a sublunar being, she exists in phases of herself. Such an inescapable figurality is part of the urban condition, as if the city were

15. See "Denys L'Auxerrois," in Walter Pater, *Imaginary Portraits* (London: Macmillan, 1910), 47–77; and John Keats, *Hyperion*.

constituted by false or fictive language, by gossip and hearsay. The urban linguistic milieu, to which we may add journalism, salon wit, and financial speculation, constitutes the world of footloose language. In *Diana*, language becomes a commodity, sold to propitiate the household god Debit; to accumulate objects; and, most insidiously, to obtain the good opinion of the man Diana loves, Percy Dacier.

But London is also the place where the appropriately "arrowy" wit of Diana strikes home, and where the creative activity of writing occurs. While Diana bemoans her "London cabhourse" of a pen, she is also afforded some means of independence and self-realization as a result of her authorial activity. She becomes, in partly hidden ways, the author of herself as well. The metaphor of writing is as potent as that of reading in this novel.[16] Cut off from her origins, refusing the socially defined roles thrust upon married and unmarried women, Diana sets out upon an enterprise of self-creation. Letters, which ought to be self-revealing documents, turn out to be misleading; it is only as the writer of fiction that Diana can make herself real.

At this point, it would seem as if the issue is resolvable into a paradox centering on the ambiguous powers of language to create and destroy. Immaterial, it nevertheless becomes, in the world of time, a commodity. This is most strikingly manifest when Diana sells a political secret to the newspaper editor Tonans, thus betraying her lover. Her night journey (as Hecate) through London into his journalistic heart of darkness surely symbolizes the way in which she has betrayed herself to the word. Earlier, she writes that she takes refuge in metaphor. Is language, then, inevitably a form of self-betrayal or displacement, even when it constitutes one's very being? Meredith's Hesperidean ideal is contradictory. Those western islands are figured in the glorious pastoral sunsets, which are nevertheless autumnal and strangely premonitory of a kind of death. This motif punctuates the text and culminates in the final scene. Diana has returned from a wedding trip, a cruise on the yacht *Diana*. (Earlier, she voyages on the *Clarissa*, with its evocation of that beleaguered and self-inscribing lady.) Redworth, Diana's husband, poor in the "pleading language" but nevertheless the source of metaphor, as Diana remarks, plays old Sol to her moon. When her friend Emma says that she hopes to be a

---

16. On the theoretical significance of reading in Meredith's novels, see Judith Wilt, *The Readable People of George Meredith* (Princeton: Princeton University Press, 1975).

godmother, Diana is silent—and the novel ends.[17] The Hesperidean, the source of metaphor, the figure for unity and closure, may also be the metaphor for silence, as if the text were willing its own end. Closure would then amount to a form of cancellation. To abandon one's London circus animals—or cab horses—is to embrace a form of death-wish, located ambiguously in text or in "character." If the act of narration prolongs life by displacing it into language, the moment of death affords, as Benjamin notes, closure and meaning.[18] The irony for Diana is surely doubled: beyond the already ironic division into author and mother, where the life of one is preceded by the death of the other, lies the loss of that very meaning that the moment of death should have ensured. Here the heart, the mind, the source—all unities, all forms of closure— exclude themselves from the register of language.

IV

The modes of negation, displacement, and suspension in the depiction of character, necessarily metaphorical, are so prevalent that they question the adequacy of conventional, quasi-referential approaches as well as the displacement of character into narrative functions. Both depend upon a notion of language that fails to take into account the specularity, the "passivity," the self-effacement, as if the writing of character involved a willingness to be viewed "under erasure." There have always been Inn signposts without Inns behind them: this is the stock-in-trade of the novelist, especially the urban novelist. The more difficult issues concern characters who are defined metonymically in the contexts of their drawing-rooms filled with *bibelots* but who then reappear in the contextless darkness of the theater. It seems that a novel's referentiality, insofar as character is concerned, must be largely intratextual. Or there is the presence of a Diana, her voice and beauty, which can only be disseminated into the written. There is, finally, the sheer power of the passive figure, whose passage through the city may

17. Diana's twitch of the fingers is conventionally interpreted as confirmation of her pregnancy. Apparently Diana has had to choose between motherhood and literary creativity. The subtext notwithstanding, Meredith championed the cause of thinking women, especially in his later novels and letters.

18. See Walter Benjamin, "The Storyteller," in *Illuminations*, trans. Harry Zohn (New York: Schocken Books, 1969).

transform site into insight but who achieves his or her artistry at the cost of identity. Something like a residual will, a lonely proper name, wanders through these fictional mazes carrying negation and inscription as its baggage, impediments to sheer annihilation and conveyers of enigma. An adequate critical terminology for character would have to go beyond metaphors limited to either ontological or functional dimensions. It would have to take into account the negative figuration that is inextricable from the concept of character. The suspension of figure, moreover, would imply that character is not so much subject as it is subject to the city, which would now appear not only as the site of encounters but as the site of those negative figures. The forms of alienation and resistance to the city may then be transferred to the realm of an urban art that, out of denial itself, weaves its veil of fiction.

6

The
Empty
Spaces
of
the
Urban
Sublime

*T*he deepest fascination of the spectacle [of the crowd] lay in the fact that as it intoxicated him it did not blind him to the horrible social reality. He remained conscious of it, though only in the way in which intoxicated people are 'still' aware of reality. That is why in Baudelaire the big city almost never finds expression in the direct presentation of its inhabitants.[1]

The crowd, Walter Benjamin remarks, solicits the attention of the nineteenth-century writer more than any other subject. Its signification,

1. Walter Benjamin, *Charles Baudelaire: A Lyric Poet in the Era of High Capitalism*, Trans. Harry Zohn (London: New Left Books, 1973), 59.

however, is legion: street masses, the physical crowd, the collectivity of workers, the reading public, the consuming public. Responses to the crowd are equally varied, ranging from the casual ease of the flâneur to the dismay and apprehension of a journalist at the turmoil, from the perception of the crowd as offering shelter to the fugitive or as absorbing and obliterating those whom one seeks, from distancing the crowd by self-absorption to finding in it a specular image. Where a Nancy Lord removes herself from the crowd at the top of the Monument, a Jamesian narrator hears it as an underground murmur, portending revolution: as opposed to the narcissism of the one, a visual fade-out heightens hearing or apprehension. Baudelaire's response—in Benjamin's account—sharpens the paradoxes of representation; as soon as the crowd becomes a spectacle, an image that by definition presses itself upon vision, it removes itself from direct presentation. Intoxication is the fulcrum by which the spectacle neither "blinds" nor permits direct presentation. An intensified sensory awareness, a celebration and abstraction of the visible: both bespeak an aesthetics of indirection, an inverse logic of the sublime in which description and continuity are suspended.

Baudelaire's awareness of the indirection of urban representation is similar to authorial consciousness in nineteenth-century English novels in which the city is a receding referent. The conditions for its entry into narrative stipulate that the city, both conceived of as a totality and approached through its discrete objects, its characters, and its activities, appear through the mediation of figures. The array of figures from horizontal metaphors to hyperbole, figures that transform, negate, and displace, deepens the mysteriousness of the city. Narrating the city becomes tantamount to a form of concealment, insofar as it is predicated upon the deviation and the errancy that are inherent in figuration itself: a personified city that "casts its veil" intensifies the process by veiling its figurality.

Nor does urban fiction desert the culture from which it springs. Its metaphors are figures for a culture, sometimes celebrated, whose contradictions, crises, and obscurities disrupt the public celebration of urban growth and progress. Representation is necessarily charged with the political. To foreground the visual is often to posit a knowable stasis or an unerring advance of civilization. But the apparent candor of the visual is in reality exclusive. The reverse then also holds for representation: abstraction and figurality are unsettling and culturally charged.

One theoretical mode that frames the recessive referentiality of the city is that of the sublime. The sublime appears in a composite form, crossing from an experiential to a rhetorical mode. Here it will encompass (1) both the evocation of the visual or the material and its subsequent loss, an antithetical process that involves a shift from the taxonomical to the image-in-depth; (2) a turn to the urban subject with a concomitant doubling and self-distancing as she is caught in the sublime mode; (3) an exploration of the incommensurabilities and the agonistic issues of power involved in that mode: the sublime becomes politically and culturally fraught, engendering a deep suspicion of urban order and constraint.[2] Two tropes play major roles here: those of empty spaces and of surfaces and depths. After exploring texts of James, Wordsworth, and George Eliot, we come finally to focus on Dickens, whose early sketches mark an entrance to narrative fiction and whose late novels, especially *Our Mutual Friend*, trace a more fully developed aesthetics of the city.

Let us start with an episode in *The Prelude* that contains an exemplary urban fiction. It occurs in Book X, when Wordsworth has returned to Paris a month after the September massacre of 1791. Looking out of his hotel window, he sees the empty square, late the scene of violence, imagines it as remembered violence, and then tries to sleep. His sleep, however, is crossed by apocalyptic dreams of natural violence turning upon itself and of Macbeth crying " 'Sleep no more!' "[3] As in earlier episodes, there is a nearly scandalous compulsion to naturalize human events, or to figure human events as scandals vis-à-vis nature.[4] The image for those events is the city square, now void of presence but evocative of what amount to political primal scenes. It seems, however, that events can become texts only by their removal

2. Cf. Jean-Francois Lyotard's discussion of the aesthetics of the sublime in *The Postmodern Condition: A Report on Knowledge*, trans. Geoff Bennington and Brian Massumi (Minneapolis: University of Minnesota Press, 1984).

3. See William Wordsworth, *The Prelude, 1799, 1805, 1850*, ed. J. Wordsworth, M. H. Abrams, and S. Gill (New York: W. W. Norton 1979), Book X, lines 79–88 (1850 version).

4. See *The Prelude*, Book VII, where the passage on the Blind Beggar is introduced by the epic simile of "the black storm upon the mountain top." In *The Prelude*, Book VI, lines 422–35, the expulsion from the Grande Chartreuse evokes the protesting voice of nature.

from urban contexts; or, following Benjamin, that the site of an encounter takes precedence over the encounter itself. This is articulated
space, a square bordered by structures; its center missing, it mediates
the passage into memory or the text of memory. The scene is legible
as an image not only of the emptying out of the city, with its symbolic
and representational implications, but also of the immateriality of the
city as a textual agent. Visual objects seem to be stumbling blocks to
narrative: it is not enough to invest them, as Lukács desires, with social
or historical significance in order to recuperate them into narrative
structures. What the artist of the city needs is space or its polar antithesis, the profusion of signifiers. What Wordsworth saw as the stuff
of alienation in Book VII—mysterious street signs and costumes—
figures as more than the limiting image of writing or the scandalous
scene of revolution. Wordsworth's estrangement from the material city
prefigures the transformation of city into text. The city becomes the
scene of writing, for which the sublime provides the plot.

I

Although the narrative of the sublime varies from theory to theory, we
may identify some common moments: (1) the encounter with a sublime other—object, scene, sound, event—whose distinguishing attributes are its limitlessness and/or sensory obscurity, attributes that
separate it from the realm of the ordered and the contained; (2) the
ensuing bafflement or "blockage" in which the mind becomes aware
of its inability to "grasp" the other and its inadequation or discontinuity
with the natural world; (3) the subsequent turn in which the mind,
aware of this incommensurateness, then becomes cognizant of its
freedom from the world of the senses.[5] This third moment seems like
an advance, whether to sheer transcendence or to political freedom.
Such an interpretation, however, idealizes the turn, glossing over possibilities of resistance or loss. The emotions associated with the sublime (which Burke generally subsumes under fear, but which Kant

---

5. See Edmund Burke, *A Philosophical Enquiry into the Origin of our Ideas of the
Sublime and Beautiful*, ed. James T. Baldwin (Notre Dame: University of Notre Dame Press,
1968); Immanuel Kant, *The Critique of Judgment*, trans. James Creed Meredith (Oxford:
Clarendon Press, 1952, 1978); and Friedrich von Schiller, *Naive and Sentimental Poetry and
On the Sublime*, trans. Julias A. Elias (New York: Ungar, 1966).

transmutes to a negative pleasure) afford one index of the strength of resistance. This resistance may also propel Burke's countermove (in response to the strength of the other and the resulting terror) toward self-preservation, in which the self assumes the role of a disinterested spectator. This latter situation becomes a precondition for the development of a moral aesthetic. What is also important is that the tensions involved in these central discontinuities, whether of subject/other, fear/observation, involvement/disinvolvement, bespeak a scenario of power. To project the sublime onto the city, to conflate the labyrinth with the abyss, is to set the stage for modern struggles of subjectivity. The rewriting of the sublime in nineteenth-century fiction, in which the city is a privileged site, in conjunction with changing ways of figuring subjectivity, foregrounds the agons that are suppressed in classical versions of the sublime. The reduction and conflation of this summary, therefore, should not obscure the changing configuration of the theory.

The narrative of Wordsworth's post-September massacre sojourn in Paris intimates that not only material objects but space itself, through memory or imagination, can play an agentive role. In order to do this, the city must shift from literal mise-en-scène to figurative scene of writing and abandon the position of signified in order to adopt the role of signifier or personification. Divided from itself, figurative and thus already fictive, the city enters narrative. In a kind of urban dreamwork, it fashions memories of urban encounters, both public and private, texts to be interpreted; in its self-distancing, it becomes a city of signs and palimpsests.[6] Various metaphors for the city, especially the totalizing ones, anticipate this shift; many of these, however, ground the city, insist upon its concreteness and its mass even while representing it as wilderness or as flood. (Paradoxically, the narrative metaphors insist more upon the pictorial or scenic analogy than do the religious, nonfictional ones: apocalyptic floods that threaten the modern Babylons at least project a form of narrative.) These metaphors prefigure a still more radical transformation. The question of finding a language adequate to its urban referent recedes before the problem of how the discourse of the city signifies. Not only is it more difficult

---

6. Cf. Walter Benjamin, *Das Passagen-Werk*, in *Gesummelten Schriften*, v.1 and v.2, ed. Rolf Tiedemann, (Frankfurt am Main, Suhrkamp, 1982).

to represent the historical city in visible modes—how does one picture a network of communications, be it journalistic (as in *New Grub Street*) or financial (as in *The Whirlpool*)?—but the novels turn from the visible to the veiled, to that which is hidden within labyrinthine depths.

¶Cities share qualities with sublime landscapes that authorize the transfer from a natural to an urban sublime scene. Architecturally speaking, there are indications not only that the Victorian city itself was perceived as sublime, but that the designs of buildings as, indeed, of grand thoroughfares, were conceived in terms of an aesthetics of the sublime.[7] In the earlier part of the century, the large number of pictorial "sketchbooks" of London focus upon the city's public, often monumental structures.[8] In painting, John Martin's representation of Milton's Pandemonium as an urban structure evokes the city's sublime, if demonic potentialities. In novels the monuments rise imposingly above the equally imposing mass of the city: the Monument itself, the dome of the British Museum, the spire of St. Paul's shining golden above the flow of the London crowd. In Manchester, "the great metropolis of machinery," Coningsby moves "among illumined factories with more windows than Italian palaces, and smoking chimneys taller than Egyptian obelisks." In that "wonderful city," steam-engines cause sensations comparable to what one feels before an earthquake, and factory "chambers" are "vaster than are told of in Arabian fable."[9] Science surpasses art, fable, even irony, in supplying sublime sensations. Athens becomes the has-been: historically and geographically distant, already experienced as sublime, it is to be superseded by Manchester. Such novelty and exoticism, however reduced in the world of the dandy, also constitute the sublime object in the city. (There is an intimation here of an underside in which the stakes for the "sublime," perhaps inauthentically, must continually be raised.

7. See Nicholas Turner, "The Awful Sublimity of the Victorian City," in *The Victorian City: Images and Realities*, ed. H. J. Dyos and Michael Wolff, 2 vols. (London: Routledge and Kegan Paul, 1973), 2:431–47.

8. See, for example, Rudolf Ackermann, *The Microcosm of London*, 3 vols. (London, 1808), and *Select Views of London* (London, 1816), with prints by Rowlandson and Pugin. A list of prints is revealing: Bartholomew Fair, Billingsgate, Bow-Street Offices, Bridewell, Carlton House, the Royal Cockpit (Bird-Cage Walk, St. James's Park), Cold-Bath Fields Prison, the Court of Chancery. Not all of the structures are monumental, strictly speaking. Nevertheless, the architecture tends to dominate the groups of figures, as in the print of the Corn-Exchange, Mark-Lane. London appears as a city of grand buildings and institutions, often imposing on the inhabitants. If this is a microcosm, the city it represents is entirely public.

9. Benjamin Disraeli, *Coningsby*, (New York: Century, 1904), 143, 144.

Otherwise grandeur could be superseded by mere novelty, if not ennui, or by a lapse into the minor keys of the dandaic sublime.) If Manchester is a wonder of the world, how much more will London be one, whose size alone, confirmed by the sublime statistics of growth, entitles it to the exclusive appellation of "the metropolis."[10]

In the first moment of the scenario for the sublime, the mind confronts an object or landscape characterized by such qualities as vastness, extent, depth, height, darkness, or obscurity. The urban counterpart, in addition to the monumental structures, is the labyrinthine interior of the city, which represents extension coiled in on itself. The city has its own dark and obscure areas as well. One may, to be sure, object that all these sublime qualities are subsumed under the natural precisely because it is not art and not human, and that the inclusion of structures made by man simply blurs the dialectic of the sublime experience. Yet art creeps into the texts of theories of the sublime, in Kant's passage on St. Peter's and in Burke's requirement of self-distancing from the sublime, which turns it into a spectacle, as well as in his many illustrative allusions to the sublime language of literature.[11] The city can be relegated strictly to the domain of art only if one takes into account its most formal structures; the city's art is more like the street music of the slums, inhabited by the natural. The transfer of the spatial as well as the sensory terminology of theories of the sublime is mediated by art, by all those metaphors that ostensibly naturalize the city by invoking floods, deserts, forests, seas. The city is potentially sublime because it is analogous to those vast natural objects or scenes that have already been identified as sublime. Here the ambiguity of "identify" is crucial. Such natural metaphors, however, make fictions of what is sublime about the city and confirm the displacement inherent in the process of representation.[12]

10. On London's growth, see Asa Briggs, *Victorian Cities* (New York: Harper and Row, 1970).

11. See the *Critique of Judgment*, 100. Burke discusses the power of words to excite ideas of the sublime in *A Philosophical Enquiry*, Part 5, 163–77. See also the commentaries on Burke in Frances Ferguson, "The Sublime of Edmund Burke, or the Bathos of Experience," *Glyph* 8 (1981): 62–78; and Ronald Paulson, *Representations of Revolution* (New Haven: Yale University Press, 1983). Jacques Derrida's discussion of Kant in "Parergon" (*The Truth in Painting*, trans. Geoff Bennington and Ian McLeod [Chicago: The University of Chicago Press, 1987], 15–147) also calls attention to the intervention of the human in the *Critique of Judgment*.

12. Cf. Kristen Ross's discussion of the pitfalls of easy naturalizing in *The Emergence of Social Space: Rimbaud and the Paris Commune* (Minneapolis: University of Minnesota Press, 1988).

Such an easy transition from the natural to the urban scenario would be consonant with the narrative implicit in Kant and Schiller, which ends with a triumph of the subject, his freedom from the exigencies of the sensory world achieved, and his transcendence assured.| The difference between urban and natural is reduced to virtual sameness: all we know is that what can happen in the country can happen in the city as well.|Terror and anxiety, bafflement and blockage, repressed passions and suspect motives play an almost unduly large role in responses to the city, however.|Representations of the city tend to be far more paradoxical as well: vitality is dispersed, the present scene is crossed by the exotic or exoteric metaphor or mediated by memory, or the density of crowds is juxtaposed with the emptiness of squares and streets. The opening of *Bleak House* presents an exemplary scene for this dissemination, where the apostrophe to London precedes the breaking down of objects in the fog. If the sublime object undergoes disarticulation, if it loses its aura, the subject experiences, in relation to that object, shock, confusion, repression. The apparently triumphant narrative discloses grounds for disharmony. The incommensurability and discontinuity between subject and object persist; events lose their public shape within the anxieties of privatization, and the transfer of power that lies at the heart of the sublime experience results in diminution.[13] Wordsworth's London episode is not necessarily less sublime in this light: the empty space from which he draws his meditation on revolution refigures the abysses from which arise the sublime experiences of the Simplon Pass and Mount Snowdon episodes. Nevertheless, the problematic of revolution, which edges into his private anxieties, remains strangely unsettled in its urban contexts.

Urban "triumph," in fact, is frequently associated with space or distance. The New Jerusalem of the Book of Revelations provides the model in *Jude The Obscure* for Jude Fawley's vision of Christminster on the horizon:

> Through the solid barrier of cold cretaceous upland to the northward he was always beholding a gorgeous city—the fancied place he had likened to the new Jerusalem, though there was perhaps more of the painter's imagination and less of the

---

13. Cf. J. Hillis Miller's comment on the "entropy" represented in the first chapter of *Bleak House* in *Charles Dickens: The World of His Novels* (Bloomington: Indiana University Press, 1969).

diamond merchant's in his dreams thereof than in those of the Apocalyptic writer. And the city acquired a tangibility, a permanence, and hold on his life. . . .

In sad wet seasons, though he knew it must rain at Christminster too, he could hardly believe that it rained so drearily there. Whenever he could get away from the confines of the hamlet for an hour or two, which was not often, he would steal off to the Brown House on the hill and strain his eyes persistently; sometimes to be rewarded by the sight of a dome or spire, at other times by a little smoke, which in his estimate had some of the mysticism of incense.

When the day came when it suddenly occurred to him that if he ascended to the point of view after dark, or possibly went a mile or two further, he would see the night lights of the city. . . .

The project was duly executed. It was not late when he arrived at the place of outlook, only just after dusk; but a black north-east sky, accompanied by a wind from the same quarter, made the occasion dark enough. He was rewarded; but what he saw was not the lamps in rows, as he had half expected. No individual light was visible, only a halo or glow-fog overarching the place against the black heavens behind it, making the light and the city seem distant but a mile or so.[14]

Christminster's blurred lights suggest that what appears is, most likely, an apparition; in one sense the entire narrative of *Jude* demonstrates the phantasmic quality of the city of Jude's desire. Even here, in this first moment of vision, the elusive and deceptive lights in the uncertain distance transmute Christminster into a symbol of the unattainable. What the gaze sees is an object re-presented in the language of desire or apocalypse.

Small wonder, then, that the bifurcation and inadequation often point to a specularity, a problematic suspension, hesitation, or lack of closure, if not to loss or ruin. Here is a passage from *Middlemarch*, in which the city appears as its own double, separated from itself as well as from Dorothea Brooke:

The weight of unintelligible Rome might lie easily on bright

---

14. Thomas Hardy, *Jude the Obscure*, ed. Norman Page (New York: Norton, 1978), 20.

nymphs to whom it formed a background for the brilliant picture of Anglo-foreign society: but Dorothea had no such defence against deep impressions. Ruins and basilicas, palaces and colossi, set in the midst of a sordid present, where all that was living and warm-blooded seemed sunk in the deep degeneracy of a superstition divorced from reverence; the dimmer yet eager Titanic life gazing and struggling on walls and ceilings; the long vistas of white forms whose marble eyes seemed to hold the monotonous light of an alien world: all this vast wreck of ambitious ideals, sensuous and spiritual, mixed confusedly with the signs of breathing forgetfulness and degradation, at first jarred her as with an electric shock, and then urged themselves on her with that ache belonging to a glut of confused ideas which check the flow of emotion.[15]

Neil Hertz identifies in this passage, with its "persistent emphasis on the scene's at once soliciting and resisting comprehension, linked to the rhythms" of the sentences, the "elements" of an experience of the sublime,[16] with its release in a "shock" and a "glut of confused ideals which check the flow of emotion." We may add to this account the double source of confusion. First, the "Titanic life" of the past is "set in the midst of a sordid present," not only as simple juxtaposition, though that is a factor, but also as the image of a prior, more heroic life that is variously imprisoned in or alienated from the present. Conceptually, the image is chiastic: vitality set over against or checked within the ruins of art, and art as what remains of that vitality "sunk" in the degeneracy of a present life. All that is intelligible of this confusion is the text of an agon in which past and present, art and life, the sordid and the spiritual, struggle. Even this minimal intelligibility depends upon the observer, whose connection with the scene is contained in the rhetoric of repetition and transfer: Dorothea's "deep impressions" against the "living . . . sunk in deep degeneracy"; "this vast wreck of ambitious ideals . . . mixed confusedly with the sign of breathing forgetfulness" against Dorothea's "glut of confused ideas." The loss of "reverence," which will soon move from the historical to

15. George Eliot, *Middlemarch*, ed. Gordon S. Haight (Boston: Houghton Mifflin, 1968), 143–44.

16. Neil Hertz, "Recognizing Casaubon," in *The End of the Line* (New York: Columbia University Press, 1985), 90.

the personal, bespeaks the loss of aura in the "shock" resulting from Rome's degeneracy. The moment of sublime confusion is premonitory not only of the deferring of the sublime into a narrative in which Dorothea will realize her freedom, but also of the loss of the sublime, of high, sacred emotions to the mundane. The ambiguous space of Rome therefore prefigures a double move of disengagement of the mind and of loss of a sacred text or pattern for living. There is a third, more familiar mode of confusion, in which the urban text constitutes a projection of Dorothea's disappointed ideals and thwarted emotions concerning her marriage to Casaubon (upon which she had earlier projected ideals still intact and emotions still vital). Insofar as Dorothea is aware of her feelings but not clearly aware of their significance, we may observe a form of repression "imprisoned within" or written upon the city, feelings displaced into urban discourse. Here, too, the city assumes primary agency as its sites dominate the imagination.

Let us turn to an episode in *Bleak House*, in which London, embedded in a setting of the natural sublime, wears a mantle of metonymic sublimity. Esther Summerson views London from St. Albans:

> It was a cold, wild night, and the trees shuddered in the wind. The rain had been thick and heavy all day, and with little intermission for many days. None was falling just then, however. The sky had partly cleared, but was very gloomy—even above us, where a few stars were shining. In the north and north-west, where the sun had set three hours before, there was a pale dead light both beautiful and awful; and into it long sullen lines of cloud waved up, like a sea striken immovable as it was heaving. Towards London, a lurid glare overhung the whole dark waste; and the contrast between these two lights, and the fancy which the redder light engendered of an unearthly fire, gleaming on all the unseen buildings of the city, and on all the faces of its many thousands of wondering inhabitants, was as solemn as might be.
>
> I had no thought, that night—none, I am sure—of what was soon to happen to me. But I have always remembered since, that when we had stopped at the garden-gate to look up at the sky, and when we went upon our way, I had for a moment an indefinable impression of myself as something different from what I then was. I know it was then, and there, that I had it. I

> have ever since connected that feeling with that spot and time. . . .[17]

The setting is prototypically pre-sublime: the vast natural panorama is wild, dark, and gloomy, although there is an "awful" light to the north. London contributes its own play of light in the "lurid glare" that overhangs the "dark waste" between town and city. The city seems at its most sublime when, aside from its "redder light," it is unseen or when the light of "fancy" displaces literal light: Esther projects her own wonder onto the city-dwellers. What is even more striking is Esther's sense of herself, in that play of lights, as "something different from what I then was." That sense appears in a passage marked by repetition: "I had for a moment an indefinable impression. . . . I had it." These phrases appear within "I have always remembered since. . . . I know it was then. . . . I have ever since connected with feeling," along with the repeated insistence upon that spot and time. Sense of self within impression within memory; or, self within spot and (of) time: Esther's sense of herself as other is imaged in the divided sky, in the separation of town and city by the "dark waste" of memory or time. Esther habitually projects her stories onto landscapes, but what earlier suggested a benign unfolding under the orderly regimen of the little housekeeper, the Dame Durden of *Bleak House*, now evolves into the more terrifying narrative of self-division. Memory is figured in a landscape marked by antithesis and transference. The "indefinable" in Esther corresponds to the "unseen" in the city, a city estranged by time and darkness as the self is estranged from itself by those terrible repetitions. What opens up within the apparent containment of the city as a sublime image is both an ocular disparity—unseen houses projecting their lurid glare—and a fissure bespeaking, oddly enough, the transferential relation between the self and the sublime image. A conventional image of passion, fiery light, places it within the city as that which cannot be represented or structured. Its only shaping, however minimal, occurs within the repetitions of Esther's narrative. Her obscure sense of possible sublimity is both anticipatory on the level of *fabula* and memorial on the level of *sujet*. Esther's doubled, repetitive, and uneasy sense of self also has the lineaments of the uncanny: at home in Bleak House, she cannot be at home in the city. The site of the uncanny, it marks her self-repression.

17. Charles Dickens, *Bleak House* (London: Oxford University Press, 1956), 429.

What happens when wonder collapses into a moment of confusion? At one point in *Bleak House*, Jo the crossing-sweeper, always pressed to be "moving on," stops to eat at a corner of Blackfriars Bridge in London:

> And there he sits, munching and gnawing, and looking up at the great Cross on the summit of St. Paul's Cathedral, glittering above a red and violet-tinted cloud of smoke. From the boy's face one might suppose that sacred emblem to be, in his eyes, the crowning confusion of the great, confused city; so golden, so high up, so far out of his reach. There he sits, the sun going down, the river running fast, the crowd flowing by him in two streams—everything moving on to some purpose and to one end—until he is stirred up, and told to "move on" too. (207)

Heights, mass, the totalizing natural metaphors: all these ought to catalyze a sublime experience. (The crowd's metonymical relation to the river is itself a metaphor for temporal urban experience.) The awesome otherness of nature distances the immediacies of the city, but only to represent confusion or obliteration. What is so conspicuous in Jo is the absence of awe: he is stirred up not by the scene, but by some unidentified civic agent. Jo's perplexity in London culminates in his utter confusion:

> It must be a strange state to be like Jo! To shuffle through the streets, unfamiliar with the shapes, and in utter darkness as to the meaning of those mysterious symbols, so abundant over the shops, and at the corners of streets, and on the doors, and in the windows! To see people read, and to see people write, and to see the postmen deliver letters, and not to have the least idea of all that language—to be, to every scrap of it, stone blind and dumb! (168)

With no possibility of decipherment, perplexity folds upon meaningless signifiers. This prior moment, an extreme counterpart to Wordsworth's alienation among urban signs,[18] should be commensurate with Kant's mathematical sublime. What is missing, of course, is Jo's

18. See *The Prelude*, Book VII, lines 158–67.

consciousness, in which the sublime moment is baffled or dispersed among city streets. We may compare these passages to one in the *Critique of Judgment*, in which "bewilderment or [a] sort of perplexity . . . seizes the visitor on first entering St. Peter's in Rome": "For here a feeling comes home to him of the inadequacy of his imagination for presenting the idea of a whole within which that imagination attains its maximum, and, in its fruitless efforts to extend this limit, recoils upon itself, but in so doing succumbs to an emotional delight."[19] The recoil (an aftereffect of the labyrinthine coils of the city) is attended by the recognition that no standard of sense, no sensible object, can be commensurate with the workings of the supersensible faculty of reason. The sublime experience attests to the supremacy of our cognitive faculties, of our humanity and of our subjectivity. The sublime in nature or in a building such as St. Peter's is attributed to an object only by a process of subreption or displacement. Displacement, or a turn to metaphor, is therefore a sign of the active consciousness if not of the artist of the city, then of the subject in the scene.

One may question, then, whether Jo's undeveloped subjectivity is at all representative, whether his experience of the city belongs to some category of the antisublime. What articulate experience can there be for someone in such "utter darkness," upon whom the city seems to have cast not a veil but a blindfold? As in the passages on the poor in the urban sketches, there is a separation in which large metaphors, the language of the sublime, even the rhetoric of sympathy overleap a part of its very object. The confusion of the city does not impress Jo alone: both Esther and the third-person narrator, the two most authoritative consciousnesses in the novel, are sensitive to it, as the opening chapters indicate. Nevertheless, the sublime resides less in Jo, who as a contained figure cannot read signifieds, than in the third-person narrator, in whose cumulative phrases and obsessions with reading and writing, a reformulation of the sublime appears. The political imagination as well belongs to the narrator. At this point, the scenario widens to accommodate a Longinian element. The deferral of the sublime, so apparent in Jo, reaches to Esther. Her vision of the city rises up as she is on her way to see Jo, who has been lost and rediscovered, terribly ill. Nursing Jo, Esther will catch his illness. Thus a double figure of contagion and the dubious sublime, centered in Jo, spreads from the city; despite Esther's insistence upon the cog-

19. *Critique of Judgment*, 100.

nitive states of memory and of knowing, she doesn't know and she cannot see. (Her illness temporarily makes her blindness literal.) Jo's illness is traced to a pestilential graveyard in the city: in some crossed figure or catachresis, contagion and the sublime spread, the latter to be denied immediate resolution as if it were the function of narrative to suspend it.

There is a comparable irony in *New Grub Street*, where the dome of the British Museum crowns human intellectual achievement and covers human failures, as the hacks who work there disperse their writing into a vast communicative network. The blindness of Alfred Yule, editor and hack, then corresponds to Jo's illiteracy.

The novels of Dickens, Eliot, Hardy, and Gissing concur, then, in several assumptions about the role of the city. The first of them posits a doubleness in the city that figures the specular relation of perceiver to object. Objects would be sources of the sublime if one could only perceive them that way: the fault, when there is one, lies in the confused perceptions of the subject. (The etymological meaning of "confusion," a pouring together, suggests that objects may be confused, or perceptions alone may be, or both objects and perceptions may be "poured together" through the mediation of the text.) A second assumption is that urban objects tend to be mystifying, to resist the gaze, and that their obdurateness is a factor in their possible sublimity. A step in opening the city to narrative, the giving over of oneself to its mystery, which a number of Dickens's sketches foreground, gestures toward the sublime. Conversely, objects may be sublime because we make them so by displacing our own sense of our cognitive faculties, our subjectivity, onto them. The mysteriousness of objects is potentially uncanny, insofar as they represent otherness and yet, simultaneously, mean us.[20] A third assumption is that sublime rhetoric results from confusion: what cannot be resolved within the jumble of experience, at the level of the fabular, is sustained or shaped at the level of narration. But then the verbal sublime would appear to be the transformation of the natural or experiential sublime into figures or signs. It is at this point that the larger theoretical turn to the figurative runs parallel to what Neil Hertz has called the "sublime turn," as well as to the turn in the representation of the city. Each instance of gazing

20. I borrow the phrase from its not entirely different context in Geoffrey Hartman's "Spectral Symbolism and Authorial Self in Keats's 'Hyperion,' " in *The Fate of Reading* (Chicago: University of Chicago Press, 1975), 57.

at the city disturbs its surfaces: the city is transformed into apparitions, ruins, confusion, into light itself. Modern theories of the sublime tend to foreground the loss that precedes the ultimate triumph: resolution is less ideal, more tensional.[21] Representation of the city does not accede to the advent of signs without acknowledging that those signs, those texts, figure the hidden and the repressed. Before we examine the ways in which *Our Mutual Friend* presents this problematic, let us explore one more turning of the urban sublime.

II

One of the consequences of the bifurcated structure of the sublime experience, in which self and world, subject and object, interior and exterior are set into relations of alterity, is that both the innocent idealisms of the idea of the city and its negations are rendered problematic. The idealization of Manchester as an Athens of the north, like the characterization of London as Babylon or its slums as the Slough of Despond, functions primarily as a set-piece whose narrative consequences will be undermined. The monolithic urban metaphors evoke the metonymies and contiguities of narrative that then qualify them.

If narrative qualifies the representation of the city, so does the observer. It is the spectator who recognizes the powerful nature of the object and validates its sublimity by responding with the appropriate terror or awe. Surprisingly, however, the sense of spectacle accompanies the experience of powerful emotions. The passage from Benjamin that opens this chapter indicates as much, but the argument appears as early as Burke, for whom the sublime experience entails the distancing or even exclusion of subject from scene: "When danger

---

21. See, for example, Harold Bloom, "Freud and the Sublime: A Catastrophe Theory of Creativity," in *Agon* (New York: Oxford University Press, 1982), 91–118; Walter Benjamin on the concept of the aura in *Illuminations*, (trans. Harry Zohn [New York: Schocken Books, 1969]), especially "On Some Motifs in Baudelaire," 186–92 and "The Work of Art in the Age of Mechanical Reproduction," 220–24. Neil Hertz's "A Reading of Longinus"(*The End of the Line* [New York: Columbia University Press, 1985], 1:20) compares Benjamin with Longinus: "each evokes a catastrophe [involving a loss in European culture], yet each seems equally concerned with a recurrent phenomenon in literature, the movement of disintegration and figurative reconstitution I have been calling the sublime turn" (591).

or pain press too nearly, they are incapable of giving any delight, and are simply terrible; but at certain distances, and with certain modifications, they may be, and they are delightful, as we do every day experience."[22] Paradoxically, the sublime experience in relation to mountain or city depends upon one's separateness, just as the sublimity of a great action, like a revolution, depends upon one's position as spectator rather than participant. Consequently, the spectator perceives those great actions or objects as elements of theater. The spectacle achieves its effects in part because it is perceived as if it were a representation, rather than "the real thing." To be a spectator is now to be an interpreter as well, in a transaction involving gazer and scene.[23] The passages we examined before seemed predicated upon a closer relation, in which self seemed inextricable from urban scene. Yet Esther's self-consciousness presupposes a metaphorical self-distancing parallel to her actual distance from the city, and Dorothea's suppressed vitality is separated by time from the "Titanic" vitality of an earlier Rome. The difference is one of degree.

The vicissitudes of the sublime are strikingly implicated in the thematics of revolution, which threatens to tear the fabric of urban life but which is experienced as spectacle. At the same time, it is appropriated into a figurative discourse that joins public and private life. Although revolution is not merely an urban phenomenon, it plays a significant urban role in several novels, among them Scott's *The Heart of Midlothian*, Disraeli's *Sybil*, James's *The Princess Casamassima*, and various works by Dickens. Revolution or the threat of revolution, social and political, comes to seem inherent in urban life. In the novels it works contrapuntally against alternating rhythms of progress and stagnation in English political life; it also engenders defensive fictional strategies of privatization and abstraction. The crowds and riots of *A Tale of Two Cities* or *Barnaby Rudge* appear in a more domesticated form in Dickens's novels of contemporaneous life. In *Sybil*, the closure of its romance form as well as the political gesture of aristocratic social concern quell the threat of social unrest. To these strategies of neu-

---

22. *A Philosophical Enquiry into the Origin of our Ideas of the Sublime and Beautiful*, 40.

23. Cf. Hannah Arendt's comment that "only the *spectator*, never the actor, can know and understand whatever offers itself as a spectacle. . . . [A]s a spectator you may understand the 'truth' of what the spectacle is about, but the price you have to pay is withdrawal from participating in it" (*The Life of the Mind: One: Thinking* [New York: Harcourt Brace Jovanovich, 1977, 1978], 92, 93).

tralization, *The Heart of Midlothian* adds historical distancing. It is in *Bleak House*, however, that both the political rhythm and the turn to privatization emerge with particular strength. Sir Leicester Dedlock's fear of "opening the floodgates" and his consequent immersion in the status quo (even, rhetorically speaking, in the stasis of his name and in the repetitive names of the Doodles and Boodles who run the country), represent a fear of revolution that is effectively sublimated by metaphorical transpositions. Although they seem to be strategies of political or social containment, the reduction to caricature makes such containment suspect. Sir Leicester's official politics meet chiastically with the private world of Lady Dedlock, whose freezing moods—and rare melting ones—cover her traumatic and socially disreputable past. When this past eventually becomes public (albeit in a limited way), the two areas meet. Although freezing and melting are metaphorical for the most part (they become literal in the snowstorm that provides the setting for Lady Dedlock's flight and death), they inevitably naturalize the political. Lady Dedlock's ascent to the aristocracy enacts a revolution of sorts, providing a site for the displacement of political anxieties. Under such conditions revolution, itself repressed, becomes the figure for repression. This reading should not remove the political from scrutiny, however, inasmuch as it foregrounds the defensive strategies that "freeze" political life.

Revolution may act as the figure for repression on the narrative level too. If the representation of revolution is preeminently visual, then to suppress such a representation would be to shift the grounds of narrative from the mimetic to the metaphorical, and from the spectacular to the specular. In an episode in *The Princess Casamassima*, loss is succeeded by restitutions of various sorts, including internalization and self-recognition. With the help of a small inheritance, Hyacinth Robinson travels to Paris. There he encounters his double political and aesthetic heritage. The Gallery of Apollo in the Louvre reveals the cultural side with the force of an epiphany; walking the streets of Paris or sitting in its cafés, Hyacinth imagines his grandfather fighting in the Revolution. Each of these constitutes an imaginative leap for him, a denial of the passage of time and of his mundane activities as a bookbinder. In each case he can conceive of some form of heroism involved with the splendor of art as well as with political action. If all "Paris struck him as tremendously artistic and decorative," he also locates the barricade where his grandfather "must have fallen. . . . [I]t had bristled across the Rue Saint-Honoré very near to the Church of

Saint-Roch."[24] Nor are the city's contradictions lost on him: "He had his perplexities and even now and then a revulsion for which he had made no allowance, as when it came over him that the most brilliant city in the world was also the most bloodstained" (2:121). But even that "perplexity" is resolved: "the great sense that he understood and sympathised was preponderant, and his comprehension gave him wings—appeared to transport him to still wider fields of knowledge, still higher sensations" (2:121). We may recognize in that single sentence a brief account of the sublime: a moment of perplexity followed by a release of the soul. The moment is made ironic by Hyacinth's inability to sustain such a comprehension on a mundane or temporal level, his inability to reconcile aesthetic with political commitments. There is a still longer passage in which mundane contradictions are resolved into a grasp of the sublime:

> The nightly emanation of Paris seemed to rise more richly, to float and hang in the air, to mingle with the universal light and the many-voiced sound, to resolve itself into a thousand solicitations and opportunities, addressed, however, mainly to those in whose pocket the chink of a little loose gold might respond. Hyacinth's retrospections had not made him drowsy, but quite the reverse; he grew restless and excited and a kind of pleasant terror of the place and hour entered into his blood. But it was nearly midnight and he got up to walk home, taking the line of the Boulevard toward the Madeleine. He passed down the Rue Royale, where comparative stillness reigned; and when he reached the Place de la Concorde, to cross the bridge which faces the Corps Legislatif, he found himself almost isolated. He had left the human swarm and the obstructed pavements behind, and the wide spaces of the splendid square lay quiet under the summer stars. The plash of the great fountains was audible and he could almost hear the wind-stirred murmur of the little wood of the Tuileries on one side and of the vague expanse of the Champs Elysées on the other. The place itself— the Place Louis Quinze, the Place de la Révolution—had given him a sensible emotion from the day of his arrival; he had recognised so quickly its tremendous historic character. He had seen in a rapid vision the guillotine in the middle, on the

24. *The Princess Cassamassima* (New York: Charles Scribner's Sons, 1908), 2:123.

site of the inscrutable obelisk, and the tumbrils, with waiting victims, were stationed round the circle now made majestic by the monuments of the cities of France. The great legend of the French Revolution, a sunrise out of a sea of blood, was more real to him here than anywhere else; and, strangely, what was most present was not its turpitude and horror, but its magnificent energy, the spirit of creation that had been in it, not the spirit of destruction. That shadow was effaced by the modern fairness of fountain and statue, the stately perspective and composition; and as he lingered before crossing the Seine a sudden sense overtook him, making his heart falter to anguish—a sense of everything that might hold one to the world, of the sweetness of not dying, the fascination of great cities, the charm of travel and discovery, the generosity of admiration. (2:140– 41)

The diction of the sublime, encompassing all that is expansive, great, tremendous and obscure, extends to that characteristic oxymoron, the "pleasant terror." The Revolution has become for Hyacinth a spectacle rising out of empty space; once he has envisaged its historical properties of the guillotine and the tumbrils with their victims, it becomes "a sunrise out of a sea of blood," its creative revolutionary energy transformed and naturalized by metaphor into art. Nowhere is the paradox of the classical sublime more apparent than in this double turn from grand human action to art by way of the natural metaphor. The "raw" nature of Kant now occupies the plane of representation. Hyacinth's vision is not unlike Dorothea's in *Middlemarch*, insofar as the fate of a great city and one's personal fate are rhetorically intertwined. But there is a curious passage, a visual intervention as it were, that puts the sublime in jeopardy—"That shadow was effaced by the modern fairness of fountain and statue, the stately perspective and composition"—and draws Hyacinth to the beauties of this world. "Modern fairness" presumably effaces the shadowy spirit of destruction, although there is enough ambiguity to suggest that it effaces the entire surge of revolutionary energy, even transported to the domain of imagination. The poignancy of the moment results not simply from the intolerable pressure to weigh the revolutionary or political against the aesthetic, which has so preoccupied Hyacinth, but from the unstable achievement of the sublime imaginative insight.

There is still another crucial motif, figured as ruin in *Middlemarch*

and emptiness in *The Princess Casamassima*. Hyacinth's walk toward
the Place de la Concorde progresses into isolation, away from "the
human swarm" toward quiet and darkness. It is not the human swarm,
so apt to conjure up the revolutionary crowd, but the antithetically
empty square that initiates vision. Like Wordsworth nearly a century
earlier, James incorporates revolution or history only as an absence.
Hyacinth's experience contains an allegory of repression in which the
recovery of self and its sublime powers is possible only through the
distancing and mediation of history, and then only precariously. Ironically, the image of the French Revolution supersedes the memory of
later revolutions (Paris is "the most bloodstained" city) and prefigures
the estrangement of self from city represented in the construction of
Paris in the latter part of the nineteenth century.[25]

Hyacinth is a worker who stands at the edge of his class, a softened
figure of the revolutionary whose consciousness guarantees a bridge
to all that he is not. In turn, his liminal position makes him less threatening. The urban poor incur authorial ambivalence, as we know: the
language of apocalypse both characterizes their extremity and serves
as a figure for revolution. To fear the revolutionary figures inscribed
in crowds, in Chartists, in factory workers and in single sinister figures
roaming the streets, is not only to mask compassion but to cast social
change as a threat and to shift responsibility to the other.[26]

In this context, Jo's experience gazing at the summit of St. Paul's
exceeds urban alienation and confusion. Jo cannot read the Cross—
and it is left indeterminate whether it means as much as "confusion"
to him, whether he is aware of his own state of mind—any more than
he can read London's street signs. His repeated " 'I don't know noth-
ink,' " his phonetic word-twisting ("inquest," for example, becomes
"inkwich"), his telling confusion of Lady Dedlock with her maid Hor-
tense and Esther: all these are signs of the plight of the urban poor,

---

25. See Walter Benjamin on Haussmann, in *Charles Baudelaire: A Lyric Poet in the
Era of High Capitalism*, 174: "Meanwhile, as far as the Parisians were concerned, he alienated their city from them. They no longer felt at home in it. They became conscious of the
bohemian character of the great city." The drive to create a monumental Paris produces
the estrangement that is in turn a part of sublimation. See also T. J. Clark's comments on
the consequences of this estrangement for representation in *The Painting of Modern Life:
Paris in the Art of Manet and His Followers* (Princeton: Princeton University Press, 1984),
23–78.

26. See, for example, the accounts in *Mary Barton* and *Sybil*, in which the workers
present such threats to the middle and upper classes. Sir Leicester Dedlock's terror of
opening the floodgates frames the fear of revolution in hyperboles that collapse into irony.

whose illiteracy is more than literal. No wonder that the representation of this group often tends toward the grotesque, which may be understood as a partial or incomplete version of the sublime.[27] Jo may be included in the crowd while he is kept "moving on," but he is denied any developed subjectivity. No capacity to grasp symbols, no symbolic stage, is possible for one denied access to writing. As London's counterpart to the natives of Borioboola-Gha—those objects of Mrs. Jellyby's frantic and misdirected philanthropic activities—Jo is cast as a primitive and as pure object. If we turn to the totalizing metaphors that enter so often into the rhetoric of the urban sublime, they assume sinister dimensions. To characterize the city in terms of great natural forces or objects (and the passage on St. Paul's offers a fair example) and thus to place Jo as a primitive in nature, is to incur severe consequences. First, it refigures the cultural situation as a natural one in which it is easy to establish or perpetuate charity: in that case, one may continue to pity Jo, who will always remain an object. Second, the exclusion of Jo from subjectivity denies him important parts of the urban experience. His baffled consciousness limits experience and skews the representation of the city toward modes of catachresis. Gazing at the Cross, he creates a complex narrative stoppage that he can unblock only by moving on.

What is latent in the idea of the urban sublime, then, is that it is a privileged experience, in aesthetic, social, psychological, or rhetorical terms. The universal accessibility that Kant posited (and to which Wordsworth would theoretically have subscribed) becomes relegated to the domain of idealisms. The sublime appears as a form of privileged awareness, as the parodic use of the term in the fashionable world suggests. Social privilege need not be aristocratic, as we see in Esther or in Dorothea, in direct narration or indirect discourse. Nevertheless, the sublime cannot be a commonplace mode; its rhetoric is allied with forms of urban power. Against the moment in which response to a sensory phenomenon is succeeded by an awareness of one's supersensible powers, there is balanced a second, in which awareness is held forth as a narrative possibility and then quelled. Consciousness would then reside, or be residual, in the artist of the city or his surrogates, such as Hyacinth Robinson.

27. Cf. the discussion of the grotesque in Gogol, in Donald Fanger, *Dostoevsky and Romantic Realism*, 115–26; and in Ronald Paulson, *Representations of Revolution, 1789-1820* (New Haven: Yale University Press, 1983), 168–211. There is a brief discussion of the conceptual link between the sublime and the grotesque on 168–69.

III

Urban novels, especially in the latter part of the nineteenth century, thematize the turn away from the visible, the ordered, or the contained. Their tropes vary, from the sunrise of revolutionary energy to the twilight of entropic dark mounds. One particularly important trope, however, is that of surfaces and depths, which finds an illuminating theoretical setting, as well as some helpful supplementary images, in Foucault's concept of the doubles.[28] In his discussion of the doubles in *The Order of Things*, Foucault points to the way in which the conditions of representation change in the nineteenth century, so that the governing image of the tabular defers to the concept of depth. *Our Mutual Friend* offers an exemplary text, not only for Foucault but also for Freud's essay on "The Uncanny."[29] We find a further doubling there, in the pairing of the *heimlich* with the *unheimlich* as well as in the psychoanalytic concept of the double. That concept itself is related to the play of surfaces and depths in Dickens's novel. It is in "The Uncanny," Harold Bloom writes, that Freud presents indirectly his theory of the sublime: thus we may return to the theoretical framework with which we began.[30] Dickens's symbolic field is coextensive with the city (the country appears as the dream of the city), a place in which the precariousness of selfhood (already apparent in the passages from *Middlemarch* and *Bleak House*) is all too evident. Suppose, in addition, that we think of the city in Lacanian terms, as the site of the discourse of the other: then the very otherness of the city would provide a route to understanding the unconscious of the subject. Such an urban surface would be denser, more metaphorical, more skeptical about its own visibility. But let us begin with Foucault.

¶The advent of the modern subject marks the nineteenth century, according to Foucault. It is man who shapes the very conceptions by which he may be understood. Knowable as an empirical being, at the same time he formulates the conditions for that knowability. His newly

28. See Michel Foucault, "Man and His Doubles," in *The Order of Things* (London: Tavistock, 1970), 303–43.

29. Sigmund Freud, "The Uncanny" in *The Standard Edition of the Complete Psychological Works of Sigmund Freud*, trans. and ed. James Strachey, 24 vols. (London: Hogarth Press, 1953–74), 17:217–56.

30. "Freud and the Sublime," in *Agon*, 101. It is, Bloom writes, "the only major contribution that the twentieth century has made to the aesthetics of the Sublime." The Sublime is, he continues, one of Freud's "major *repressed* concerns."

prominent capacity for self-reflection locates an "element of darkness," an "obscure space" or "abyssal region" in which the unthought, the unconscious, constitutes the other. That "new" self-consciousness, moreover, provokes an awareness of one's location in history and a concomitant search for origins, which in turn recede by dint of the very quest to find them. To be a creature with form, self-understanding, and a history is to have one's dimensionality, one's depths, predicated upon limitation: one's initial undeterminedness will be subject to determination by the other, from the outside. Foucault's term for this set of contexts in which the subject both determines himself and is determined by the other is *doubles*. The doubles ensure that man becomes a subject, but they also prevent him from being fully known to himself. The representation of man-as-subject, then, would have to take account of his indeterminacy, of the paradox of an increased self-knowledge that includes the awareness of what one does not or cannot know about oneself. We cannot think of the doubles as directly antithetical, however; the otherness of the unthought would be separated from the *cogito* or the thought not by transparency—that would be a contradiction in terms—but by displacement and distortion. In effect, the more one knows about the subject, the more the subject seems to be relegated to a liminal position, from the perspective of representation. How can the subject, understood as a creature in and of depth, be spread across the very representational surface for whose constitution he is responsible?

Our Mutual Friend begins with a passage that is remarkable for its presentation of this problematic of the visible. The passage is crossed with the breaking of a surface, with the negations of identity, and with disturbing figures of repetition. A boat is floating on the Thames:

> The figures in this boat were those of a strong man with ragged grizzled hair and a sun-browned face, and a dark girl of nineteen or twenty, sufficiently like him to be recognizable as his daughter. The girl rowed, pulling a pair of sculls very easily; the man, with the rudder-lines slack in his hands, and his hands loose in his waistband, kept an eager look out. He had no net, hook, or line, and he could not be a fisherman; his boat had no cushion for a sitter, no paint, no inscription, no appliance beyond a rusty boathook and a coil of rope, and he could not be a waterman; his boat was too crazy and too small to take in cargo for delivery, and he could not be a light-

erman or river-carrier; there was no clue to what he looked for, but he looked for something, with a most intent and searching gaze. The tide, which had turned an hour before, was running down, and his eyes watched every little race and eddy in its broad sweep, as the boat made slight headway against it, or drove stern foremost before it, according as he directed his daughter by a movement of his head. She watched his face as earnestly as he watched the river. But, in the intensity of her look there was a touch of dread or horror.

Allied to the bottom of the river rather than the surface, by reason of the slime and ooze with which it was covered, and its sodden state, this boat and the two figures in it obviously were doing something that they often did, and were seeking what they often sought. Half savage as the man showed, with no covering on his matted head, with his brown arms bare to between the elbow and the shoulder, with the loose knot of a looser kerchief lying low on his bare breast in a wilderness of beard and whisker, with such dress as he wore seeming to be made out of the mud that begrimed his boat, still there was business-like usage in his steady gaze. So with every lithe action of the girl, with every turn of her wrist, perhaps most of all with her look of dread or horror; they were things of usage.[31]

The passage depicts the threshold on which the optical meets the hidden and invisible. Gaffer Hexam gazes intently at the river, and Lizzie gazes intently at him. Balancing watching with horror, the looks are, like the rowing, "things of usage." The irony of that phrase, bespeaking the unstable combination of dread-full repetition and business practice, only points up the energy of the gaze.[32] The boat is "allied" to the river's bottom: the figures in the boat share in that metonymical relation. Lizzie's manifest horror has to do with her father's unsavory occupation of retrieving dead bodies from the river, but it is ambiguous whether that horror is existential, in the face of death, or moral, because between the river and the police station to which they are brought, bodies are picked clean of valuables. (Gaffer is described more than once as a "bird of prey.") In this respect,

31. *Our Mutual Friend* (London: Oxford University Press, 1967), 1–2. Compare Gaffer's loosely knotted kerchief with the tie-knots of "Seven Dials" in *Sketches by Boz* (London: Oxford University Press, 1969).

32. Cf. Benjamin's discussion of the gaze in "On Some Motifs in Baudelaire," 190.

Lizzie's horrified gaze is complicit; the river is, as Gaffer says, " 'meat and drink' " to her. The uncanny is inscribed in this scene, insofar as "homely" meat and drink are derived from the sinister aspects of the river and thus inhabited by the "unhomely," while "usage" acquires the force of involuntary repetition and is itself invested with dread. |The uncanny, Freud writes, "is undoubtedly related to what is frightening—to what arouses dread and horror."[33] The metaphorical transformation into the body is both a repetition and a closing of the circle: the gaze turned outward, the river turned inward—or, if one prefers, a "sinking" of self into the outward scene, repeated by the hidden figure in the river as well as by the visible figures in the boat. Gaffer's ties to the river are both literal and figurative, metonymical and metaphorical. A recessive figure of the savage, he is also the businessman searching for his stock in trade of drowned bodies. The catalogue of negations concerning his "business" identity allies him to the other businessmen of the city who traffic in equally indefinable or nonexistent financial matters. While this concealed alliance of the disreputable with the bourgeois is a familiar theme in Dickens's novels, it is not the social satire or the thematics that matters so much here as it is the language of negation. In consequence, the flora and fauna of the city are located in a wilderness of which the river is one pole, the "suburban Sahara" of Holloway another. The gloom and the absence of the object mark this regressive loss of aura, while Lizzie's look of "dread or horror," intensified by repetition, traces the sublime in its moment of vanishing. This opening scene composes a rebus that contains clues to the rest of the novel. There are no surfaces that are not in some sense ruptured by the depths. In this scene alone, there are multiple transgressions: the violation of surfaces by depths, of the body by the outside, of the moral law by the economic. The very structure that separates surfaces and depths, exteriors and interiors (that which is "normally" held in a tension represented by the gaze) is violated by an excess or "slime" that is thematic and ideological, narrative, figurative, and psychological.

The collapse of excess or the degeneration of the sublime into slime involves more than a bad pun. It includes the retreat from the visual, which is figured in both Mr. Venus's shop and the image of the mounds. The mounds or dust heaps are the piles of refuse that the elder John Harmon collected and that, sifted, have yielded enough to

---

33. Freud, "The Uncanny," 219.

amass a fortune. (Their indeterminate content and form link Harmon's occupation with those of Gaffer Hexam and the various financial speculators and moneylenders.) As an urban image, they represent a point of separation from (if not an ironic comment upon) the growth and vitality that characterized the architectural enterprise in nineteenth-century London.[34] Against the major building projects, from the Regents Park houses to the Venetian Gothic structures in the City to the massive blocks of flats, we may set the motif of ruin or loss, whose limiting image is the dust mounds. Heaps of broken images, the mounds rise as indefinite forms in the urban landscape: "certain tall dark mounds rose high against the sky" (55). Dickens does not describe them at length, although they are the object of discourse and concern, the hiding-place of at least one significant will, a source of wealth, a significant element in the plot, and a massive symbol. In a compensatory movement, their absence at the level of description is restored by a symbolic shorthand. They are, however, the antithesis of those most sublime of objects, mountains. The mounds belong rather to the grotesque, in a line of images that includes Wordsworth's London perceived as a "monstrous ant-hill."[35] Out of the low life of the river dredgers and refuse collectors comes the figure for a narrative of the urban sublime, as powerful in its way as the classical sublime.

If the mounds preside over that threshold where the seen shades over into the unseen, so in its own way does the shop of Mr. Venus. Silas Wegg approaches it through the streets of Clerkenwell, away from the shops where "artificers" work in precious stones and metals:

> [N]ot towards these does Mr. Wegg stump, but towards the poorer shops of small retail traders in commodities to eat and drink and keep folks warm, and of Italian frame-makers, and of barbers, and of brokers, and of dealers in dogs and singing-

34. Two good accounts of Victorian architecture are John Summerson, *Victorian Architecture: Four Studies in Evaluation* (New York: Columbia University Press, 1940); and Donald J. Olsen, *The Growth of Victorian London* (London: Batsford, 1976). Olsen comments on the attempt to make London orderly and predictable. He notes, however, that although a great deal of energy was devoted to the "provision of pleasures," the "providers" were kept out of sight as much as possible, in sweatshops, in City counting-houses (325). Moreover, he compares London to "a vast baroque opera or masque" (326). There is, then, significant historical background for the contrary subtexts in the novels. See also Donald J. Olsen, *The City as a Work of Art: London. Paris. Vienna* (New Haven: Yale University Press, 1986).

35. *The Prelude*, Book VII, line 149.

birds. From these, in a narrow and a dirty street devoted to such callings, Mr. Wegg selects one dark shop-window with a tallow candle dimly burning in it, surrounded by a muddle of objects vaguely resembling pieces of leather and dry stick, but among which nothing is resolvable into anything distinct, save the candle itself in its old tin candlestick, and two preserved frogs fighting a small-sword duel. Stumping with fresh vigour, he goes in at the dark greasy entry, pushes a little greasy dark reluctant side-door, and follows the door into the little dark greasy shop. It is so dark that nothing can be made out in it, over a little counter, but another tallow candle in another old tin candlestick, close to the face of a man stooping low in a chair. (77–78)

After the detailed catalogue of the street, nothing is resolvable on the interior, with the exceptions of the candlesticks, the source of dim light, and the grotesque frogs. Despite Mr. Venus's trade—he stuffs or "articulates" animals and other figures—the description of his shop lacks articulation. Nor is there anything grammatically articulate about his survey of his shelves:

'My working bench. My young man's bench. A wice. Tools. Bones, warious. Skulls, warious. Preserved Indian baby. African ditto. Bottled perparations, warious. Everything within reach of your hand, in good preservation. The mouldy one a-top. What's in those hampers over them again, I don't quite remember. Say, human warious. Cats. Articulated English baby. Dogs. Ducks. Glass eyes, warious. Mummied bird. Dried cuticle, warious. Oh, dear me! That's the general panoramic view.'[36]

All these "warious" items exist, so to speak, side by side, or on a hierarchy of shelves, but without much explicit relation to one another. Everything is in some state of preservation, whether good or mouldy. The "panoramic" view, encompassing what is visually obscure, requires enumeration, some approximate form of identification. The items in the shop, geographically as well as generically various, are

36. *Our Mutual Friend*, 81. Cf. Walter Benjamin on the genre of "panorama literature" in Paris, in *Charles Baudelaire: A Lyric Poet in the Era of High Capitalism*, 35. Mr. Venus then stands as the parodist of both panoramas and panorama literature.

so represented as to be referentially unstable. The objects arrayed in the general obscurity are quite literally figures of dismemberment and reduction, at the same time that they supply a virtual allegory of taxonomy. The obscure shop in the heart of London stands as a visual text opposed to the vast enterprise of Mayhew's *London Labour and the London Poor*, as well as the more casual sketches of such writers as Sala. He and Mayhew attempt to make London "accessible" in any district, at any hour: London becomes their panoramic text, visible, comprehensible, and neutralized. As in the contemporaneous physiologies of Paris, "[i]nnocuousness was of the essence."[37] Even when such sketches approach the dark parts of London, they proffer a form of reassurance in what amounts to a reversion to the picturesque. In Mayhew and Sala, taxonomy is part of the process of making visible; what a man does is what he is. The structure of Dickens's London, on the other hand, arises from self-creation and dissolution. The unstable metaphors of river, urban desert, and mirror are not merely visual: they are metomymies of occupation as well. What a man does is what undoes him.

Articulation or taxonomy is at best a suspect enterprise. Mr. Venus's work comprises the preservation of various items, heterogeneous and often grotesque. After articulation they are shelved to form an array of discrete items, a panorama looming through the darkness of his shop. It would not be difficult to read this section as a parable for the pitfalls of urban fiction, in which objects detached from their contexts, without narratives, serve as admonitions of the neutralizing effects of articulation. In light of Dickens's predilection for the grotesque, the catalogue, and the suspended narrative, such warnings serve as moments of self-reflection in which urban narrative encounters itself. While the facts that Dickens had figures of dueling frogs on his writing desk and that the shop is modeled after one that Dickens found in St. Giles[38] may suggest that objects do find narrative homes, one should remember that the frogs are forever suspended in a solution and that the shop, not unlike the secondhand clothing shop in "Reflections in Monmouth Street," recedes into darkness. But Mr. Venus is also one

---

37. *Charles Baudelaire; A Lyric Poet in the Era of High Capitalism*, 36. See also Karlheinz Stierle, "Baudelaire and the Tradition of the Tableau de Paris," *New Literary History* 11 (1980): 345–61.

38. See Stephen Gill's notes to Charles Dickens, *Our Mutual Friend* (Baltimore: Penguin, 1971), 899. Gill cites John Forster's *The Life of Charles Dickens* (2 vols. [London: J. M. Dent, 1966]), as well as Dickens's letter of 25 February 1864.

of the most grotesque versions of the artist of the city, a kind of *bricoleur* obscured within its heart, continually articulating the forms of life that the city's denizens bring to his shop. There is a considerable distance between the loss of aura and the darkness of the shop, yet Mr. Venus and his unhappy love life—his ladylove cannot forgive him for articulating figures, those of adult men and women, so close to her own—parody the conflict between the original work of art, (here the human body) with its aura, which is lost in the mechanical reconstruction. Mr. Venus has the impulses of an artist, although his work is limited to reproduction of the materials on hand. The narrative turn, via Silas Wegg's walk, away from the finer crafts with their ties to high life, to the craft of a lower life represents an aesthetic choice that belongs as well to the artist of the city. That choice is sometimes abortive or grotesque, as the "panorama" on the shelves shows. Representation is a risky business; but then risk is a hidden figure, or figure of hiding, that runs through many of Dickens's novels and renders representation problematic even as it becomes an enabling figure for narrative.

IV

The parodic taxonomy that emerges in the treatment of Mr. Venus and his shop represents the slippage away from order and containment that is foregrounded more briefly and more starkly in the police station episode near the beginning of *Our Mutual Friend*. Dickens's detectives can be complex, although in this novel they foreclose the very investigation that should constitute their business. *Our Mutual Friend* begins with the breaking of a surface and the retrieval of a dead body from the Thames. The mystery concerning the body is unusual, in that, the characters are not mystified at all, but simply assume that the body is that of the younger John Harmon. Nor are readers mystified for long: they realize fairly soon that the body is not that of John Harmon. Its real identity is only a minor narrative question, not quite a subject for mystery. We start with the presence of the body and the double absence of the subject, and with the beginning of displacement as John Harmon, viewing his supposed dead self, adopts successively the personae of Julius Handford and John Rokesmith. It seems that the surface has been broken only to re-form at another level where mystery is bracketed. So obvious is the mystery that the detectives are relegated to metaphor almost as soon as they appear: the Police Station is a monastery, the Night-Inspector an Abbot, the episode "solved" and summed up in a colloquial but scholastic paragraph, as if the dead man had fallen not so much into the river as into an already written plot, a text that had been waiting for him.[39] The function of the police seems to be merely to inspect, to account for, and to privilege the visible and thus ensure social stability. We might call this minimal interpretation. Never have narrative, the city, and society seemed so structured. Yet stability is achieved only at the cost of repression. It is what the Night-Inspector overlooks, here figured as the voice of the madwoman crying in her cell, that breaks the surface twice as narrative excess:

> [T]hey found the Night-Inspector, with a pen and ink, and ruler, posting up his books in a whitewashed office, as studiously as if he were in a monastery on top of a mountain, and no howling fury of a drunken woman were banging herself against a cell-door in the back-yard at his elbow. . . . Then, he finished ruling the work he had in hand (it might have been illuminating a missal, he was so calm), in a very neat and methodical manner, showing not the slightest consciousness of the woman who was banging herself with increased violence, and shrieking most terrifically for some other woman's liver.[40]

Detection is a nearly universal activity in Dickens's novels, carried on unofficially as well as officially. But official detection is apt to be questionable. If it is not perfunctory as in the Harmon incident, then it is marred by other factors. Official detection seeks social stability, aided by the visible and by a drive toward coherence.[41] But the Night-Inspector, society's secondary reviser, cannot have the last word. Even Sloppy, that gangling, good-natured creature, knows that the police have "different voices." The privileging of surfaces and the ordering

---

39. See *Our Mutual Friend*, 24–27.

40. *Our Mutual Friend*, 24. Cf. the voice of the woman crying in the night in *Sketches by Boz*, 55–56.

41. For a different view of the police in Dickens's novels, cf. D. A. Miller, "Discipline in Different Voices: Bureaucracy, Police, Family, and *Bleak House*," in *The Novel and the Police* (Berkeley: University of California Press, 1988), 1–32.

of official accounts are opposed by the violence and excess, by the uncanny itself, that occupy the city. The artist of the city seeks them, rather than the scholastic texts of a Night-Inspector.

Let us glance at the narratives of both John Harmon and Eugene Wrayburn. Even in the beginning, the excess—the voice of the mad-woman—has already appeared as displacement, in John Harmon's self-removal. It will soon appear as deferral. Accompanying his friend Lightwood (the solicitor in charge of Harmon's will) to the scene, Eugene Wrayburn has a glimpse of Lizzie. His desire for her is suppressed and deferred throughout most of the novel; what cannot be accounted for in visual terms still plays over its surface.

Even these two phenomena, displacement and deferral, invite that second-level, harmonious interpretation: John Harmon, as his own double John Rokesmith, protects his interests as a guardian spirit, deferring identification until he inspects the bride his father has willed for him. In Otto Rank's terms, he is guarding against his own extinction by casting it into the realm of the inauthentic, although such tacit self-acknowledgment seems to drain the double of its uncanniness.[42] Eugene's more complex deferral of desire betrays an accompanying death-wish insofar as he courts the antagonism of Bradley Headstone, his demonic rival for Lizzie's affections. There is a clear parallel to the "masterplot" of Freud's *Beyond the Pleasure Principle*, in which Peter Brooks has found a model for narrative: the death instinct seeks the organism's end by necessarily devious routes.[43] Plot, constructed out of deferred desire, seems either to appear as personification or to remove desire from the conscious subject. This form of displacement, in which the subject is realized in the other, offers a fruitful ground for interpretation. In a formulation that has affinities to Foucault, Lacan notes, "The symbolic function presents itself as a double movement within the subject: man makes an object of his action, but only in order to restore to this action in due time its place as a grounding."[44] The "equivocation" and reversal that Lacan finds in the symbolic function identify subjectivity as a transaction. It is within this notion of a double movement that we may locate both the surfaces and the abysses of *Our Mutual Friend*.

42. See Freud, "The Uncanny," 234–35.

43. See Peter Brooks, "Freud's Masterplot," in *Reading for the Plot* (New York: Knopf, 1984), 90–112.

44. Jacques Lacan, "The Function and Field of Speech and Language in Psychoanalysis," in *Ecrits*, trans. Alan Sheridan (New York: Norton, 1977), 73.

It is within this theoretical context as well that we may identify strategies of doubling. The first is that of self-distancing, in which the assumption of a persona permits the self to become an observer of both oneself and others. When John Harmon takes on the role of the grave, efficient secretary, John Rokesmith, in order to observe Bella Wilfer, he gains more than the advantage of being unrecognized. His otherness is predicated upon his apparent lack of financial means, so that he is valued, or not valued, for himself. The narrative pun here is doubled by his unassuming assumption of a judgmental stance that a potential husband could not take openly toward his intended bride. Harmon's allegory of value and judgment is played out upon some larger canvas on which, as himself, he is both visible and invisible: he is the threshold figure, validated by the concept of the double, par excellence.

The second strategy arises in the quests for origins, in which closure is elusive. John Harmon seeks along the waterfront, a marginal area, the "origins" of his newly acquired pseudonymity, itself the result of his narrow escape from murder and the ensuing death of his assailant, upon whose body Harmon's papers are found. Wandering through the maze of streets and alleys in Limehouse Hole, among the "too abundant" flights of stairs and rooms, Harmon seeks the "scene of his death": "And, like most people so puzzled, he again and again described a circle, and found himself at the point from which he had begun" (365). The scene of death is thus a profoundly mystifying scene of origin. Harmon's eventual reconstruction of the episode that enables him to be reborn constitutes a self-origination that will eventually recede to a still earlier origin. That one is not biological but social, to be found in the accumulated dust of the mounds that represent his father's fortune and his will.

Harmon's search emblematizes one of the modes in which representation binds self to city. Another appears in the accounts of the Harmon murder, which find their way into several texts that are not easily meshed. To Mortimer's dinner-table account of the older Harmon's will, we may add the Inspector-Abbot's sequel: "No clue to how body came into river. Very often was no clue. . . . How was it he had totally disappeared on leaving ship, till found in river? Well! Probably had been upon some little game. Probably thought it a harmless game, wasn't up to things, and it turned out a fatal game" (24–25). The indirect discourse, with its frequent omission of the subject, its knowing but empty game metaphor, and its compressed narrative, tidies up matters. Then the murder drifts into public accounts, the ballads. Beneath the family saga, the case for detection, and the popular ballad, there lies the subtext of the nonmurder and the self-deferral, which John Harmon narrates to himself in his autobiographical musings. This subtext also contains a burial, or surface-depth metaphor. It would be too facile to say that Harmon's is the original text, the text of self-presence, to which the other versions appear as fictions. By that logic, all the novel's other self-presenting texts, in which characters in effect narrate their own histories to themselves, would be equally authentic. Rather, *Our Mutual Friend*'s odd couplings, extending into even stranger series, bespeak an undifferentiation of self and world, or self and world-as-text. In this context, so antithetical to taxonomical order and clarity, the uncanny appears not only within the problematic consciousnesses of the characters, but also as an effect produced by the text.

Freud's discussion of the Sandman in "The Uncanny," where substitution is a major symbolic strategy, plays out a related scenario of dislocation. For example, the lawyer Coppelius, Coppola the optician, and the Sandman substitute for each other and for "the dreaded father at whose hands castration is awaited."[45] Although it would be possible to read *Our Mutual Friend* as a text "about" castration, that is not our concern here. Nor, for the moment, must every chain of displacements lead to the father, despite the array of strong fathers ranging from Gaffer Hexam to John Harmon. Against Freud's originating figure we may pose the possibility of a greater uncertainty, in which the self becomes incapable of resolution. Mortimer Lightwood's source is outside himself: he "founded himself" (285) upon Eugene Wrayburn when they were schoolboys. But to himself Eugene is an " 'embodied conundrum' " (286), a riddle he has given up trying to solve. (He is also incapable of resolution in the sense of firm determination.) *Our Mutual Friend* contains a dizzying round of selves seemingly founded upon external sources: upon others, upon texts (Boffin creates a deliberately inauthentic self out of the texts of misers' lives), upon cultural systems (Mrs. Boffin's Fashion and the Veneering circle's fashionable surfaces), upon the beliefs of others (the Lammles each believe in the other's financial worth; customers of Pubsey and Co. believe that the gentle Riah is a rapacious moneylender). Selfhood now seems to be a temporary endowment from the world.

45. Freud, "The Uncanny," 232.

The traffic moves in both directions, however. If the Boffins emerge from their culture, they also parody it. Parody here stands as a distorted form of interpretation. The related figure of catachresis surely informs the interpenetration of self and world: the Veneerings and their mirror, Twemlow and the dining table, Silas Wegg and his wooden leg, the Hexams and the river. That material culture is marginally situated: along the river front, "vessels . . . seemed to have got ashore, and houses. . .seemed to have got afloat . . . bowsprits staring into windows, and windows staring into ships" (21), just as the dust mounds in Holloway image the disintegration of material culture. The world is represented in a state of perpetual transition and refiguration.[46] If characters are fundamentally interdependent with a world construed in both material and social terms, if they emerge from river slime and mirrors, from the eyes of others and from the signifying systems of society, then, like the beggars in *Little Dorrit*, they solicit their world for identities that stand just beside them.

At this point, the descriptive premises of Dickens's world involve a swift turn to metaphor (albeit founded in metonymy), especially metaphors that involve forms of interpenetration, dissolution, or corruption. The restitution of the "panoramic view" in the dark mounds or the mutual gaze of vessels and houses defies taxonomic articulation: the parodic interior of Mr. Venus's shop is, after all, not a bad index of those premises. The corruption extends to language. Harmony Jail, derived from the older Harmon's adversarial isolation, presents the paradigmatic sign of linguistic and imaginative corruption:

> . . . Mr. Wegg's conversation was jolted out of him in a most dislocated state.
>
> "Was-it-Ev-verajail?" asked Mr. Wegg, holding on.
>
> "Not a proper jail, wot you and me would get committed to," returned his escort; "they giv' it the name, on accounts of Old Harmon living solitary there."
>
> "And-why-did-they-calitharm-Ony?" asked Wegg.
>
> "On accounts of his never agreeing with nobody. Like a speeches of chaff. Harmon's Jail; Harmony Jail. Working it round like." (54)

Here, if anywhere, the Name-of-the-Father is a floating signifier. But

---

46. Cf. Donald Fanger, *Dostoevsky and Romantic Realism*, 83–86.

it is also a part of the representational staging in which the city's internal deserts and murky river waters and society caught in a kind of mirror stage—one thinks of the mirror passage in which the Veneerings are transfixed without the pronouns that confer subjectivity[47]—lose their solidity within the instability of metaphors. Corruption is linked to the shop of Mr. Venus, which in turn stands at a threshold where the seen shades over into the unseen. Here we may recall Benjamin's comment on the absence of the city in Baudelaire's poems, which nevertheless presuppose its "presence" throughout. Analogously, Dickens's texts allow the phenomenal presence of the city to slip in order to pay homage to its mystery and complexity, but at the same time to subordinate it to its figurative recreation. To the dissolution of urban objects as a form of urban impressionism, in which urban light dominates and idealizes the material scene,[48] we may compare the vision of light as a trace of the unseen city in *Bleak House*, as well as the empty squares of *The Prelude* and *The Princess Casamassima*. Where direct description, as an approach to the real and a commitment to the scene, is ideologically charged, what would be gained by distancing or idealizing? Urban narrative may counter the overwhelming phenomena of the city (the signs and spires that so confuse Jo, or the labyrinthine streets that oppress Esther) with the clearing of a space. The urban sublime, now construed as a counterthrust to the drive to describe, involves a kind of textual repression. What remains is a trace or aura in which the subject, the artist of the city or a narratorial consciousness, encounters the city in the space of writing.

V

What emerges in this account of urban description, then, is its tendency to estrangement of the very objects, scenes, or events to which

---

47. *Our Mutual Friend*, 10–11.

48. Cf. Michael Riffaterre's comments on *Bleak House* in "Intertextual Representation: On Mimesis as Interpretive Discourse," in *Critical Inquiry* 11 (1984): 155–56. Realism, he writes, "seems to be built exclusively on the representation of squalor. The pressure of this ideological bias, of this overwhelming aesthetic and ethical constant, makes for quite a dramatic, almost operatic contrast, when London is transfigured into a midsummer night's dream—a moonlit sublimation of the object. . . ."

it refers, by metaphor, or by a reversion to the perceiving subject. It is this notion that evokes the idea of the uncanny, in which the familiar is estranged by the process of repression. If we return once again to the opening scene of *Our Mutual Friend*, we can see the elements of the uncanny distributed through it: the dread, the primitivism, the intensity of the gaze (this last, as Freud points out, is evidence of animistic thinking, as in the child's belief that her dolls would come to life under a concentrated gaze). Yet the full force of the uncanny appears later, in the relation between the schoolmaster Bradley Headstone and the barrister Eugene Wrayburn, the former filled with passion, the latter with ennui, both attracted in unexplainable ways to Lizzie. The two are doubles, linked by their mutual antagonism: "Through the ensuing dialogue, those two, no matter who spoke, or whom was addressed, looked at each other. There was some secret, sure perception between them, which set them against one another in all ways" (288). When Lizzie, fearing Bradley's importunities as well as his murderous impulses toward Eugene, disappears from London, Bradley stalks Eugene through the city's dark streets, hoping that Eugene will lead him to her hiding-place. Aware of the pursuit, Eugene leads Bradley on fruitless chases that simply exacerbate Bradley's passion:

> Looking like the hunted and not the hunter, baffled, worn, with the exhaustion of deferred hope and consuming hate and anger in his face, white-lipped, wild-eyed, draggle-haired, seamed with jealousy and anger, and torturing himself with the conviction that he showed it all and they exulted in it, he went by them in the dark, like a haggard head suspended in the air, so completely did the force of his expression cancel his figure. (544)

The uncanny lies not in the venting of passion—it has been apparent, however suppressed, all along—but in the indeterminacy of roles, in the terms of deferral, suspension, and cancellation, in which Bradley "means" Eugene and returns, repeatedly, as a figure for all that illicit desire which Eugene has repressed. His intentions toward the lower-class girl are still ambiguous, and this figure is in part a term for moral evasiveness. There are, moreover, some resemblances to the Coppelia story that Freud recounts in "The Uncanny": Nathaniel's irrational passion for the doll Olympia, which makes him forget his "sensible" betrothed, finds an analogue in the two men's irrational desire for Lizzie, whose marginal class status puts her in the place of an object. No doll herself, she dwells in the house of the dollmaker Jenny Wren.

Although Freud's reading of Hoffman's narrative centers upon castration anxiety and familial relations, Dickens's narrative focuses upon illicit passion and a crossing of familial relations with societal law. The various plots of *Our Mutual Friend* link the personal with the social. Desire erupts in the darkness and mystery of river and streets. Where personal passions are played out in these dark settings, the personal becomes public, the *heimlich* becomes *unheimlich*. This is an urban fantasy, a projection of desire in which the city is the scene of suspended violence and disruption. We may recall Benjamin's thesis about the way in which arcades interiorize city streets. Whatever other role they play in a commodity society, they stabilize or make continuous the relation of dwelling to street. Insofar as the arcades are the projection of a collective dream of economic life, however, they are as vulnerable as any urban setting. The uncanny presents an underside in which interior and exterior reveal the threat of one to the other: the stabilities of bourgeois society are undermined by the threat of class mobility, as well as by the threat of material decay that (like self-consuming anger) can efface the world of objects.

The representation of the uncanny requires, according to Freud, a setting of "common reality" that would relate to forms of thought that have been repressed or surmounted: repressed desires and primitive forms of thought, including animism and projection. In Dickens the enigmas of the self are invested in city sites, where estrangement is marked by the permeability of self and object-world, by the play of doubles, by the deferment of self-knowledge into the opacity of metaphor and the emptiness of city streets. Similar scenarios appear in the novels of Elizabeth Gaskell and George Gissing.

Here, finally, we may return to the uncanny as a theory of the sublime. Freud opposes the uncanny to the sublime and almost offhandedly allows that dread and darkness may belong to the uncanny in fiction.[49] Yet surely the uncanny inhabits Wordsworth's urban dreams or Esther's hesitant self-recognition, to the point of destabilizing or unnaming: in that indeterminacy, the city becomes the site of the discourse of the self. In his writing on Baudelaire, Benjamin makes the city's empty streets the site from which "poetic booty" has been

49. Freud, "The Uncanny," 219–20.

wrested.[50] The empty spaces of the urban novelists are often marked by afterimages, figured in the glow of the horizon, in dreams, in writing.

Theories of the sublime involve transactions: a mutual gaze, a transfer of "energy" from physical object to perceiving mind, from the scene of culture to the scene of writing. Benjamin's aura represents the ritual values of a past in which distance between gaze and object does not preclude the ability of the object to return the gaze.[51] The aura is lost in the reproduction of the proliferating signs of advertising as well as in the experience of shock, exemplified in the factory worker at his machine and the passer-by in the crowd. Shock is at once abrupt and given to meaningless repetition: its effects appear in the factory workers who populate the pages of *Mary Barton* and *North and South*, of *Alton Locke* and *Sybil*, as well as in Jo, the passer-by in *Bleak House*. While Hyacinth Robinson represents the urban figure in whose imagination the city retains its aura after he has distanced himself from the crowd, his death results from the intolerable aporia that opposes art to class politics. If the crowd and the machine provide the constitutive images for the modern city, the aura is poised against them as the quality that is always vanishing, but that never completely disappears.

If the loss of aura is so distinctive a feature of the advent of modernity, it is equally important in the interiorization of the urban sublime. The repositioning of the sublime or the auratic into a perceptual transaction prepares the way for the discreet work of memory. The storyteller "is the man who could let the wick of his life be consumed completely by the gentle flame of his story," Benjamin writes. This is the "basis" of his "incomparable aura."[52] The pressure of memory within the "blockage" of the sublime encounter also foregrounds that which is implicit in earlier theories of the sublime: the imprint of the artist.[53] As the artist of the city, he leaves his traces on the text: auratic loss receives textual compensation. If representation necessarily entails the subversion of the material city, the artist's resistance to that loss informs urban narrative. The dark mounds and the river's depths of *Our Mutual Friend* figure that resistance. The former constitute a narrative pun of sorts, insofar as they represent the refuse-all of objectivity. The river, from which the wrong bodies and thus the wrong

50. Cf. "On Some Motifs in Baudelaire," 165.
51. "On Some Motifs in Baudelaire," 188.
52. "The Storyteller," 108–9.
53. Neil Hertz makes this explicit in "A Reading of Longinus."

characters are retrieved, becomes the exemplary figure of the abyss—
from which narrative emerges as a kind of mistake—and the pre-figure
for Conrad's image of London as the "monstrous town . . . cruel devourer of the world's light."[54] Out of the low life of the river dredgers
and refuse collectors comes the figure for the narrative of the urban
sublime. It is the bourgeois figures who represent the excluded middle,
confined, like the Veneerings, to surfaces or to the parodic anxieties
of origin, as in Twemlow's cogitations on his relation to Veneering:
"The abyss to which he could find no bottom, and from which started
forth the engrossing and ever-swelling difficulty of his life, was the
insoluble question whether he was Veneering's oldest friend, or new-
est friend" (7).

VI

One crucial experience in which the loss of aura is inscribed is that
of shock, exemplified in the response of the passer-by to the crowd.
Some of the great set-pieces of urban fiction are almost marginal in
this context because the crowd as well as the passer-by is motivated:
neither Richard Mutimer's demagoguery (in *Demos*) nor John Hewitt's
Sunday-night harangues (in *The Nether World*) would qualify. Even
the street markets (in *Workers in the Dawn* and *Thyrza*) with their
random activity signify the vitality of street life and at least the remnants
of a community. It is the largely unmotivated crowd that fills the city's
streets in *Dombey and Son*, *Bleak House*, and *Little Dorrit*, and to
which the passer-by has no clear relation, that poses the problem for
representation. This is the crowd that seems merely superficial or
exotic to Wordsworth, though even the exotic is a complex trope for
casting the crowd as irreducibly other, for making it seem alien, bar-
barian, or threatening. Sala's linguistic difficulties with London's
crowds also represent shock. How would we then interpret the comparative absence of crowds in Dickens's later novels? To be sure,
Arthur Clennam and Little Dorrit leave the church after their marriage
and go "quietly down into the roaring streets, inseparable and blessed;
and as they passed along in sunshine and in shade, the noisy and the
eager, and the arrogant and the froward and the vain, fretted and

---

54. Joseph Conrad, *The Secret Agent* (Garden City, N.Y.: Doubleday, 1953), 11.

chafed, and made their usual uproar."[55] This final sentence of the novel makes blessedness a condition of protection from the crowd; the antithetical, quasi-allegorical language closes on the condition of otherness. It is this very condition that makes the experience of shock possible for everyone who is unblessed. Otherwise, Dickens's strategies for presenting the crowd suggest that, like Baudelaire, he makes it a hidden figure: empty sites, as in the Sabbath emptiness of the London Arthur returns to; the naturalizing metaphors, as in the flow of the crowd; catalogues of objects (although these may be further qualified by forms of negation or the evocation of what is absent). To these we may add the crowds of signs so oppressive to Jo, as well as the advertisements of *In the Year of Jubilee*. All these attempt to reduce the experience of shock by strategies of emptying or figuration. Such transference achieves some form of restitution or sublimation.

A scenario for the sublime then takes on this shape: The initiating object or scene rises up before the beholder and against narrative; the object's metaphorical richness is signified but not constituted by its materiality: the initial paradox is that its visual strength will be superseded. The function of the object or scene is paradigmatic, in that the turn away from the material image toward figuration deepens the mystery that is so much a part of the representation of the city in fiction. The sublime moment, predicated upon discontinuity, becomes a means of negotiating the transition from the presence of the city to its representation, as if acceptance of the sublime entailed a willingness to abandon the quest for the referent. That moment of transition implies, however, the loss of a prior presence and of the aura and all that it implies of the meaning that accrues to objects, whether it is that of a subtext formed by the past or that arising from the trace of the artist's hand. But that loss may not be so dire, insofar as the empty spaces offer blanks for the intervention of memory and consciousness. We need Benjamin's remark that the crowd is assumed even when it doesn't appear in the text of Baudelaire's poems. We may observe further, however, that the obliteration of the crowd provides, in city spaces, the blank page, palimpsest, or mystic writing-pad on which may be inscribed public memorials or private memories, on which national and individual histories may cross. The empty square is the figure for the site that remains, yielding to the gaze of a Wordsworth

---

55. *Little Dorrit* (London: Oxford University Press, 1967), 826.

or a Hyacinth Robinson those memories that they could never otherwise have had.

The underside of the sublime appears in the experience of shock, which we may now relate to the sensationalism in novels of the city that so alarmed Ruskin. What is mechanical and meaningless repetition for Benjamin—a form of incipient trauma—appears in Ruskin as the sensations that reduce to sameness.[56] But while for Ruskin the content condemns the form, for Benjamin the form redeems the content. From the very recalcitrance of the materials, the artist of the city wrests his texts. In those texts, predicated upon repression and loss, the city exerts its mysterious fascination.

---

56. See John Ruskin, "Fiction, Fair and Foul," in the *Works of John Ruskin*, 39 vols., ed. E. T. Cook and Alexander Wedderburn (London, 1903–12), 34:268–72.

Index